Spotlight
CANADA

Spotlight
CANADA

J. Bradley Cruxton
W. Douglas Wilson

Toronto   Oxford University Press   1980

Canadian Cataloguing in Publication Data

Cruxton, J. Bradley.
  Spotlight Canada

Bibliography: p.
Includes index.

ISBN 0-19-540347-9

1. Canada - History - 20th century.*   I. Wilson,
W. Douglas.   II. Title.

FC600.C78   971.06   C79-094872-9
F1034.2.C78

*For
Dianne and Mary
with love*

*With thanks
Tilly and Richard*

© Oxford University Press (Canada) 1980

Designed by Michael van Elsen
Illustrations and maps by Margaret Kaufhold
Two-colour line conversions by Michael van Elsen

ISBN 0-19-5403479
  345678-54321

Printed in Canada by
Hunter Rose Company Limited

CONTENTS

These symbols are used throughout the book to identify major themes in Canadian history.

 Canada and the World

 Economics

 Technology

 Politics

 People and Lifestyles

 Labour

 Canada and Britain

 Multiculturalism

 War and Peacekeeping

 Women

 Regional Development

 National Identity

 Canadian/American Relations

 English/French Relations

1
THE TWENTIETH CENTURY DAWNS

In the evening hours of 22 January 1901, a tired old lady died. She was Victoria, Queen of England and Empress of India. For sixty-three years Victoria had ruled nearly one quarter of the globe. A quarter of the human race were her subjects, including 5.3 million Canadians. Her Empire stretched around the world, carrying with it British laws, customs, and language.

Queen Victoria had always tried to keep things as they were. Though her husband, Albert, had been dead for thirty-nine years, the Queen left his room exactly as it had been. Albert's clothes were laid out as if he were alive. Victoria even ordered that hot water for shaving be brought to his room every morning. Now Victoria herself was dead, and with her death came the end of an age.

Among the subjects who watched her funeral procession, very few people could remember a time when she was not their queen. But now that Victoria was dead, people sensed that nothing could ever be the same again. Her eldest son 'Bertie' became King Edward VII. He was popular, confident, and progressive in his thinking. He stood for change. Edward was a new king in a new century. That is why it is hard to choose a more significant day for the end of the 19th century, and the real beginning of the 20th century, than 22 January 1901.

WHAT WAS IT LIKE TO LIVE IN CANADA IN 1901?
WHAT WOULD STRIKE US MOST IF WE WERE ABLE TO STEP BACK IN TIME?

Horses played a significant role in everyone's life. When a baby was coming into the world the doctor's horse-drawn carriage informed the whole community of the news. Similarly, the undertaker's sleek black horses pulled the ornate hearse to the cemetery at the end of a person's life. Horses were always in the picture. Farmers used them to pull their ploughs and town dwellers kept them for transport. Every business – the bakery, the dairy, the coal company – had to have horses to pull its delivery wagons. Horse-drawn streetcars were still in use in many Canadian towns and cities. Montreal and Toronto, however, were beginning to make the switch to the electric railway. The sight of horse-drawn fire engines racing through the streets was an

Yonge Street, Toronto, 1900.

exciting thing to behold. There were traffic jams in larger cities and people were run over, though there was nothing to match the traffic accidents of today. A more common cause of excitement was when a horse ran away and had to be stopped by a policeman or a brave passerby.

By the turn of the century the bicycle craze swept Canada. One in every twelve persons owned 'a wheel'. The police force in many cities found the bicycle useful for patrolling city streets. Bicycles were cheaper to purchase and operate than horses, which had to be fed and housed. For many ordinary city residents a bicycle solved the problem of transit within the city. People could now live farther from their place of work and get to their job more easily. Yet bicycles were more than transportation, they were romance. Couples honeymooned on them. On summer Sundays the roads were dusty from cyclists heading into the countryside for picnics. A new sense of freedom and mobility had been given to those willing to take up the sport.

The automobile was just being introduced into society. Henry Ford had founded the Detroit Automobile Company in 1899, nine years after Daimler started his company in Germany. King Edward VII was an enthusiastic supporter of 'horseless carriages' and helped to make them popular. In Ontario the first

Fire Engine, 1912.

motorist was John Moodie of Hamilton, who imported a $1000 Winton from the United States in 1898. However, it was not until the 1920s that the automobile was no longer considered a rich man's toy. Not until the development of the assembly line did the price of a car move within the grasp of nearly everyone. Certainly no one at the turn of the century foresaw the problems of accidents, parking, and congestion which the new invention would bring.

It was not until 1903 that the American brothers, Orville and Wilbur Wright, successfully flew the first airplane. That flight, on the beach of Kitty Hawk, North Carolina, lasted just twelve seconds. But the Wright brothers proved that a machine that was heavier than air could fly. The air age had begun.

Meanwhile in Canada Alexander Graham Bell, the inventor of the telephone, also worked on the problem of flight. At Baddeck, Nova Scotia, he formed a group known as the Aerial Experiment Association (A.E.A.) with four young men. In 1908 Casey Baldwin, a member of the A.E.A., flew a plane they had built, 'Red Wing', a distance of 97 metres. The 'White Wing' was flown for 310 metres and set a new world's record. In the A.E.A.'s third plane, the 'June Bug', Douglas McCurdy flew the first figure eight in history. By the summer of 1909 McCurdy was making flights of 32 kilometres over the water at Baddeck in the 'Silver Dart'. The 'Silver Dart' was the finest and most easily flown aircraft of its day. McCurdy and Baldwin tried hard to convince the Canadian government of the military value of an air force. However, when the 'Silver Dart' crash-landed during the flight trials, military officials rejected the idea of using airplanes in warfare. Thirty years later the Canadian government asked McCurdy to become the director of government aircraft production during World War II.

Around the turn of the century the telephone was being used increasingly. In Brantford, Ontario in the summer of 1874, Alexander Graham Bell developed the idea of having electricity carry the sound of the human voice. He succeeded in sending a voice over wires and called his invention the telephone. By 1890 the number of telephones in Montreal numbered 3000. By 1910, it had increased to 30 000. Household needs could now be ordered by telephone and delivered to the home. Small storekeepers could hire young men with bicycles to deliver packages throughout the city. Party lines were the rule in those days. All calls had to be channelled through the telephone exchange. Operators sitting at boards connected the parties. The telephone had a great social impact because it provided new opportunities of employment for women as operators.

In 1901, at Signal Hill in St. John's, Newfoundland, Guglielmo Marconi received the first radio signal sent across the Atlantic Ocean. The following year, with the backing of the Canadian government, Marconi built a wireless station at Glace Bay, Nova Scotia. From here he set up official trans-Atlantic wireless communication. However, another twenty years elapsed before radio broadcasting began as a means of mass entertainment. In the first years of the 20th century, people were more dependent on home-made entertainment such as the piano, banjo, and amateur theatrical productions. The phonograph or gramophone was coming in, but the thick, flat discs sounded scratchy and tinny. Not until the invention of electrical recording in the 1920s did the sound of the records become more musically exact, and not until the 1950s was it possible to play the whole of a major composition on one record.

The first movie theatres were opened in the early years of the century and soon sprang up all over. The movies were known as silent movies because dialogue was shown on the screen as captions. A pianist or a small orchestra accompanied the film and provided important sound effects. It was twenty years before talking films arrived. Canada's own Mary Pickford made her first film in 1909, and Charlie Chaplin made his in 1911.

Another common form of entertainment was professional sport. Baseball was the most popular in the United States,

Tom Longboat, 1907.

where the World Series began in 1903. In Canada at this time tremendous attention was focused on Tom Longboat. This young Indian boy was born on the Six Nations Reserve near Brantford, Ontario. By 1906, at the age of nineteen, Tom could outrun a horse around a 19 kilometre course. The next year he raced the tough, hilly course of the Boston Marathon. Against 125 opponents, Longboat set a record of 2 hours, 24 minutes, 24 seconds in this marathon, battling snow, rain, and slush. This record was not surpassed until the course of the Boston Marathon was changed to make it easier. Each time Tom Longboat ran, crowds flocked to see him. At Madison Square Gardens he took part in the 'race of the century'. Tom arrived for the race accompanied by Indian chiefs in traditional dress. He raced against an English professional runner, Alfie Shrubb. At the 39th kilometre Longboat passed Shrubb and went on to win the race. Longboat was proclaimed the world's best long-distance runner. Tom later enlisted in the Canadian army and fought overseas in World War I. He died in 1949 back on the Six Nations Indian Reserve.

In the early 1900s other changes were taking place in industry, science, and every aspect of life. Bathrooms and modern conveniences became more common. Electric washing machines could now be bought to take some of the drudgery out of wash-

Poor Children, 1908.

day. Other gadgets included sewing machines, electric hearing aids, and vacuum cleaners. For Canadians, all of these gadgets could be purchased from the Eaton's Catalogue by those who could afford them. Eaton's opened its first store in 1869 in Toronto, and published its first mail-order catalogue in 1884. This book was considered by several generations to be the most popular book in Canada. Rural families particularly depended on the catalogue for everything from fence posts to fashionable hats. For Canadian children and adults alike Eaton's catalogue became a 'wish book' that they could gaze at for hours dreaming about the things they hoped to buy some day.

At the turn of the century Canada became more and more urbanized. The factories were in the cities, and workers were needed in the factories. When farmers began to use machinery, fewer workers were needed on the farms. They moved to cities looking for work. The farmer was turning into a factory worker, and in the already crowded urban centres they found both work and lodgings. This serious problem of overcrowding in many Canadian cities was further complicated by the rapid increase in the number of immigrants coming to Canada. In one year alone 96 000 immigrants arrived, and many of them settled in Montreal, Toronto, or Winnipeg. Often the accommodations to house this great influx of people were pitifully inadequate. Immigrants were forced to live in slums and work in basement or attic factories. Urban poverty and related problems of high unemployment and poor housing became very serious.

RURAL AND URBAN POPULATION IN CANADA

	RURAL	URBAN	TOTAL
1871	2 967 000	722 000	3 689 000
1881	3 215 000	1 110 000	4 325 000
1891	3 296 000	1 537 000	4 833 000
1901	3 357 000	2 014 000	5 371 000
1911	3 934 000	3 273 000	7 207 000

Perhaps the thing that would strike you most if you were to step back into the Canada of 1901 would be the inequality between man and man and between man and woman. People were divided by their work and by their class. In those days the rich really were rich, and taxes were so low that they were left with almost all of their money to spend. Most of it went on clothes, houses, horses, and carriages. Sir Henry Pellatt was a prime example of the wealth in Toronto. Pellatt is reported to have made $17 000 000 in the Toronto Electric Light Company and mining stocks. In 1910 he sank $2 000 000 into the building of Casa Loma, a palatial home in Toronto. Casa Loma contained thirty bathrooms, three bowling alleys, fifty-two telephones, and the world's finest indoor rifle range. The stables had mahogany stalls and Persian rugs, and Pellatt once had a custom set of false teeth made for his favourite horse.

The Palm Room in Casa Loma, 1914.

Toronto Store, 1910.

The average Canadian at the turn of the century still lit a kerosene or gas lamp and cooked on a wood stove. Most townsmen, at least on a Sunday, wore a high starched collar and a derby hat called a bowler. The women shopped every day, scrubbed clothes on a washboard, put up pickles and fruit preserves, and beat their rugs with a wire whip.

At the lowest end of the economic ladder were the immigrants and newcomers. They were often forced to live in terrible conditions, crowded into basement rooms where sanitation was poor and ventilation was worse.

There was also the inequality between man and woman. For a respectable woman to enter a tavern, a pool room, or even a bowling alley was unthinkable. To go to a concert or the theatre alone was frowned upon. Women in Canada had just begun to fight to get as good an education as men. Women in professions such as medicine were still a rarity. Women tended to work in stores and factories, and girls from poorer families became domestic servants. Girls from wealthy or middle-class families had to choose between nursing and teaching as a possible career. The early 20th century was still very much a man's world, run by men for men. In New Zealand and Australia women had recently won the right to vote (1893 and 1902 respectively). But in Canada women had no say at this time in the government of the country.

But some Canadian women were working very hard to improve their situation in society. In 1876 Dr. Emily Stowe had formed the Toronto Women's Literary Club. This name was deceiving. The purpose of this club was to teach women their rights and to help them secure these rights. It persuaded the

Women Telephone Operators, 1910.

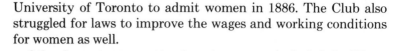

University of Toronto to admit women in 1886. The Club also struggled for laws to improve the wages and working conditions for women as well.

Other important organizations for women included the Women's Christian Temperance Union (W.C.T.U.) whose aims were to combat the problems created by alcohol in society. These women were concerned about the number of wives and children being beaten, abused, or neglected by drunken husbands or fathers. They dedicated themselves to fighting the evils of alcohol. Nellie McClung, Canada's great woman social reformer, got her start in the W.C.T.U. McClung argued that women should have exactly the same freedom as men, and she led in the fight for women's rights. With such dedicated workers the 20th century would obviously bring about great changes in the role and status of women.

Digging Deeper

Learning to Make Useful Notes

Every history student should learn how to keep a good set of notes. Your notes should be clear, concise, and complete. Writing notes will help you to remember what you have learned. Good notes will assist you to study for tests and examinations. Notes are certainly easier to remember than many pages of a textbook.

Writing notes from a text requires several skills. You have to select your material and put it together in a logical way. Many words have to be reduced into a few. The main idea has to be kept and expressed in such a way that in six months you can still understand what you have written.

Note-making skills that you learn now will be very valuable to you in the future. Most adults have to do some paperwork at some point in their lives. They need to be able to summarize reports or to make written reports out of minutes taken down in summary form. They need to be able to pick out the important parts of an argument and record them in such a way that they can recall these points when necessary. In an office, in a store or business, or in a profession, note-making skills are essential.

Here are some guidelines to help you make notes on part of the chapter you have just read. The questions will assist you to draw out the most important ideas and information for your notes. Gradually you should be able to sit down in front of a text and write good notes without any help at all. Then you will have really mastered the skill of good note-making.

Make notes on WHAT IT WAS LIKE TO LIVE IN CANADA IN 1901 following these guidelines.

a) Read the section "What Was It Like to Live in Canada in 1901?" from pages 9 to 12. In two sentences write down a general summary of what this passage is about.

b) Read the first paragraph. What is it about? Give the paragraph a subheading. Under your subheading write notes on the following: Give seven examples of how horses were used in Canada at the turn of the century.

c) Read the second paragraph. What is it about? Give the paragraph a subheading. Under your subheading write notes on the following: What changes did the widespread use of the bicycle have on the ways Canadians lived?

d) Read the third paragraph. What is it about? Give the paragraph a subheading. Under your subheading write notes on the following: Make a note of the early events of the development of the automobile, including
   i) inventors in the 1890s;
   ii) why early cars were a rich man's toy;
   iii) what event made cars more available to people.

c) Read the fourth and fifth paragraphs. What are they about? Give the paragraphs a subheading. Under your subheading briefly describe each of the following events:
   i) the flight of the 'Silver Dart';
   ii) the flight of Orville and Wilbur Wright;
   iii) Canadian military officials reject the use of airplanes;
   iv) Alexander Graham Bell forms the A.E.A.

2

THE GOLDEN AGE OF LAURIER

Sir Wilfrid Laurier campaigning.

In 1896 Wilfrid Laurier entered the House of Commons in Ottawa to the sound of cheering and applause. He made his way to the seat Sir John A. Macdonald had occupied for nineteen years. Now Laurier, the leader of the Liberal party, was the new prime minister of Canada. The next fifteen years were known as the 'Golden Age of Laurier'.

Laurier had once said that the 19th century belonged to the United States, but that the 20th century would certainly belong to Canada. As the 20th century dawned, it looked as if Laurier might be right. The world-wide economic depression of the early 1890s began to clear and prosperity started to return to Canada. Once again factories began to hum, people had jobs, and there were markets for Canadian products. Good times returned, and for the next fifteen years things went well for Canada. It certainly was a 'Golden Age' for most Canadians, and for the Liberal party.

Laurier was Canada's first French-Canadian prime minister. He brought to this high political office his great gifts as a person and as a politician. He was born near the village of St. Lin in the province of Quebec on 20 November 1841. Laurier's family was deep-rooted in Canada. His first Canadian ancestor was a member of the Carignan-Salières regiment which had accompanied Jeanne Mance and the Sieur de Maisonneuve when they founded Montreal in 1642. Members of Wilfrid Laurier's family had settled the land and explored the continent. His ancestors had lived through the conquest of Quebec by the English in 1760. Like all French Canadians they must have watched nervously as English troops, with their foreign language and religion, marched into Quebec. After the conquest, many French-Canadian families, like Laurier's, moved into rural areas in order to protect and maintain their French-Canadian way of life.

Wilfrid Laurier's character was shaped by his rather unusual background. When he was eleven, his father did a surprising thing. He decided to send young Wilfrid to school in the English-speaking settlement at New Glasgow, an hour's drive by calèche from St. Lin. There the boy studied English and became fluently bilingual. He lived with the Murray family who were Scottish Protestants. In his free hours Wilfrid used to clerk in John Murray's store and practised speaking English with the customers. In this way Laurier learned a great deal about the ways and religion of English-speaking Protestants. He also learned to be tolerant of people different from himself. In later years, as prime minister of a largely English-speaking Canada, this knowledge was extremely useful. Often Laurier told students that they owed it to themselves to be able to read and speak both languages of Canada. He added that he was grateful to his own father for giving him the chance to do so.

When Laurier was thirteen, he was sent to a French-speaking school, the College de L'Assomption. This school was run by Roman Catholic priests who were very demanding. The day began for the boys at 5:25 a.m., and bedtime came at 8:00 p.m. Most of the time in between was spent learning Latin, Greek, French literature, philosophy, history, and mathematics. This rigorous training was designed to prepare boys for careers as priests, doctors, or lawyers. Laurier chose to study law at McGill University in Montreal.

In 1861 McGill was the only university in Quebec where a student could learn English law as well as French law. Wilfrid did well in his courses at McGill and graduated in 1864. He was invited to give the valedictory address. He spoke to a large audience about the role of the lawyer in the nation. In his speech he touched on a concern that was to dominate his life. 'Two races share today the soil of Canada,' he said. These people had not always been friends. 'But I hasten to say it, and I say it to our glory, that race hatreds are finished on our Canadian soil. There is no longer any family here but the human family. It matters not the language people speak, or the altars at which they kneel.'

Following graduation, Laurier opened a law practice at Arthabaskaville, Quebec, a small town on the south shore of the St. Lawrence River. Here he pleased the townspeople with his honesty, his courage, and his sense of fair play. Eventually they chose him to represent them at the provincial government at Quebec City in 1871. Three years later he was elected to the federal government in Ottawa, and in 1887 he became the leader of the Liberal party. In Parliament Laurier impressed everyone as an excellent speechmaker. Macdonald admired his political opponent and recognized him as one of Canada's most promising politicians.

State dinner at Government House, 1912.

Probably Laurier's greatest gift to Canada was his ability to see both English and French points of view. His main aim was to keep both language groups together and to make sure each treated the other fairly. Laurier's sense of fair play helped him to work out compromises that would be acceptable to both English and French Canadians.

Laurier used all his skills of compromise to solve the Manitoba Schools Question. When the Red River settlement became the province of Manitoba in 1870, most of the people living there were French-speaking and Roman Catholic. They had been promised that they could have Roman Catholic schools kept up by money raised from public taxes. Over the next twenty years, large numbers of English-speaking Protestants, many from Ontario, had moved into Manitoba. The French Canadians in Manitoba gradually became a minority. By 1890, most of the members of the Manitoba provincial Parliament were English-speaking Protestants. They passed an act to set up a single school system that would not be connected with any church. All citizens of the province, whatever their religion, would pay for the school system through their taxes. The government would no longer support separate, Roman Catholic schools. Roman Catholics themselves would have to pay for separate schools if they wanted to have them.

In 1896 the Roman Catholic school supporters complained to the federal government in Ottawa. Laurier tried to find an answer that would satisfy both sides. He said that Manitoba had the right to decide its own education and schools. This pleased the majority in Manitoba and Protestants in the rest of Canada. But he also persuaded the Manitoba government to allow religious instruction to be given in the last half-hour of the school day. Also, in schools where there were more than ten children speaking French or another European language, a teacher of that other language must be hired. This part of the compromise satisfied the French Roman Catholic people in Manitoba and Quebec. It also pleased the other minority groups who were moving into Manitoba from Europe.

In 1897, Laurier and his wife Zoë journeyed to London, England. They went to take part in the celebration of Queen Victoria's Diamond Jubilee. Queen Victoria had ruled for sixty years, and a great celebration was planned to honour the event. Dignitaries from all parts of the British Empire had come to honour the Queen. The greatest parade that London had ever seen

Queen Victoria's Diamond Jubilee procession.

moved through the streets towards St. Paul's Cathedral. During it, some of the loudest cheers were reserved for Sir Wilfrid Laurier and the North West Mounted Police. The day before the parade, the Queen had knighted Laurier.

Before he returned to Canada, Laurier wanted to visit France. It was the country of his forefathers, and he had never been there before. In two brilliant speeches in Paris, Laurier won over the French as he had the British. He said, 'French Canadians have not forgotten France ... Here in France people are surprised at the attachment French Canadians feel for the Queen of England. We are faithful to the great nation which gave us life [France], and we are faithful to the great nation which has given us liberty [Britain].'

Sir Wilfrid Laurier returned in triumph to Canada. Canadians had never received more respect from other nations of the world. Now the Prime Minister had to turn to tasks at home.

Digging Deeper

1 What qualities and characteristics did Laurier possess that prepared him for the position of prime minister?

2 Compare the characteristics and background of Prime Minister Laurier and another French-Canadian prime minister (Louis St. Laurent or Pierre E. Trudeau).

3 What were the advantages for Canada of belonging to the British Empire?

4 The following words have been used by Wilfrid Laurier's friends and enemies to describe him. Use a dictionary to make sure you understand the meaning of all the words. Make two lists, one for those descriptions that are complimentary and another for those words that are not:

appeasing	humane	stubborn
charming	liberal	tolerant
clear-sighted	nefarious	traitorous to
compromising	pro-British	French Canada
elegant	reasonable	
eloquent	responsive	

Which words would *you* use to describe Wilfrid Laurier? As you study this unit, you may wish to revise your list, or add words of your own.

What kind of a man was Wilfrid Laurier? Read the following quotations for some clues.

'He was always ready, even anxious, to talk to any of his followers no matter how trivial the subject. One of the things that endeared him to the younger members of the party was his habit of meeting us in the corridors, inviting us into his office to smoke a cigarette, and passing five or ten minutes in asking us how Bill Jones was in such and such a village, how so-and-so was and how he was getting along, and inquiring about our own studies and our interests. After ten minutes' talking we returned to the House ready and eager to do anything we could for our leader.'

– C.G. Power, Liberal M.P. for Quebec West

'I am branded in Quebec as a traitor to the French and in Ontario as a traitor to the English. In Quebec I am branded as a jingo* and in Ontario as a separatist. In Quebec I am attacked as an imperialist and in Ontario as an anti-imperialist. I am neither. I am a Canadian.'

– W. Laurier, Saint John, New Brunswick, 1911

At a giant outdoor meeting in Edmonton, Laurier paused suddenly in the midst of his speech to regard intently an upper-floor window from which a child leaned too far. 'Is that little one safe?', he enquired. The child was retrieved and the speech resumed.

Laurier thought English, French, Scottish, Irish, and others could all survive and Canada would still be strong just like a cathedral – 'a harmonious whole, in which granite, marble, oak and other materials were blended. This cathedral is the image that I hope to see Canada become... I want the marble to remain the marble; I want the granite to remain the granite; I want the oak to remain the oak.'

'When Sir Wilfrid Laurier arrives at the Gate of Paradise, the first thing he will do is to propose a compromise between God and Satan.'

– Henri Bourassa

After laying the cornerstone of the University of Saskatoon, Laurier told of having a long chat that morning with a very talkative newsboy by the name of John Diefenbaker. 'Well, Mr. Prime Minister,' the boy said after a half hour had passed, 'I can't waste any more time. I have to deliver my papers.'

*war-lover

3
THE BOOM IS ON!

By the 1880s the Canadian prairies were ready to produce large amounts of wheat. The buffalo had disappeared from the plains, treaties had been made with the Indians, who surrendered most of their lands for settlement, and Riel's last rebellion had been crushed. Law and order had been established by the North West Mounted Police. Most important, a railway had been built to bring in settlers and to carry their harvests to the markets of the world. Though the Dominion Land Act had provided free homesteads since 1872, not very many settlers had yet arrived. All that was needed were people to grow the wheat.

From 1881 to 1896 settlers took up only 56 000 homesteads in the West, and abandoned 16 000 of these. In 1896, only 16 835 immigrants came to Canada, the lowest number since 1868. In fact, during the previous fifteen years, the number of Canadians going to the United States was greater than the number of immigrants coming to Canada. Then everything happened at once. The new prime minister, Laurier, and a new immigration minister, Clifford Sifton, took office in Canada. The Canadian Pacific Railway joined the government in the country's biggest advertising campaign. It was to sell 'the Golden North-West' to people in Britain, the United States, Europe, and eastern Canada.

Clifford Sifton was an aggressive Manitoba lawyer, newspaper publisher, and politician. He was a super salesman with enormous confidence in the West's potential. But the West needed people to develop its natural resources and to provide markets for manufactured goods from the East. Like any good salesman he believed in advertising and persuaded the government to spend money in an attempt to 'sell Canada'. The Immigration Branch concentrated on looking for settlers from three main areas – Britain, the United States, and Europe.

Advertising in Britain for Settlers

One of the best ways to promote the West in Britain was through pamphlets. These booklets were full of pictures of wheat fields and new homesteads in the glorious Canadian West. They described the great opportunities available in Cana-

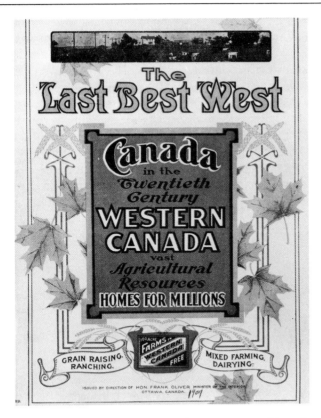

The Last Best West

Canada in the Twentieth Century

WESTERN CANADA

vast Agricultural Resources

HOMES FOR MILLIONS

160 ACRE FARMS IN WESTERN CANADA FREE

GRAIN RAISING. RANCHING.

MIXED FARMING. DAIRYING.

ISSUED BY DIRECTION OF HON. FRANK OLIVER, MINISTER OF THE INTERIOR OTTAWA, CANADA. 1907

da, how you could get free land, and how you could make a fortune.

Many of these pamphlets were given to schools in Britain. Teachers sometimes gave the pamphlets as prizes at the end of the school term, and even used them as readers. Many boys and girls read the booklets and dreamed of adventures in Canada.

Another way of promoting Canada was the exhibition van. This wagon travelled about Britain showing samples of wheat, vegetables, soil, Canadian animals and birds, and pictures of western life. In a single year the exhibition van visited 513 different villages, travelled 2900 kilometres, and was inspected by almost 2 000 000 visitors.

Then there were the magic lantern shows that projected slide pictures of life in Canada. Pictures of herds of cattle, trainloads of settlers, and men threshing unusually large crops were shown in every British village. Following the lantern show a lecturer explained how the Canadian government offered sixty-five hectares of free land.

British newspapers helped to spread the word about Canada. There were full-page advertisements, paid for by the Canadian government and the railroads, and editorials describing Canada. The Canadian government also brought English newspapermen to Canada on free trips to see for themselves what Canada was like. They were lavishly entertained, and as a result went back to England and wrote enthusiastic reports about Canada. They encouraged British farmers and workers who were thinking about moving to the United States to choose Canada instead.

Some people complained that all this advertising was overdone. Gradually, though, it became more realistic, and told the truth about the harsh as well as the good side of life in the West. British settlers in Canada were asked a series of questions about climate, storms, soil, water, and winters in their districts. Their answers were published in British papers together with their names and addresses. This helped to provide an honest picture of what homesteading life was really like.

British immigrant family, 1908.

NUMBER OF IMMIGRANT ARRIVALS FROM BRITAIN
1897 - 1905

1897	11 383
1898	11 173
1899	10 660
1900 (Jan. to June)	5 141
1901	11 810
1902	17 259
1903	41 792
1904	50 374
1905	65 359

Advertising in the United States for Settlers

Sifton was also anxious to recruit American farmers to settle the West because they were used to farming the dry, wide plains, and they knew how to grow crops where there was limited rainfall. He opened immigration agencies in the United States in Chicago, Kansas City, St. Paul, and other large western cities. Three hundred agents travelled through the United States to spread facts about the Canadian West. These agents received a commission for every American family they persuaded to move to Canada. As salesmen the agents were hard to beat. When the Oklahoma Indian Reserve lands were put on the market in 1904, enterprising Canadian agents pitched their tents right beside the American land office. They competed for business, offering the land-hungry farmers better land and free homesteads in Canada.

Eventually the advertising paid off, and the Americans began to come north to Canada. One reason for this was that land was selling in the United States at $250 or more per hectare. An established American farmer could sell his farm at a good price. Then he could come to Canada where he would receive sixty-five hectares free, and buy good land from the railroad or Hudson's Bay Company for a few dollars per hectare. This way he could buy machinery and horses, and still have lots of money left over! To many American farmers it seemed like a very good deal.

Sifton and the C.P.R. brought free-loading American editors to the prairies by the trainload. They then went back home and wrote glowing reports about life in the Canadian west.

Most of the settlers who came to Canada from the American West bought large farms and quickly became successful. Since all the good farm land in the United States had been taken up, many Americans saw Canada as the new frontier. Thousands began to head northwards.

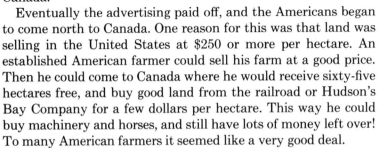

NUMBER OF IMMIGRANT ARRIVALS FROM THE UNITED STATES 1897 - 1905

1897	2 412
1898	9 119
1899	11 945
1900 (Jan. to June)	8 543
1901	17 987
1902	26 388
1903	49 473
1904	45 171
1905	43 543

Advertising in Europe for Settlers

Clifford Sifton once described the kind of immigrant Canada was looking for in Europe:

> The peasants, the men in sheepskin coats, are the ones that are wanted here in Canada. When I speak of quality, I have in mind something that is quite different from what is in the mind of the average person. I think that a stalwart peasant in a sheepskin coat, born on the soil, whose forefathers have been farmers for ten generations, with a stout wife, and a half dozen children, is good quality, as an immigrant. I do not care whether or not he is British-born. It does not matter what his nationality is.

Sifton also advertised in the crowded rural areas of central and eastern Europe. He wanted people like the Ukrainians, Doukhobors from southern Russia, Poles, and Germans because they were solid peasant farmers who could survive the tough prairie environment.

Galician immigrant family, 1911.

Advertising in Europe for settlers posed serious problems for the Immigration Branch. Most European countries were not pleased that Canada was attracting large numbers of their people. Some, like Germany, made it illegal for agents to advertise for potential immigrants. Sifton responded to this challenge by making an arrangement with a secret organization of German steamship agents known as the North Atlantic Trading Company. These agents found and interviewed peasant farmers anxious to come to Canada, and also arranged for their transportation. The company was paid $5 per head for farmers and domestic servants, and $2 per head for dependent children. There was no shortage of farmers wanting to escape the overcrowding and lack of political freedom in Europe.

Sifton did not encourage orientals, blacks, Jews, and city-dwellers to come to Canada because he believed they would not make successful prairie farmers. This policy was known as selective immigration. It meant that some groups were encouraged to come to Canada, while others were not. Like most Canadians of his day, Sifton wanted to keep Canada Anglo-Saxon (British). Some other people would be allowed to come to Canada only if he thought they would make good farmers.

NUMBER OF IMMIGRANT ARRIVALS IN CANADA FROM OTHER COUNTRIES 1897 - 1905

1897	7 921
1898	11 608
1899	21 938
1900 (Jan. to June)	10 211
1901	19 352
1902	23 732
1903	37 099
1904	34 786
1905	37 364

The Canadian government set aside large areas or blocks of land where immigrants from one country could settle. This helped to overcome the loneliness and isolation that many settlers in a new country would feel. European immigrants were not always warmly welcomed into Canada. Newcomers' languages and customs were different. Many people thought they were inferior because they were not British. Some French-Canadian nationalists even accused the government of bringing in foreigners in an attempt to outnumber and thus destroy the French way of life in Canada.

In many places non-English speaking settlers were shunned and ridiculed, and suffered forms of discrimination. A black American settler in Alberta recalled:

A house of sod and logs in Alberta, 1910.

When we were very young they opened the school and because we were a black family, my oldest sisters and brothers could not go to school. Mother took one of the girls over to see what would happen, and they would not open the door.

In time, however, when the new immigrants proved they were good neighbours and excellent farmers, they were gradually accepted in their districts.

Canadian trade unionists also objected to the flood of immigrants coming into the country. They complained that the foreigners were willing to work for lower wages and in terrible working conditions. They believed that immigrants took jobs away from Canadians. Sir William Van Horne, chairman of the Canadian Pacific Railway, disagreed with this point of view and argued for an open-door immigration policy. He said in 1906, 'Let them all come in. There is work for all. Every two or three men who come into Canada and do a day's work create new work for someone else to do.'

Reasons for Success

In addition to Sifton's advertising campaign, a number of other factors helped draw immigrants to Canada.

1. About the time Clifford Sifton took office, the world-wide depression began to end. Now families could afford to think about taking up homesteads.

2. There was a great deal of good free land available in Canada.

3. The countries of Europe at this time were becoming more

and more industrialized. People were leaving the farms to go into the cities to work in factories. Since fewer farmers were producing food in Europe, these countries needed to buy food from Canada and the United States.

4. The Canadian government had a large staff of officials waiting in Canada to help the immigrants once they arrived. There were medical doctors to inspect them and interpreters to help in filling out forms. Temporary housing was provided in large immigrant halls. Other officials were there to help settlers locate homesteads, or to provide the names of farmers looking for hired help. Trains provided by the government took colonists out west. The Immigration Department wanted to get people settled as quickly and efficiently as possible.

5. In Europe the demand for Canadian wheat increased, almost doubling the price of wheat. Growing wheat became more profitable for the Canadian farmer.

6. A remarkable new strain of wheat, called 'Marquis', was developed by Charles E. Saunders at the government's experimental farm in Ottawa. It suited the Canadian growing season because it took just 100 days to ripen for harvest. Marquis wheat was called 'the discovery of the century'. Now farmers could be sure they had a type of wheat that could withstand the cold and would ripen before the frost hit in the fall. More northern areas of the prairies could be opened up for settlement.

7. Several new tools were invented that made wheat farming more efficient. For example, the 'chilled steel' plough could cut through tough prairie sod which had been baked by the hot sun. Steel discs were then pulled across the turned sod after plough-

ing to chop up the lumps. At harvest time, reapers were pulled through the fields to cut down the grain. These were followed by binding machines that could tie rope or wire around a sheaf of wheat. Then the sheaves of wheat were carried by wagon to the threshing machine which separated the wheat from the straw.

At first, all the machines were driven by horses or oxen. But by the 1890s the steam engine brought great changes to farm machinery. Now tractors, threshing machines, and binders could be propelled by steam power.

Grain elevators were soon built in every town on the prairies. Here wheat could be stored until it was shipped out by rail. The railway boxcar was developed so that large amounts of grain could be moved in bulk to the Great Lakes or ocean ports. From there the wheat could be sent to Canadian or world-wide markets by steamers.

8. Canada now had a transcontinental railroad by which grain could be shipped to markets. Steam-powered ocean vessels transported the wheat to Europe cheaply and quickly.

9. Most important of all, millions of Europeans left their native lands between 1900 and 1914. They were looking for new homes and better opportunities all over the world. As a result Canada experienced the greatest wave of immigration in its history. Not only did the number of people grow rapidly, but the make-up of the population changed as well. By 1912, almost one-fifth of the population was not of British or French origin.

Because of the influx of settlers, the West advanced rapidly. Roads and railway branch lines were built, and towns and villages sprang up. Regina, Edmonton, Calgary, and Saskatoon, which had been small, isolated outposts on the prairies, became large and thriving trading centres. Almost overnight, the plains changed from a wilderness life of trapping to the business of growing wheat to feed the world.

GROWTH OF CANADIAN POPULATION 1851 - 1971

1851	2 737 000
1861	3 330 000
1871	3 690 000
1881	4 325 000
1891	4 833 000
1901	5 371 000
1911	7 207 000
1921	8 788 000
1931	10 376 000
1941	11 507 000
1951	14 009 000
1961	18 238 000
1971	21 568 000

As the population of the West grew, two new provinces were created. In 1905, Alberta and Saskatchewan became the newest members of Confederation. In thirty-eight years, Confederation had grown from the joining of four provinces in eastern Canada to the union of nine provinces coast to coast.

Digging Deeper

Role play: You are government agents attempting to encourage settlement in the Canadian West. Divide into three groups – the first to work in Britain, the second in Europe, and the third in the United States. On large sheets of paper design posters to attract settlers from your area of the world.

1

In the early years of the 20th century, forecasting Canada's population growth was a favourite pastime. 'Fifty million people by 1950,' said Sir Wilfrid Laurier. Donald Smith of the C.P.R. predicted there would be at least eighty million by the end of the century. Using the table 'Growth of the Canadian Population 1851-1971', compare Canada's population today with the predictions made around 1900. Suggest reasons why Canada has fewer people than enthusiastic Canadians thought it would have by now.

2

Use the charts in the chapter to discover the total number of immigrants who came to Canada during each year from 1897 to 1905. On large sheets of paper plot graphs to show these yearly totals.

3

If any of your relatives came to Canada between 1896 and 1914, find out what you can about where they came from, how they travelled here, where they settled, and what they did after their arrival in Canada.

4

Sometimes the new immigrants were not warmly received in Canada. How did some Canadians react to the presence of the new settlers in their midst? How do you think the new immigrants felt when treated like this? Suggest reasons why some Canadians may have held these views. Evaluate the fairness of the treatment of new immigrants in a new land.

5

How do Canadians treat immigrants who come here today? Why would some sections of the Canadian public oppose an 'open door' immigration policy? Refer to newspapers and magazines, such as *Macleans*, for information on these issues.

6

4
PROSPERITY AT LAST!

With the rush of settlers to Canada, the West developed rapidly. Towns sprang up, roads were built, and railway lines branched out. Regina, Saskatoon, Calgary, and Edmonton mushroomed in size almost overnight. Grain elevators used to store the harvested wheat quickly began to dot the plains. On every side were endless fields of grain. Prosperity had arrived! The West was booming!

By 1901 the quantities of wheat being hauled out of the prairies became so great that the Canadian Pacific Railway could not handle all the business. The C.P.R. was jammed with traffic at its Winnipeg bottle-neck each year as the crops were shipped out. Many farmers had resorted to shipping out their grain on American railroads. The time had come for a new transcontinental Canadian rail line.

In 1903 the Laurier government announced its willingness to support a railway-building campaign. Two powerful railway groups were eager to go ahead. Ontario-born railway promoters William Mackenzie and Donald Mann had been building short lines in the West. Their railroad, the Canadian Northern, was at first only a western network. Now they wished to extend into a transcontinental system from coast to coast. The Grand Trunk Railway was a central Canadian line which tended to follow the St. Lawrence River. The directors of the Grand Trunk now suggested building from Moncton, New Brunswick to the British Columbia coast. Thus the Grand Trunk Pacific would give Canada a third transcontinental railway.

The sensible approach would have been for the two companies to combine their efforts and create a second transcontinental railway from the East to the Pacific. But the Grand Trunk Pacific and the Canadian Northern were rivals, and they refused to pool their resources in spite of Laurier's pleading. Finally Laurier gave in and promised both companies government funds and support for their projects.

Because they would be competitive, two new transcontinental railways did not make economic sense. Yet their construction pleased most Canadians. Farmers in the West were quite displeased with the high freight prices and poor service of the C.P.R. They welcomed the building of two new lines. Laurier's railway building policy was also applauded in Ontario and Que-

Train Station, 1910.

bec. Here industries would be kept busy supplying the steel, rail-way cars, and everything else that railway construction required. The Maritimes were also happy because the railway building boom would provide thousands of jobs constructing and maintaining the line. All regions would benefit from the improved communication the two new lines would provide in many parts of Canada.

There began in 1903-4 the greatest railway boom in Canadian history. One in three wage earners in eastern Canada worked for a railroad or a company making railway supplies. Thousands of men found jobs surveying the routes, clearing and grading the land, and laying the ties and the track. Between 1904 and 1914, 18 200 kilometres of new lines were added in Canada.

Railway building became the greatest single factor in the industrialization of Canada at this time. Gigantic quantities of steel, timber, dynamite, spikes, tools, and bridge-building mate-rials were needed. Orders poured in for new freight cars and locomotives. Hundreds of grain elevators, docks, and warehouses had to be built as well. Every little town had its station, and in Montreal and Toronto the huge Windsor and Union Stations were constructed for the increasing throngs of railway passen-gers. Grand hotels such as the Chateau Laurier in Ottawa, the

Empress Hotel in Victoria, and the Chateau Frontenac in Quebec City were erected to provide luxury living for travellers.

The accident rate reached an all-time high as inexperienced engineers roared their engines out of control, collided head on, or started so abruptly that passengers fell off the back platform of the train. A major disaster occurred on 29 August 1907. A huge railway bridge was being built across the St. Lawrence River 13 kilometres above Quebec City. On the day of its completion, with thousands watching, the southern section of the bridge suddenly collapsed. Tonnes of twisted steel sank to the bottom of the St. Lawrence. The crash killed 60 workmen and injured 11 others. It was a dramatic sight as a priest crawled out on a girder to administer the last rites to a man caught in the wreckage. There were no devices capable of cutting metal quickly in those days, and the trapped man drowned as the water rose inside the girder.

CAUSES OF RAILWAY ACCIDENTS	KILLED	INJURED
Struck by engines	53	35
Injured in collisions	33	77
Derailing of engines, cars	18	24
Injured when coupling cars	12	24
Falling from trains and cars	22	49
Falling from trains and run over	26	3
Catching foot and run over	5	5
Run over by trains in other ways	47	23
Boiler explosions	3	5
Blasting and dynamite explosions	20	12
Suffocated by coal gas	6	1
Crushed between cars, engines	10	16
Crushed in roundhouses and shops	2	5
Striking objects on moving trains	1	2
Striking objects on electric car	-	2
Injured by falling snow and rock	4	-
Injured by electric shock	2	-
Struck by falling freight	1	8
Falling from ladders	-	2
Falling in other ways	4	13
Injured by tools	-	2
Injured by a saw	-	1
Injured by machinery, belting	-	1
Injured by an elevator	-	1
Unclassified	4	29

January 1905, *Labour Gazette*

Train Wreck, 1910.

Eventually it seemed as if the whole railway boom would come crashing down like the Quebec bridge. Rapidly rising costs of production had put the railway companies heavily into debt. When World War I broke out in 1914, the stream of settlers travelling to the West suddenly stopped. British and foreign investment in railway building projects dried up. Many parts of the new routes closely paralleled the C.P.R. lines. There simply was not enough business to support three lines in Canada. The new railway companies were on the verge of going bankrupt. The Canadian government had no choice but to bail them out of their financial difficulties. After the First World War, the federal government took over the Grand Trunk Pacific and the Canadian Northern lines and merged them into a system we know today as the Canadian National Railway. The C.N.R. is still owned and operated by the federal government.

GOLD IN THE KLONDIKE

In the summer of 1896 George Carmack and two Indians, 'Skookum' Jim and 'Tagish' Charlie, were fishing for salmon on the Bonanza Creek just off the Klondike River. In the gravel bed of the creek they spied several nuggets of gold. They drove stakes into the ground to mark their claim and hurried to register their discovery with the Mounted Police. There was gold on the Klondike!

The discovery of gold in the Yukon sent prospectors crazy with excitement. Thousands of men and a number of women from all over the world headed to the scene of the strike, the junction of the Yukon and Klondike Rivers. Today the town of Dawson City sits on this site. From as far away as the gold fields of California and central Australia people came to the Klondike.

Most miners came into the gold fields over the treacherous route known as the 'Trail of '98'. Follow the route on the map on page 46. They went by boat to Skagway; they climbed more than 1000 metres through the Chilkoot Pass in the Coast Range to the headwaters of the Yukon River. The Chilkoot Pass was so steep that pack animals could not be used. Men had to carry their loads of supplies on their backs, repeating the trip again and again until all their goods were on the top of the pass. It was an amazing feat of human endurance! Once, when an avalanche of snow fell, sixty-five people were killed. After crossing the Chilkoot Pass, prospectors built rafts and boats and floated downstream on an 800 kilometre voyage to Dawson. During the winter of 1897, 22 000 people were checked through the Chilkoot Pass by the North West Mounted Police. Each person was required by the Mounties to carry a year's supply of food, tents, equipment, and clothing. The goods weighed about a tonne in all.

Prospectors had staked out all the creeks around the Klondike by 1899. At first they just shovelled gravel into a pan and washed it with water. The gold nuggets were picked out of the

Dawson, 1899.

pan and stuffed into the miner's poke (pouch). Later they rigged up rockers, a kind of baby's cradle about 1.2 metres long and 0.6 metre wide, with a strainer at the bottom. One miner shovelled in gravel while his partner poured in water and rocked the cradle. The water ran through the strainer to a second strainer, usually a woolly blanket that caught the gold dust. In larger operations men built sluice boxes and directed the water of the creeks and rivers through them. The gold was collected at the end of the sluice in a 'mud-box'. When the gold was collected, it was once again washed, dried, and then weighed. This was done at least once every day, and even more frequently in areas of rich deposits.

Dawson boomed, and within two years grew from a few shacks to a flourishing city of 25 000. It was known as a 'rip-roaring gold town' with saloons, music halls, hotels, and restaurants. By the time the gold rush died down in 1904, over $100 000 000 worth of gold had been taken from the creek beds. Huge fortunes were made. 'Big Alex' MacDonald staked half of Claim 30 on the Eldorado Creek for a sack of flour and made $20 000 000. He spent it almost as quickly, and died penniless in a log cabin. Another prospector brought his bride along to the Yukon. Whenever she needed money, she just panned the muck the men were digging up and nearly always found nuggets worth a few dollars!

In 1898 the Yukon was made a territory by the Yukon Act and given its own government. Four years later it received the right to send one member to the federal Parliament in Ottawa. Gold had sent the Yukon leaping ahead of the rest of the Canadian North.

Ontario also had a mining boom. Legend has it that in 1903 a railway worker named Alfred LaRose threw his hammer at something he thought was the eyes of a fox shining in the light of his campfire. The next day to his amazement he discovered that the hammer had hit a silver vein. His luck resulted in the world's largest silver deposit. The Timmins brothers paid LaRose $30 000 for his claim. News of the strike spread quickly and suddenly the town of Cobalt became the centre of a flourishing mining area. Thousands of small claims were staked and 584 mining companies were formed in the region. Only twenty-nine companies actually struck it rich, but those mines made many millions of dollars. The silver veins of Cobalt lay right on the surface, and not much more than a pick, shovel, and burlap bag were needed for equipment. By 1914 these mines had yielded $115 000 000 worth of silver, and silver became the second most important mineral mined in Canada.

The discovery of silver at Cobalt started exploration throughout the Canadian Shield. Up to this time the Shield was consid-

Real-estate office.

ered a wasteland of bare rock and blackflies. But attitudes
changed when silver was found at Elk Lake in 1906 and Gow-
ganda in 1907. Gold was discovered at Porcupine in 1909. That
same year a young man named Benny Hollinger and his pal
Alex Gillis decided to try their luck on the Canadian Shield.
They set out with $250 between them and discovered a mine
near Timmins that was to become the second biggest gold producer in Canada. The Dome and McIntyre Mines were also
established in the same area, and by 1914 the annual production
of gold in Ontario was over $6 000 000.

The settlement of the West, the wheat, railways, and mining
booms all combined to make Canada's economy leap ahead
between 1900 and 1914. All regions of Canada shared in the
prosperity to some degree. Rails and locomotives were built in
the steel mills of the Maritimes. Ploughs, binders, mowers, furniture, and clothing for thousands of new settlers were manufactured in the factories of Quebec and Ontario. Lumber for railway
construction came from British Columbia. There was gold in the
Yukon and rich silver and gold mines in Ontario. These were
indeed golden years of prosperity for Canada!

In the early 20th century Canada became a major exporting
nation. Wheat was still Canada's most important export, but it

was followed in order by lumber, cheese, fish, silver, flour, livestock, and meat products. Between 1891 and 1911, Canada's exports tripled in dollar value. Canada was on its way to becoming an important international trading nation.

Digging Deeper

The railway building boom assisted all aspects of the economy in Canada. Draw two columns in your note book. In the left hand column make a list of all the materials that would be required for the railway boom. (Remember that railways are more than trains and track.) In the right hand column make a list of the industries that would benefit from making these materials for the railway boom.

1

Why were the North West Mounted Police requiring prospectors to carry in so many supplies? Make a list of the equipment and supplies you think you would need to survive for a year and mine for gold in the Yukon.

2

Four Victorian Order nurses were sent to the Klondike by Lady Aberdeen, wife of the Governor-General. Lady Aberdeen had organized the public health nursing service in 1897. What functions could the Victorian Order nurses provide in Dawson City? How would the presence of the four nurses in Dawson City bring favourable publicity to their newly formed organization?

3

Read some of the poems of Robert Service, such as 'The Trail of '98' and 'The Spell of the Yukon'. What reasons does the poet suggest for the 'gold fever' that sent thousands of men into the Klondike looking for gold?

4

5

CANADA: BETWEEN BRITAIN AND THE UNITED STATES

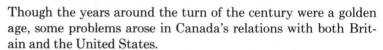

Though the years around the turn of the century were a golden age, some problems arose in Canada's relations with both Britain and the United States.

Difficulties first came with Britain. The great issue of Laurier's day was imperialism. Imperialism was a policy of having colonies and building an empire. Colonies provided a source of raw materials, a market for manufactured goods, a great deal of prestige, glory, and military strength for the mother country. In the later days of Queen Victoria, imperialism triumphed in Britain. There was a tremendous feeling of pride that Britain had extended its rule over many countries and colonies. What was to be Canada's place within the British Empire? In England and in English Canada, the imperialist movement was very strong and popular. As prime minister, Laurier had to walk a tightrope. Most French Canadians were anti-imperialists and felt little sense of pride or responsibility in belonging to the British Empire. Laurier had to frame policies that would be popular in both English and French Canada.

The Boer War

In 1899 war broke out in South Africa, where the discovery of gold and diamonds had attracted many British settlers. Trouble developed between the British and the Boers, who were the descendents of the early Dutch colonists. While the war did not directly concern Canada, the British government asked Canada to send soldiers as 'proof of the unity of the Empire'. Many Canadians were anxious to take part. English Canada said 'Yes' to the imperialist request, and French Canada said 'No'. Quebec politicians such as Henri Bourassa argued that Canada should not get involved in any of Britain's imperialist wars. Bourassa was a French-Canadian nationalist who wanted people to think of themselves as Canadians, rather than as members of the British Empire.

Laurier tried to provide a solution through compromise that would satisfy both the English and the French. The compromise worked out by Laurier was that Canada would not send an official army to South Africa. Canada would equip and transport 1000 volunteers, but they would be part of the British forces once they arrived in Africa. In the end Canada sent about 7300 volunteers to South Africa and spent $2 800 000 in their support.

Laurier's compromise did not fully satisfy anyone. Imperialists felt that Canada had let Britain down while many French-Canadian nationalists felt Laurier had done too much. In spite of the differences in attitude to Laurier's compromise solution, his government was returned to power in the election of 1900.

The Alaska Boundary Dispute 1903

Canada and the United States came into conflict over the border between Alaska and Canada. When the United States purchased Alaska from Russia in 1867, the deal included the 'panhandle'. This was a strip of coastline extending south from Alaska as far as Prince of Wales Island. The wording of the old treaty was fuzzy, but no one cared very much until the discovery of gold in the Yukon. As thousands of prospectors flooded into the Klondike during the Gold Rush, the ownership of the land through which they passed became very important.

The old treaty set the boundary of the panhandle along 'the summit of the mountains situated parallel to the coast'. The Americans said that this meant a boundary line following the jagged coastline. This would mean that seaports such as Skagway, Dyer, and Juneau would be in American territory. The Canadians argued that the boundary should be measured from the mountains nearest the ocean. This would give Canada direct access to the Pacific Ocean by way of several deep inlets. Gold could be brought out of the Yukon and supplies brought in without passing through American ports. The Americans were determined to keep as much land as they could. President Theodore Roosevelt threatened to send troops to Alaska to protect the American claim.

Eventually it was decided to submit the boundary dispute to a court of six judges. Three judges were appointed by the United States, and Roosevelt made sure these three men thought that the American claim was right. Three judges were chosen by Britain. Two of the judges appointed by the British government were Canadians; the third was Lord Alverstone, an Englishman.

After a full month of discussion the tribunal decided 4 to 2

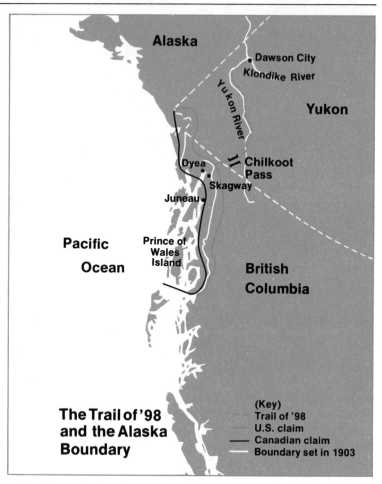

The Trail of '98 and the Alaska Boundary

(Key)
Trail of '98
U.S. claim
—— Canadian claim
Boundary set in 1903

against Canada. Lord Alverstone had sided with the Americans. Britain was facing growing problems with Germany in Europe, and was therefore not willing to risk losing its friendship with the United States at this time.

When the decision was announced, Canadians were outraged. There was hostility towards the United States because Canadians thought they had been bullied by their much more powerful southern neighbour. At the same time Canadians felt bitter resentment towards Britain and Lord Alverstone. It appeared that Britain had let Canada down in this confrontation with the United States. The reaction in Vancouver was so hostile that the *Victoria Colonist* reported on 23 October 1903 that some hot-headed citizens had pledged 'they will not sing 'God save the King' again until England has justified itself in the eyes of Canada.'

One good thing did come out of the Alaska boundary dispute. It was decided in 1909 to set up the International Joint Commission to settle peacefully any future disputes that might arise between Canada and the United States. This permanent commission would deal with all matters concerned with boundary waters or rivers along the Canadian-American border. In the future this commission would solve many controversies between these two North-American neighbours in a friendly manner.

Imperial Relations and the Naval Crisis

In 1902 and 1907 important meetings were held of all member countries of the British Empire. At these conferences Joseph Chamberlain, the British Colonial Secretary, argued for his idea of imperial federation. Chamberlain wanted one imperial parliament in Britain for the whole Empire to handle matters of trade, defence, and foreign affairs. The parliaments of each of the colonies would be responsible for only local concerns. Laurier had steadfastly opposed the idea of a common defence and foreign policy for all of the Empire.

By 1909, however, the possibility of a war against Germany dominated Canada's relations with Britain. At a special meeting held that year, the colonial delegates heard that Britain was facing a crisis. Without help from its colonies, Britain would soon fall behind in a race with Germany to have the largest navy in the world. The British emphasized that they were now facing a major emergency. They wanted Canada and the other Dominions to contribute funds to build ships for the British navy.

This became a crisis for Canada. It was just as serious an issue between English and French Canada as the Boer War had been. Should Canada add to the British navy, or develop its own navy? Every aspect of the problem threatened to separate French and English Canadians.

Again Laurier offered a compromise – the Naval Service Bill. Canada would have a navy of its own under the control of the Canadian government. In the time of an emergency the Canadian navy could be placed under Imperial control with the consent of Parliament. Service in the navy would be voluntary. Five cruisers and six destroyers would be built immediately. Canadian naval bases would be established at Esquimalt, British Columbia and Halifax, Nova Scotia.

A storm of protest in Canada greeted Laurier's Naval Service Bill. On the one hand, Bourassa and some French-Canadian nationalists complained that this policy would mean that Canadians could be sent anywhere at any time to fight Britain's imperialist wars. On the other hand, the Conservatives, led by Robert Borden, attacked the bill. They thought Canada should make an outright contribution to the British navy. They accused Laurier of setting up a 'tin-pot Canadian navy' when an immediate contribution to the British navy was urgently need-ed. Laurier admitted that when Britain is at war, Canada is also at war. However, he made it clear that Canada would decide the extent of its participation in future wars.

Reciprocity

The last great issue that faced the Laurier government was reci-procity. Reciprocity means that an arrangement exists between two countries who have agreed to trade certain products without tariffs or taxes on them. In December 1910 a large group of west-ern farmers massed on Parliament Hill in Ottawa. They com-plained of high prices caused by high tariffs on farm products and materials. The farmers demanded a policy of free trade between Canada and the United States.

The farmers in western Canada had a legitimate complaint. In general they did not share as fully as the industrialists in the national prosperity. They had to pay high freight rates to the eastern railway companies to ship their grain and supplies. They were charged high interest rates on money they borrowed from banks. When they visited friends or relatives across the border in the western American states, they were annoyed to discover that farm machinery cost half as much as it did back home in Canada. High costs were blamed on Ontario and Quebec manu-facturers who grew rich because of the tariffs that kept out for-eign competition.

Laurier was prepared to try to do something about the farm-ers' complaints. He managed to work out a reciprocity agreement with the Americans. Canadian products of farms, fisheries, forests, and mines were to be allowed into the United States free of tariffs. Taxes on American items coming into Can-ada, such as farm implements, automobiles, building materials, and canned goods would be lowered. It was the kind of tariff deal that every Canadian government since Confederation had been trying to make with the United States. When news of the proposed agreement became known the leader of the Conserva-tive party, Robert Borden, became so discouraged that he wanted to resign. It seemed impossible that the Laurier Liberals could be defeated in the next election. But Borden was per-suaded to stay on and fight it out.

Then the tide turned. Laurier's right hand man, Clifford Sif-ton, was opposed to reciprocity. He joined seventeen other wealthy Liberals in fighting the idea. Businessmen, manufactur-ers, and bankers of both political parties were afraid that cheaper American goods in Canada would put them out of busi-ness. Canadian railway builders such as C.P.R.'s president Wil-liam Van Horne, who for years had been constructing east-west lines in Canada, feared they would be ruined if trade suddenly

A NEW FIELD FOR CONQUEST.

became north-south. Canadian nationalists felt that most Canadian natural resources should be kept at home and not shipped across the border. Anti-American feelings were still strong in Canada from the decision made over the Alaska boundary dispute.

The Americans did not help Laurier in any way. In fact they provided his opposition with all kinds of ammunition. President Taft of the United States forecast that Canada was at the parting of the ways with Britain. Another prominent American politician, Champ Clark, declared that he was all for reciprocity. Clark remarked, 'I hope to see the day when the American flag will float over every square kilometre of the British North American possessions, clear to the North Pole.'

That was enough ammunition for the Conservatives. They waved the British flag in every campaign speech during the election of 1911. They preached an anti-American policy. They warned that if reciprocity passed, it would mean a political as well as economic takeover of Canada by the United States. Borden campaigned with the slogan 'No truck or trade with the Yankees'.

In the election of 1911, Laurier's Naval Bill was also an important issue. Anti-imperialists like Bourassa joined forces with the Conservatives and supporters of imperialism to defeat Wilfrid Laurier. The Laurier government probably would have survived the crisis of the Naval Bill had it not been for the added complication of the issue of reciprocity with the United States.

UNCLE SAM—"I CAN ALMOST HEAR THEM SINGING 'THE STAR SPANGLED BANNER' IN OTTAWA, BE GOSH."

The headlines of 22 September 1911 told the election results: THE GOVERNMENT GOES DOWN TO DEFEAT (*The Globe*), CONSERVATIVES SWEEP COUNTRY, RECIPROCITY KILLED (*The Mail and Empire*).

Two issues were central in the Liberals' defeat: the Naval Service Bill and introducing free trade with the United States. French-speaking Canadians did not want to become involved in British imperialist disputes. English-speaking Canadians did not want to be taken over by American economic interests. However, a great many Canadians may have been ready for a change of government, and were willing to find any reason to vote against the Liberal government that had been in power almost fifteen years. Neither Laurier's great personal charm nor his program could save the Liberals from defeat in 1911, and Sir Wilfrid was never again to be prime minister of Canada. He died on 17 February 1919.

Digging Deeper

1

a) What were the causes of the Boer War?
b) How did English Canadians and French Canadians react to the British request for Canadian assistance in South Africa? Why?

c) Make a list of the possible solutions open to the Laurier government. What might have been the potential outcome of each solution?

d) Explain and evaluate the eventual compromise worked out by Prime Minister Laurier.

In 1903, F.H. Turnock, a Canadian journalist, discussed the anti-British feeling caused by the Alaska boundary dispute:

2

The callousness, the selfishness, and the bad faith with which Canadians consider Britain has treated Canada in this matter will long rankle in the breasts of Canadians. It is bound to affect Canada's destiny. What the ultimate outcome may be, it is perhaps too early yet to predict. But it will sensibly loosen the tie which binds Canada to Great Britain. It will quench the spirit of Imperialism which has for some time been growing in Canada. Canadians now realize how little their services in the cause of the [British] Empire have been appreciated.

Account for and describe the anti-British feeling triggered by the Alaska boundary dispute.

Role-play: Reciprocity. Assign the following roles to various members of the class.

3

  i) President of the C.P.R.;
 ii) a Saskatchewan wheat farmer;
iii) a fisherman in Prince Edward Island;
 iv) an Ontario manufacturer of farm implements;
  v) a housewife;
 vi) an owner of a meat canning factory in Quebec;
vii) a worker on the docks of British Columbia;
viii) the wife of a worker in a Canadian steel company;
 ix) a pro-British imperialist;
  x) a wealthy Conservative businessman;
 xi) a French-Canadian Liberal.

Each student prepares arguments for or against reciprocity depending on the role assigned. Then stage a public meeting in the class to debate the issue 'Is reciprocity a good policy for Canada in 1911?' A vote can be taken in the class in order to reach a consensus.

How would you have voted in the election of 21 September 1911?

4

Cartoon Study:

1. Who are the characters in the cartoons on pages 49 and 50?
2. What event is being portrayed?
3. What is the message of the cartoons?
4. Decide whether the newspapers publishing these cartoons were for or against Laurier's policies.
5. How does the cartoonist's point of view differ from your own?

Document Study:

Henri Bourassa published a pamphlet titled 'Why the Navy Act Should be Repealed [cancelled]' in Montreal in 1912.

> Let the Navy Act be repealed.
> Above all, let our system of transportation, by land and by water, be completed without a minute's loss. While we are talking 'battleships', populations, drawn to western Canada by alluring advertisements, are clamouring for the means of selling and shipping their wheat. If our politicians lose their time in trying to save the British fleet and the motherland in spite of the British people, they may suddenly awaken from their magnificent dreams of Imperialism, and be confronted with serious troubles in Canada by their neglect to secure Canada's economic safety and national unity.
> Let Canada first be looked after .... If in order to do other people's work, we neglect our own, neither the British nor the Australians will come and help us in setting our house in order.

1. What arguments does Henri Bourassa put forward for cancelling the Navy Act?
2. What help does he think Canada should give to the British Empire and why?
3. Rewrite the last paragraph in your own words.
4. Why would a French-Canadian nationalist be likely to feel this way about Britain?

Document Study:

The Kingston *Daily Standard* published the following document about reciprocity on 20 September 1911.

WORKINGMEN, YOUR JOBS ARE IN DANGER. THAT IS WHAT RECIPROCITY MEANS TO YOU!

IT WILL AT ONCE ROB OUR EAST-AND-WEST RAILWAYS OF MUCH OF THEIR BUSINESS. THE LOCAL INDUSTRIES WILL BE HIT. THE PORT OF KINGSTON WILL BE BADLY CRIPPLED. THIS MEANS THAT RAILWAY HANDS AND DOCK HANDS WILL BE DISCHARGED, AND WILL COMPETE IN OUR LABOUR MARKET. WE WILL HAVE NO MORE WORK TO SHARE: BUT MANY MORE WORKERS TO SHARE IT. COMPETITION WILL BEAT WAGES DOWN.

THEN OUR DOCK LABOURERS WILL BE OUT OF WORK; FOR OUR SHIPPING WILL GO TO AMERICAN PORTS. AGAIN, LABOUR ON THE MARKET WILL CUT WAGES.

CERTAIN LOCAL INDUSTRIES WILL BE CRIPPLED OR SMASHED. AMERICAN FIRMS WILL STOP BUILDING BRANCHES IN CANADA. LESS WORK, AGAIN; AND MORE WORKERS. OUR FACTORIES WILL RUN ON SHORT TIME, AND WAGES WILL FALL.

THEN TAFT AND THE GRAIN GROWERS SAY THAT RECIPROCITY WILL LEAD TO 'FREE TRADE IN EVERYTHING.' THAT MEANS THE CLOSING OF ALL PROTECTED INDUSTRIES. IT PROBABLY MEANS THE CLOSING OF YOUR INDUSTRY.

AWAY GOES YOUR OWN JOB.

VOTE AGAINST RECIPROCITY, KEEP THE PRICE OF LABOUR UP AND THE 'COST OF LIVING' DOWN.

1. To whom was the *Daily Standard* appealing and why?
2. What arguments did it put forward to try to prove its case?
3. How convincing were these arguments and why?
4. What do you think of this type of appeal? Can you think of modern examples of this sort of appeal?

IMPORTANT THEMES
IN THIS UNIT

Economics

1. Increasing prosperity
   and growth
2. Settlement of the West
3. The wheat boom
4. New railway construction
5. Gold and silver mining
6. Reciprocity

Canada and the United States

1. Advertising for settlers
2. Alaska boundary dispute
3. International Joint Commission
4. Reciprocity
5. Election of 1911

French-English Relations

1. Early settlement of Canada
   by the French
2. The Conquest 1759-60
3. Manitoba Schools Question
4. Differences over Imperialism,
   Boer War, and Naval Service Act
5. Bourassa and French-Canadian
   nationalism

THE
LAURIER
ERA

Canada and the World

1. Advertising in Europe for
   settlers
2. Canada becomes an exporting
   nation
3. Foreign policy largely
   determined by British Empire

Women

1. Inequality between man
   and woman
2. Women organize for change

Multiculturalism

1. Cultural origins of
   settlers to Canada
2. Discrimination against
   newcomers

People and Lifestyles

1. Living in Canada in 1901
2. Differences between rich
   and poor
3. Living in the city
4. Gold Rush
5. Robert Borden, Alexander
   Graham Bell, Nellie McClung

Labour

1. Labour criticizes 'Open
   Door' policy

1896-1911

Regional Development

1. Gold develops the Yukon
2. Alberta and Saskatchewan
   become provinces
3. Wheat in the West
4. Mining in the Canadian
   Shield

Politics

1. Laurier's leadership
   as prime minister
2. 'Open Door' policy
3. Government supports
   railway building
4. Yukon becomes a
   territory
5. Laurier's compromises

Canada and Britain

1. Death of Queen Victoria
2. Victoria's Diamond Jubilee
3. Advertising for settlers
4. Imperialism
5. Boer War
6. Bitterness over Alaska
   boundary decision
7. Imperial Federation
8. Naval Crisis

National Identity

1. Canadians – still British?
2. Anti-American feelings

Technology

1. Inventions

War and Peacekeeping

1. Boer War

6
MURDER AT SARAJEVO

Sarajevo was a sleepy little city in Austria-Hungary. On Sunday morning, 28 June 1914, its citizens were getting ready to welcome Archduke Franz Ferdinand and his wife Sophia. The Archduke was an important visitor because he would someday be their ruler, the emperor of Austria-Hungary. That day the Archduke was in uniform – a light-blue tunic, black trousers, and a hat topped with large green ostrich feathers. Sophia looked beautiful in a high-collared white dress and a white hat.

As a four-car motorcade drove the royal couple towards the town hall at 10:00 a.m., someone threw a bomb. The bomb exploded against the hood of the dark-green limousine without hurting the Archduke. The tour continued. At the town hall the Archduke complained angrily to the mayor, 'I come here on a visit and get bombs thrown at me. It is outrageous!' Both the mayor and chief of police assured the Archduke there would be no more danger. The visitors' cars moved on to the governor's palace. Several minutes later, a nineteen-year-old, Gavrilo Princip, stepped up to the car and fired two shots from a pistol at point-blank range. The first shot hit the Archduke in the throat; the second hit Sophia in the stomach. Franz Ferdinand, blood pouring from his mouth, saw that his wife was wounded. 'Sophia,' he cried, 'don't die! Keep alive for our children.' However, both died on the way to the hospital.

Archduke Franz Ferdinand and his wife Sophia.

Meanwhile, Gavrilo Princip swallowed poison. The poison failed to work. Within minutes Princip and five others were rounded up by the police. They were members of a Serbian terrorist group known as the Black Hand. Their plan had been to murder the Archduke and then to commit suicide. As it turned out, three of the terrorists were hanged and three others, including Princip, died in prison.

That day a friend of the assassins sent a message to the Serbian capital. It read, 'Excellent sale of both horses.' Members of the Black Hand in Serbia knew exactly what this code meant. What they could not know was the terrible effect those two shots would have on world history.

The shots fired that day were the immediate cause of World War I. However, in explaining an historical event as complex as a world war, there are many background causes to be investigated. No single cause ever adequately explains why an historical event happened. There are always a number of causes to explain something as complicated as a world war. To understand World War I, some of the causes must be traced back to the late nineteenth century.

THE BACKGROUND OF WORLD WAR I

The countries that went to war in 1914 were Britain, France, and Russia on one side, and Germany and Austria-Hungary on the other. France and Germany had been enemies for centuries. Each had tried to find other countries to be its friends or allies in case of future wars. Just as two or three children sometimes band together for safety or protection against a bully on their street, so countries also banded together for protection against threatening enemies. The process of banding together is called forming alliances. France had allied itself with Russia and Britain in what was known as the Triple Entente. Germany, on the other hand, made the Triple Alliance consisting of itself, Austria-Hungary, and Italy. These countries of the Triple Alliance were also known as the Central Powers. When the war did start, Italy left the Central Powers to join the Triple Entente.

Thus at the time of the assassination of Archduke Franz Ferdinand, Europe was already divided into two hostile camps. The alliances were dangerous because they increased fear and suspicion among rival nations. With alliances, a war between two countries would likely involve many more!

Nationalism

Nationalism is a feeling of deep loyalty to one's nation. In Europe of the 19th century it was a powerful force helping people of the same culture to come together to form strong nations. But by the early 20th century, extreme nationalism was one of the forces causing problems. People under its spell seemed willing to take any action to help their own nation, regardless of the effect on others. They were even ready to start wars to promote the interests of their motherland.

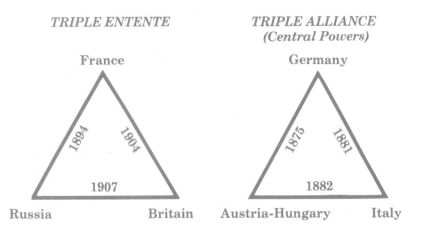

A strong feeling of nationalism existed in the small country of Serbia in the early 1900s. Serbia was a nation bordering on the Austrian province of Bosnia. Many people of Serbian descent lived in Bosnia and bitterly disliked being under Austrian control. Some Serbs and Bosnians, who thought that Bosnia should be a part of Serbia, formed the terrorist organization known as the Black Hand. Their motto was 'Union [with Serbia] or Death'. Gavrilo Princip belonged to the Black Hand which claimed responsibility for the assassination of the Archduke Ferdinand. The Austrians were also expressing feelings of nationalism when they strongly opposed the attempts of any group to break away from their empire.

Thus nationalism was causing suspicion and jealousy in the world in the early 1900s.

Imperialism

During the late 19th and early 20th centuries, the nations of Europe became more industrialized. As a result the spirit of imperialism became increasingly important. This is a policy of controlling lands far from home as colonies and building an empire. Colonies are a source of raw materials and a market for manufactured goods. They also give the mother country glory and military strength.

Kaiser Wilhelm II.

By the early 20th century, France owned large areas in northwest Africa and the Far East. Russia controlled a vast empire across northern Europe and Asia. The largest empire was owned by Britain. Its empire included Canada, Australia, New Zealand, India, Burma, Malaya, South Africa as well as parts of Africa, the East and West Indies, and islands in the Pacific. The United States had gained power in the Pacific by taking the Hawaiian and Philippine Islands. Germany also wanted its share of colonies and world markets. But by the time Germany began to build an empire, all that remained for it were some territories in Africa and the Pacific that were not particularly valuable.

Imperialism led to frequent quarrels among the great powers of Europe in all parts of the world. Arguments over colonies and trade constantly threatened peace.

Militarism

Closely related to nationalism and imperialism was the rise of militarism. Militarism is the belief in the power of armies and navies to decide issues. Leaders of the armed forces insisted that the only way to guarantee peace was by preparing for war. If a nation was strong, they argued, no enemy would dare to attack it. If a war did start, the militarized nation would be able to defend itself. This kind of thinking led to an arms race. Each country produced steel battleships, high-powered cannons, and explosives. Each tried to have a bigger and more deadly war machine than its rival. The size of armies and navies was

H.M.S. Dreadnought, a British battleship.

increased in the race to be the largest and most powerful nation in Europe. Britain was particularly upset by the fact that Germany was building a huge navy. Britain was an island. Britain depended on its giant navy to 'rule the waves' to guarantee its safety. By building a powerful navy, Germany challenged Britain's supremacy at sea.

Thus, as the nations of Europe became more militarized, they became increasingly suspicious and alarmed by each others' military power.

When Princip fired those two fateful shots on the morning of 28 June 1914, Europe was already divided into two well-armed hostile camps. In the next few weeks a chain reaction of events gradually entangled the Central Powers and the Triple Entente (or the Allies, for short) in a major war. The Austro-Hungarian government blamed the Serbian government for the deaths of the Archduke and Sophia. Austria-Hungary saw the assassination as an opportunity to crush Serbian nationalism once and for all. With Germany's support, it sent Serbia an ultimatum. An ultimatum is a demand by one government that another government accept its terms or face the threat of war. In the ultimatum the main terms that Austria-Hungary insisted on were that Serbia should

1. put down all forms of nationalist hatred against Austria-Hungary;
2. punish all those involved in the assassination plot;
3. allow Austro-Hungarian officials to enter Serbia to help crush all terrorist movements such as the Black Hand.

The Serbs were given forty-eight hours to reply to the ultimatum. The Serbs agreed to all these conditions except one. They refused to allow Austro-Hungarian officials into their country. Austria-Hungary took this as a complete refusal of its ultimatum, and declared war on Serbia on 26 July 1914. Russia, considering itself a friend and 'big brother' of the Serbs, started to mobilize its armies (get them ready for war). France, as Russia's ally, also mobilized its forces for war. Germany now felt threatened by the actions of its two neighbours, France and Russia. Germany ordered them to stop mobilizing. When they refused, Germany declared war on Russia on 1 August 1914, and on France on 2 August 1914. The German plan of attack on France was to invade through the small, neutral nation of Belgium. Up to this point Britain was not at war. However, Britain had signed a treaty guaranteeing to protect the neutrality of Belgium. When Belgium was invaded, Britain decided to act and declared war on Germany. In London, England, that evening, Sir Edward Grey, British Foreign Secretary, told a friend, 'the lamps are going out all over Europe. We shall not see them lit again in our lifetime.' By midnight on 4 August 1914, all the countries of the two alliances except Italy were at war. The world war had begun!

WAR!

In Canada the giant headline on the front page of the *Toronto Star* announced the news simply: WAR! When Britain entered war with Germany, Canada and the other countries of the British Empire were automatically at war too. The reason for this was that the colonies were still not independent. They could neither declare war nor make peace. All across Canada, in cities, towns, and villages, there was widespread support of Canada's involvement in the war. In 1914 Canada had close ties with Britain and the monarchy. It was natural that Canadians would want to aid Britain in its hour of need. Most politicians agreed.

Laurier was on record as having said, 'There is in Canada but one mind and one heart ... When Britain is at war, Canada is at war also.' Even Henri Bourassa, the nationalist spokesman for French Quebec, agreed that it was Canada's duty 'to contribute within the bounds of her strength ... to the triumph and to the endurance of the combined efforts of France and England.' In Montreal both French and English Canadians linked arms in the street and sang 'La Marseillaise', the French national anthem, and the patriotic song 'Rule Britannia'. Across Canada

Canadian Army Service Corps at Camp Niagara.

there was a strong conviction that the Allies must be supported.

The beginning of the war was welcomed with enthusiasm in Canada. Sir Sam Hughes, Minister of Militia and Defence, ordered an immense camp constructed at Valcartier, near Quebec City. When the call went out for volunteers, recruiting offices across the country were flooded with men willing to fight for a private's pay of $1 a day. Wealthy and patriotic men donated machine-guns and trucks. Everyone believed the war would be short, glorious, and full of adventure. Within the first two months, over 30 000 men had been recruited and were on their way across the Atlantic Ocean. Most thought that the war would be over by Christmas. Who could have known it would take more than four years and the involvement of another 400 000 Canadians before peace would return to the world?

The Events of the War

The war that began in August 1914 eventually became a world conflict. At first it involved seven countries, but by its end thirty countries were involved, including the United States. It was a world war in the sense that fighting was not limited to Europe. Battles were also fought in African jungles, Asia, and the Pacific and Atlantic Oceans. In Europe there were four major fronts or lines of battle which are indicated on the following map.

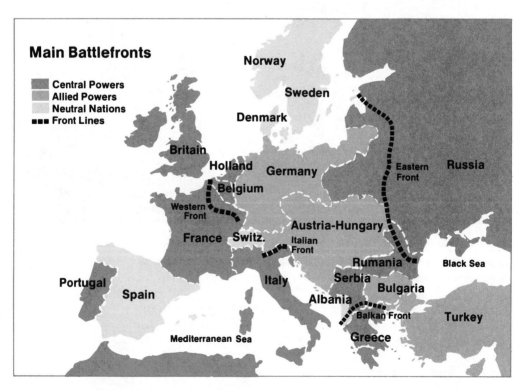

1. Locate four main fronts of the war.
2. Identify the countries that joined with the members of the Central Powers.
3. Identify the countries fighting with Britain and France.
4. Identify the European countries that had decided to remain neutral.

Canadian forces made their greatest and most significant contribution to the war effort along the Western Front.

Digging Deeper

The diagram in the text shows how the Triple Entente and the Triple Alliance were formed.
a) Which alliance was made first?
b) Which two nations formed the first agreement? In what year?
c) When was the Triple Alliance completed?
d) Which European nation was the last to join an alliance?

1

Why did the system of alliances make countries feel safer?
At the same time, how did alliances make a major war more likely?

2

When the Triple Entente was formed, Germany complained that it was being surrounded. Examine the map of Europe on page 62. How justified was Germany's complaint that it was being encircled?

3

If there had been a United Nations in 1914, do you think war could have been averted?

4

Which of the following do you consider to be the most important of the causes which brought about World War I: nationalism, imperialism, militarism, alliances, or propaganda? Why?

5

In 1914 Europe was divided into two armed and hostile camps that alarmed each other. Were the alliances the cause or the effect of the build-up of armies and navies? Is there any parallel in the world situation today? Can the arms race today be slowed down or stopped? If so, how? If not, is war inevitable?

6

When officials of Austria-Hungary proposed to enter Serbia to track down the Archduke's assassins, Serbia insisted this would violate its national sovereignty. National sovereignty is a nation's right to run its own affairs. Does this seem like a reasonable position to you? Explain your answer.

7

7

HORROR ON THE WESTERN FRONT

During August 1914 German forces swept through Belgium and into northeastern France. The Germans wanted to capture Paris before the British and Russians could fully mobilize their armies. Within a few short weeks they had advanced almost to the outskirts of Paris. The Allies moved faster than the Germans expected. Using every available vehicle – including the taxicabs of Paris – the French rushed troops to the front. With British help, the German advance was stopped at the Marne River. Gradually the Allies managed to drive the Germans back to the River Aisne. By October 1914 both sides decided to strengthen and secure their positions by digging in before winter. They dug rows of deep trenches. These were protected by machine-guns and barbed wire. The lines of trenches soon stretched several hundred kilometres from the English channel to the border of Switzerland. These parallel trenches twisted and turned across the countryside, separated in some places by only twenty-five metres. The corridor between the enemy trenches was called a no-man's-land. This strip of land was armed with buried land mines and covered with barbed-wire entanglements. Any soldier who ventured into this area was an easy target for enemy fire. Sometimes the men who died in no-man's-land could not even be buried because it was not safe to go to bring back their bodies. Often the wounded in no-man's-land could not be brought into safety. The men in the trenches could do nothing but listen to the cries of agony of their dying comrades.

The front-line trenches were dug as deep as possible until water began to seep in. Usually this was about two or more metres deep. The diagram illustrates how the firing lines were linked by traverses. This zigzag layout helped prevent enemy fire from sweeping along the whole length of the trench. From the front-line trenches, communication trenches were dug back to a line of support trenches. Here at the rear were command posts and reserve companies of soldiers. Sometimes small trenches, known as saps, probed out into no-man's-land to serve as lookout posts.

Trench warfare

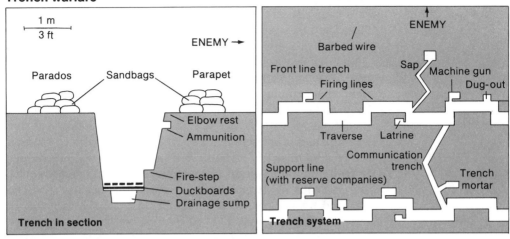

In wet weather the trenches became slippery and waterlogged. Even though wooden floorboards (duckboards) were placed in the bottom of the trenches, the men often stood in water up to their knees. The soldiers slept where and when they could, often standing up or slumped against the sandbags. At other times they crawled into crude underground dugouts carved in the walls of the trenches.

The early days there, for the first winter, oh boy, I want to tell you, primitive living alright. They were packed into a lot of dugouts, six or seven or eight men all pushed in together as tight as they could go, and wet right straight through. We never took off our shoes or our clothes, we just slept in them. But we'd take any sandbags that were halfway dry and pull them over our feet and tie them one on top of the other, four or five on each leg. Your body heat and that of the other men would more or less heat the place, provided it wasn't too drafty. And in the morning when you woke up, why the outside sandbag would be soaking wet ...

Because men were constantly cold, wet, and dirty, sickness and disease spread rapidly. Two of the most common illnesses were trench foot and trench mouth. The former was rotting of the flesh between and around the toes. The latter was a painful infection of the gums. Everyone had body lice living in their mud-caked uniforms. Rats as big as alley cats ran through the trenches feeding on the garbage and human waste. No wonder some men suffered nervous breakdowns under the stress. These were the shell-shock cases who were sometimes physically unharmed, but whose minds and will to fight were destroyed.

Meals were monotonous, with little variety. Most times they consisted of 'bully' beef (tinned corn beef), bread or hard biscuits, and hot tea. Occasionally there was stew, which was mostly vegetables and not much meat. The soldiers looked forward to packages from friends and families at home in Canada. Then they received treats of chocolate, fruit cakes, and tins of jam.

Night-time was the worst time in the front trenches. Men were tense and watchful of any signs of enemy attack. It was at night that raiding parties would creep across no-man's-land. They would cut through the barbed wire with wire cutters and make a surprise attack on enemy trenches with their bayonets.

Companies of soldiers manned the front lines and the support and reserve lines in rotation. Men in the support lines brought up food and ammunition through the communication trenches. They also dug new trenches and repaired old ones that had been damaged by shell fire. After a month or so in the trenches the units would be allowed to go to the rear for the chance to sleep in a dry place, to rest, to eat a decent meal, and above all, to bathe and clean up.

Canadian troops using a shell hole.

You know, the first baths we had, they didn't have any special bathing facilities, nor did they have any new replacement underwear or anything. But they had built these shacks out of any old boards they could get. There were cracks through the boards, and you could feel the wind coming through like nobody's business. You went into a dressing room section, and they had nails in the wall, big spikes, and you took off your stuff and hung it up on that. And then you went to a hole in the wall, and you threw in your underwear and your socks, and went into the bath house. The bath house had tubs made out of beer barrels cut in two – they were good and big, you see. There were ten tubs in this one that I'm thinking of. You worked in gangs of twenty men, two men to a tub. You were given a piece of yellow soap, like laundry soap, and you got two buckets of cold water and one bucket of hot water. The hot water was heated on an old boiler that they had out in the yard, which they fired with anything that would burn. The bath attendants filled the tubs, and the two men stood in a tub, washed each other with the soap, and sloshed themselves off. You were given three minutes, and then you had to get out. Then you went to another door where you got a towel to dry yourself. You went up to another wicket and you got a suit of underwear and a pair of socks. It was the old army game of one man, one shirt, and you never knew when you got them what size they were. You might be six feet tall and get a suit of underwear for a midget, and some other guy would get one where they had to roll the sleeves right up to his elbows. That's the kind of bath you got once in a dog's age when you came out. Otherwise, if the weather was halfway decent, and if you were out in the camp somewhere, all around that place there, there were shell holes that had been filled full of water. By that time, the mud would have settled, and the water would be clean – it would be rainwater. If you could get some sort of biscuit tin or something to scoop it out without disturbing the mud, you could get yourself enough fresh water to strip off and wash yourself right out there in the open. At least you could get some kind of relief in that way.

The men in the trenches must often have wondered what they were doing there. To remind them of home, the soldiers stuck up street signs naming their trenches 'Yonge Street' and 'Paradise Alley'. On Christmas Eve 1915, Canadian and German soldiers joined in signing 'Silent Night' across the shell-torn no-man's-land. Another soldier put his feelings this way:

It seemed to be that they [the Germans] didn't want to be there any more than we did. But it seemed to be that somebody else was manipulating the strings behind the line, and we were just put there to work out a game. It wasn't really hatred. Only sometimes you did hate, when you see your chums and your friends get shot. It would be pretty hard on you that way, and you could say you'd hate for a while, but not necessarily hate that you wanted to kill. But you had to kill or be killed, if you wanted to survive .... Sometimes at that time there, I felt, well, it's so unnecessary. A bunch of men, say a hundred and fifty yards or a hundred yards away – you could talk to them and you could hear them talking, hear them working, and here you was, you got to make an attack. And you had to kill them or get killed. And you would sometimes wonder what it was all about.

THE WAR ON THE WESTERN FRONT

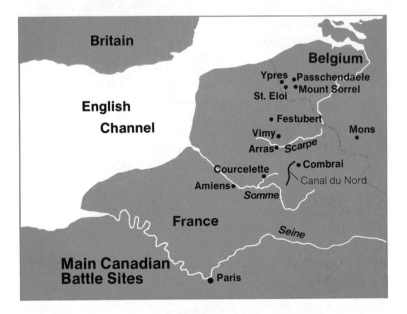

The first division of 20 000 Canadian troops took up places alongside their allies on the front lines in mid-April 1915. In the months and years that followed, they were joined by another 400 000 fellow Canadians. Some of Canada's proudest moments in the Great War are associated with battles along the Western Front. Canada's contribution will never be forgotten at Ypres, Festubert, the St. Eloi craters, Mount Sorrel, the Somme, Courcelette, Vimy Ridge, the Scarpe, Passchendaele, Amiens, Arras, the Canal du Nord, and Cambrai. A few of the major battles in which Canadians were involved are described below.

Ypres

The Canadian First Division was assigned to the front lines near the ancient city of Ypres in Belgium. Their task was to hold about three and a half kilometres of the line in the face of heavy German attack. They had only been in action for a few weeks when the Germans unleashed the first deadly poison gas. Made of chlorine, it was released from canisters when the breeze was blowing towards the Allied trenches. The chlorine gas burned eyes and throats and destroyed the lungs. Those who breathed the gas choked, gagged, gasped, coughed, and died. During the attack French-African troops positioned beside the Canadians broke ranks and fled from the poisonous gas. The Germans then came pouring through the hole in the line. The Canadians, with makeshift gas masks, managed to hold their position and eventually closed the gap in the line.

The Gas Attack at Ypres

Major-General Victor W. Odlum, commander of a Canadian battalion during the second battle of Ypres, recalls the gas attack:

I saw the whole picture of the gas attack as probably no one else did. I have never been in a battle – and I have been in many – where the men were suffering in such numbers that their crying and groaning could be heard all over the battlefield.

There were some who ran away, French, British and Canadians. These were individuals. They were young and they were terrified.

They had never seen gas before. None of us had – it was the first gas attack in history.

But not a single unit skipped out – some individuals, yes, but formations, no. In every battle someone runs away. I saw it wherever I was.

In front of us was the 8th (Canadian) Battalion: to the right were the British battalions and way to the left were French-African troops.

Suddenly we saw the gas rolling up in a brownish-yellowish bank. It was between one to three metres high and it wouldn't rise higher unless it was puffed up by the wind.

We saw the French-Africans running away choked with gas, not as a body, but as individuals. We paid no attention to them. We were sorry for them.

I went over to where the line had been broken and where there was confusion. No Canadian troops were running.

The gas was dreadful and suffering was immediate. The only thing we could do was soak our handkerchiefs in urine and hold them over our noses.

Thousands were lying around gasping and crying. They were being drowned by the gas. They didn't know how to protect themselves.

But we held our position.

The Canadians suffered dreadful casualties at Ypres. More than 5200 Canadians died, and one in five was listed as killed in action, gassed, missing, or wounded.

Later in the war even more deadly poison gases were used. Worst of all was mustard gas. This burned the skin and the respiratory tract, and caused blindness. Eventually more effective gas masks were invented that held filters through which the air could be purified.

The battle at Ypres revealed a serious problem with the rifles of the Canadian soldiers. Sir Sam Hughes insisted that Canadian forces be issued with the Ross rifle. The Ross was a good target rifle but tended to seize up under rapid-fire conditions of trench warfare. At Ypres Canadian soldiers were bitter and frustrated by the useless and inadequate weapon. Many threw their Ross rifles away in disgust, and replaced them with British Lee-Enfields obtained in any way they could get them.

Battle of the Somme

The first day of the battle along the Somme River in France – 1 July 1916 – was the most disastrous the British army had ever suffered. The Canadian corps fought as part of the British forces under the command of General Douglas Haig. For days the Allies had been pounding the German trenches with heavy gun-fire. General Haig believed that this bombardment would soften the Germans for the eventual attack. These pictures, taken at the Somme attack, record what happened in the first few minutes. At exactly 7:30 a.m. the British Officer leaped to the top of the trench, and with a wave of his cane ordered his men to go forward. The soldiers went over the top.

One man was hit as soon as his head appeared over the trench, and he fell back into the mud. The men stumbled through the barbed wire of no-man's-land heading for the German trenches. The soldiers faced a hail of German machine-gun fire. The British and Canadian attackers were mown down by the thousands. A British sergeant recorded, 'Our dead were heaped on top of each other . . . in places three and four deep.' Only a few Allied soldiers ever reached the enemy trenches. By nightfall British and Canadian casualties totalled 57 470, the heaviest ever in warfare for one day's fighting. Ninety per cent of the Royal Newfoundland Regiment were killed or wounded that day. In spite of the heavy loss of men in the first day of the attack, hardly any ground had been captured.

Despite the death toll, General Haig insisted that the attack go on. For 141 days the battle of the Somme continued. The Canadians fought so heroically at the Somme that they were marked out as storm troops, and during the rest of the war they were often brought in to lead an attack. British Prime Minister Lloyd George later wrote in his *War Memoirs*, 'Whenever the Germans found the Canadian corps coming into their line, they prepared for the worst.'

When the battle of the Somme ended five months after it began, both armies were exhausted. Casualties for both sides had reached 1 250 000, of whom 24 000 were Canadians. The British had advanced no more than eleven kilometres through shell-torn rubble. People at home were horrified and disillusioned by this massacre. Many blamed General Haig; others blamed the politicians who had started the war. To many sol-

diers the real enemy was not the Germans or the Austrians, but the war itself.

At the Somme, tanks were used for the first time in warfare. A British invention, tanks were huge armed 'land ships' weighing over twenty-five tonnes which lumbered along at less than five kilometres per hour. Their first appearance at the Somme was a bad shock for the German forces. Though they often got stuck in the mud, tanks were able to break through the barbed wire of no-man's-land. Although the British High Command did not at first appreciate the potential value of the tank, this new weapon eventually helped to win the war.

Vimy Ridge

Today a white stone Canadian war memorial stands high on Vimy Ridge. Here on Easter Monday 1917, Canada won its greatest victory. German forces had dug in on the height of land at Vimy. From this vantage point they could command control of all surrounding areas. Several unsuccessful attempts had been made by both British and French to push out the Germans. Finally, after months of preparations and weeks of heavy preparatory bombardment, 100 000 Canadians launched their attack. For the first time, all four Canadian divisions fought together. In a blinding sleet storm, they forced their way up the hill. In a few hours, the Canadians had captured the ridge. That day more ground, more guns, and more prisoners were taken than in any other Allied offensive on the Western Front in the first two and a half years of the war. It was a magnificent victory!

Four Canadians won the Victoria Cross (the most prestigious award given by Britain to its heroes) at Vimy. Major-General Currie, who led the First Division, was granted a knighthood from King George V. Tragically, 11 000 Canadian lives were lost. However, since it was the first time the Canadians had fought as a national unit, the victory was a great morale booster and a source of enormous pride. Some people said that at that moment – its first clear-cut national military success – Canada became a nation.

Passchendaele

One of the most bitter disasters for Canadians occurred at Passchendaele in the fall of 1917. Here the Canadians were ordered to advance in a sea of mud. This Belgian land had once been beneath the North Sea, and when the shelling destroyed drainage ditches, the land became waterlogged. Fighting men sometimes wept with the sheer frustration of trying to advance through the mud. Narrow duckboards were placed as pathways over the mire, but thousands of soldiers and horses who slipped into the mud were sucked in and drowned. Locomotives sank to their boilers and tanks quickly bogged down. A British official, seeing the battlefield for the first time, cried out, 'Good God! Did we really send men to fight in that?' Almost 16 000 Canadian lives were sacrificed in this insane enterprise. The offensive gained seven kilometres of mud which the Germans soon won back again.

The Last Hundred Days

By the spring of 1918, Germany's leaders realized a crisis had come. Food supplies were running short, but German submarine attacks on food ships had failed to force Britain to surrender. Now the United States had entered the war. Austria-Hungary and Turkey, Germany's allies, were on the point of collapse. The only hope for Germany seemed to be a mighty offensive on the Western Front before the United States army could arrive in Europe in large numbers. In one last desperate gamble the German generals launched a devastating attack all along the Western Front.

Thousands of Germans poured into France and were stopped only eighty kilometres from Paris. This swift advance exhausted the German troops. Supplies had failed to keep up, and the soldiers became undisciplined, looting and drinking heavily. On 8 August 1918, the battle-proven Canadians and Allies launched a counter-attack. Fresh American troops had arrived and were a great encouragement for the Allies. Now there was no stopping them! Supported by 500 tanks, the Allies swept north and east towards Germany. The Germans fought well, but they fell back steadily. Eventually France was liberated, and then Belgium. By November the Allies reached the frontiers of Germany. On 11 November 1918, at a pre-dawn ceremony, the Germans formally surrendered. Hostilities were to cease at 11:00 a.m. on that morning. For some Canadian troops the war ended on the streets of the Belgian town of Mons with General Currie taking the salute on horseback. Flags that had been hidden by the Belgians for four years while their country was occupied by Germans flew joyously. Grateful Belgians shouted, '*Vive les braves Canadians!*'

Digging Deeper

1 Use the following words correctly in a sentence to illustrate their meaning:
no-man's-land
over the top
barbed wire
crater
duckboards
sap

2 Choose a single battle, for example the Somme, Passchendaele, or Vimy Ridge. Do some research and write a detailed account of it.

3 Research and then write up the Ross rifle controversy.

4 You are a front-line soldier. Write a diary describing the conditions in the trenches.

5 Field Trip. Try to visit the National War Museum in Ottawa. As well as exhibits, it houses millions of photographs concerned with both world wars.

Or find out if you have a regimental armoury close by which you could visit. Armouries often have a museum of relics connected with their regiment's history.

Memorial plaques in local churches, town halls, and schools are valuable sources of information. Find out how many men and women from your home town or neighbourhood were killed in World War I. What was the population of your town or city at that time? It is often possible to work out what particular battles local soldiers took part in.

6 Soldiers were frequently expected to fight in intolerable conditions. For example, at Passchendaele it was almost impossible to carry on trench warfare in the mud of the battlefield. Many believed that the battle should have been stopped because of the conditions and the high number of casualties. Yet the commander ordered the fighting to continue. Would soldiers ever be justified in refusing to carry out the orders to fight? Why? Do you think military leaders were to blame for the high number of casualties? Why?

7 Research the life of Sir Arthur Currie, Canada's greatest soldier of World War I, or Sir Sam Hughes, the Minister of Militia.

8

WAR IN THE AIR, WAR AT SEA

THE WAR IN THE AIR

When the war broke out in 1914, the airplane was a new and unproven invention. The Wright brothers had made their first successful flight only eleven years before. Few military leaders had any confidence in the airplane as a weapon of war. Colonel Sam Hughes is reported to have said, 'The airplane is an invention of the Devil and will never play any part in such a serious business as the defence of a nation.'

Canada had no air force of its own, but 25 000 joined the British Royal Flying Corps. The earliest planes were usually single-seaters. Their maximum speed was between 95 and 125 kilometres per hour and they could stay airborn for only an hour without refueling. At first unarmed airplanes were used just to scout enemy troop movements behind the lines and to observe enemy strength and position. Some pilots carried pistols, rifles, and shotguns, while others threw bricks or links of rusty chain at the propellers of enemy planes!

The Germans started the war with several advantages in Europe. They had the most aircraft (400 compared to 156 French and 113 British). They had a superior plane called the Fokker, a monoplane with one set of wings. It was armed with a machine-gun whose firing mechanism was timed so that bullets did not hit its own propeller blades. The Germans also had gas-filled balloons called Zeppelin dirigibles or airships. These were used on observation missions and bombing raids. Eventually both sides used airships. By 1917, the Allies developed the Sopwith-Camel, an excellent fighter plane. Their fighting technique was to engage in aerial 'dogfights' or duels, manoeuvering their light planes to dive on the enemy from the rear.

The pilots were usually very young, daring, and brave. The percentage of men killed was higher than in any other branch of the military. In late 1916 it was said that the average life of an airman was three weeks. There were no parachutes to save those unlucky enough to be shot down. The great air aces – Germany's Manfred von Richthofen, Britain's Alfred Ball, and Canada's Billy Bishop – were a special breed of men. An ace was a fighter who had shot down at least five enemy planes. Richthofen, known also as the Red Baron, had downed eighty planes. Richthofen had icy nerves, lightning reflexes, and dead-eye aim. After each victory he ordered the date and the type of aircraft he had shot down engraved on a silver cup, until eventually the Berlin engraver ran out of space.

Few people know it was a Canadian air ace who finally shot down Germany's Red Baron. On 21 April 1918, von Richthofen, flying about the Somme Valley, spotted an Allied plane far below. He put his Fokker into a steep dive and moved in on his 81st victim. His target was an inexperienced Canadian flier, Wilfred ('Wop') May. May was helpless because his gun jammed. Fortunately, behind the German ace was another Canadian pilot, Captain Roy Brown, from Carleton Place, Ontario. Brown, in his Sopwith-Camel, opened fire on Richthofen. The Red Baron fell in a deadly spin. The dreaded German ace was dead at the age of twenty-six. Roy Brown was given the seat from the Red Baron's plane as a trophy. Today you can put your finger through the bullet hole because the seat is on display at the Royal Military Institute in Toronto.

Billy Bishop

Canadians thrilled to the victories of a reckless young pilot, W.A. 'Billy' Bishop. As a boy in Owen Sound, Ontario, Billy Bishop practised shooting at moving targets with his rifle in the woods. Now his expert marksmanship made him one of the greatest fighter pilots of the British Commonwealth. On his first day behind the front lines, he shot down a German plane. On his last day he destroyed five enemy planes. In one five-day period, Bishop destroyed thirteen planes. His total enemy kills were seventy-two.

Billy often prowled the skies alone. On one occasion he attacked a German air base near Cambrai, France. Two enemy planes rose to chase him, and Bishop shot down both of them. Two more enemy planes came up to attack the single raider. One fell from the deadly fire from Bishop's gun, and the other was driven off, out of ammunition. Billy Bishop returned safely to his home field.

By the end of the war, Billy Bishop was awarded the Victoria Cross by Britain and the highest honours of France. He was among the top three Allied air aces. He went on to become Director of Recruiting for the Royal Canadian Air Force in 1940. He died in Florida in 1956.

As a group, Canadian airmen brought down 438 enemy aircraft during World War I. Four of the top seven leading aces of the Royal Air Force were Canadians. It was a truly remarkable record!

Captain Billy Bishop.

These aces downed more than 50 enemy airplanes.

French	
Rene Paul Fonck	75
Georges Guynemer	54*

German	
Manfred von Richthofen	80*
Ernst Udet	62
Erich Loewenhardt	53*

British	
Edward Mannock	73*
William A. Bishop (Canada)	72
Raymond Collishaw (Canada)	60
James McCudden	57*
A. Beauchamp-Proctor	54
Donald MacLaren (Canada)	54
William Barker (Canada)	53

*did not survive World War I

THE WAR AT SEA

In early May 1915, the British luxury liner *Lusitania* was crossing the Atlantic Ocean on a calm sea. The unarmed ship carried almost 2000 passengers. Suddenly a torpedo streaked through the waves towards the hull of the *Lusitania*. Moments later there was an explosion, panic, chaos, and death. At sea there was a new terror. A sinister and deadly weapon had been added to naval warfare – the submarine. More than half the passengers on board the *Lusitania* that day were Americans, including many women and children. Eleven hundred and ninety-eight people were drowned. The United States, still neutral at this stage of the war, did not want to get involved with European wars. But the sinking of the helpless *Lusitania* shocked the American people and swung public opinion in the United States against Germany. Eventually it helped to bring about the entry of the United States into war against Germany.

Britain was an island and therefore command of the seas was of supreme importance to it. The country depended on its navy to keep the sea lanes open for supplies of food and raw materials. British naval policy had to make sure that supply ships got safely to British ports. At the same time the navy tried to block-ade the German coast, or control everything going in or out, so that food and war supplies could not get into Germany by sea. The German naval policy was to try to blockade Britain by means of submarines. All waters around Britain were declared a war zone. Allied merchant ships heading to British ports were to be sunk on sight by German submarines. This is what had happened to the *Lusitania* in 1915.

Both Britain and Germany began the war with strong fleets of battleships. Only once, at Jutland, off the coast of Denmark, did these two great fleets face each other. In May 1916, 149 British warships met 99 German warships head on. It was one of the most dramatic nights of the war. Within a few hours Britain had suffered greater losses both in ships and men. The German navy claimed a victory! The Germans, however, recognized the superior size of the British fleet and headed for port. After Jutland the Germans risked no more major sea battles. Their fleet remained in port. German shipyards stopped producing surface ships and started producing more submarines.

Germany's most deadly weapon was the submarine or U-boat (*Unterseebooten*). Submarines carried a crew of thirty-five men and twelve torpedoes. Torpedoes were very expensive, but could be fired underwater at a moving target. The early submarines could stay submerged for two and a half hours. However, they preferred to come to the surface and sink their enemies by gunfire. By late 1916 German submarines were sinking an average of 160 ships per month. Germany was predicting an early defeat for Britain.

By 1917 the war on the Western Front still had not been won. Germany now decided that some more drastic action had to be taken to defeat the Allies. The German navy introduced a policy of 'unrestricted submarine warfare'. This meant that German U-boats would sink any Allied or neutral ship approaching Britain.

The results of this policy were almost disastrous for Britain. In the first four months the policy was in operation, Germany sank:

February 1917 –	212 ships
March 1917 –	297 ships
April 1917 –	335 ships
May 1917 –	230 ships
Total	1074 ships

An enormous amount of much-needed cargo, as well as human lives, was being lost. An answer had to be found for the U-boat menace or Britain would be starved into surrender.

One answer was the convoy system. Instead of cargo ships sailing alone from Canada and the United States to Britain, they sailed in fleets escorted by armed destroyers. Destroyers kept constant watch like sheepdogs guarding a flock of sheep. Convoys of the necessary supplies began to get through to Britain again.

Two other methods were used to combat the threat of the U-boats. The first was the use of underwater mines which exploded on contact with submarines. The other was to employ 'Q-ships'. Q-ships were actually battleships disguised as unarmed, harmless merchant vessels. When a U-boat surfaced to attack, Q-ships would suddenly open fire from hidden guns. Many deadly U-boats were sent to the bottom of the ocean in this way.

Though the U-boats did tremendous damage to British and Allied shipping, the policy of 'unrestricted submarine warfare' backfired on Germany. The sinking of American ships by U-boats brought the United States into the war against Germany. The entrance of the Americans in 1917 helped to turn the tide in favour of an Allied victory.

Canada's main contribution to the war at sea lay in the provision of men and ships for the Royal Navy. Canadian shipyards built more than 60 anti-submarine ships and more than 500 smaller anti-submarine motor launches. Several thousand Canadians served in the British Royal Navy, in the Royal Naval Canadian Volunteer Reserve, and in the Royal Naval Air Service.

Digging Deeper

1

a) Describe the various roles played by the air force in World War I.

b) Outline the problems which might be encountered by pilots in wartime flying.

2

a) In what ways was the submarine a revolutionary new weapon?

b) Explain the defensive measures that were taken against the submarine.

3

a) Explain why Germany felt it was necessary to sink the *Lusitania*.

b) Describe the reaction of Britain and the U.S.A. to the sinking of the *Lusitania*

c) Was the sinking of the *Lusitania* a justifiable act in a time of war? Explain.

9
WAR ON THE
HOME FRONT

World War I was different from every other war that had ever
gone before it. It was total war, which meant that it involved
civilians almost as much as soldiers. This war had an effect on
everybody. And when at last it was over, life could never be the
same again.

KEEP THE HOME FIRES BURNING.

Women hold a bazaar
for war aid.

Canadians at home got behind their men overseas in many
different ways. There was a feeling that no sacrifice should be
spared to ensure a victory in Europe. Many people planted 'victory gardens' in order to produce as much food as possible. Canadians were sending large amounts of food to feed the fighting
forces as well as the civilian populations of other Allied countries. At home people were trying to waste nothing and to
reduce their own food consumption. Most people accepted 'war
bread' (bread made from inferior flour and fats instead of butter)
without too many complaints.

ADVICE TO THE HOUSEWIFE

1. Use nut-butter or margarine.
2. Remake leftover bread into new bread, cake, or pudding.
3. Instead of one beefless day, why not try for six to make up for people less patriotic?
4. Eat as little cake and pastry as you can.
5. Use oats, corn, barley, and rye instead of wheat.
6. Use ham and pork bones in other dishes.
7. Chew your food thoroughly – you will be satisfied with less.
8. All kinds of cold cereal can be saved, and when not enough to roll into balls to fry, they can be used in batter cakes and corn breads.
9. Cut each slice of bread as required.
10. Mix your own cleanser (use white sand, washing soda, soap, and chalk).
11. Fifty million dollars is thrown away in garbage cans annually.
12. Do not display the joint of meat on the table. It is an inducement to eat more than you need.
13. Do not eat both butter *and* jam with bread.

Schoolboys in Saskatchewan and other wheat-producing areas were often dismissed from school early to replace the farm workers who were overseas. Groups of women of all ages met regularly to knit socks for the soldiers and to roll bandages. Every community held card games, dances, and variety shows. The profits from these evenings were used to send cigarettes, candy, soap, writing paper, and pencils to the troops.

During 1918 the war cost Canada over one million dollars a day! Workers helped to pay the enormous costs of the war by buying Victory Bonds. Private and commercial investors loaned over one billion dollars to the government. This would be paid back with interest when the war was over. Children could also play a part by buying Thrift Stamps. Each stamp cost 25 cents and was stuck on a card. When a child had bought $4.00 worth of stamps, he or she received a War Savings Stamp. A War Savings Stamp bought before the end of 1918 could be cashed in for $5.00 in 1924.

It was at this time that the Canadian government introduced the practice of an income tax. This was supposed to be a 'temporary measure' to help finance the war. But as we know, the income tax has never been abolished. Charitable groups raised over $47 000 000 for servicemen's wives, orphans, and widows. This 'Patriotic Fund', as it was called, had as its slogan, 'If you cannot join him, you should help her.'

Agricultural and industrial production reached dramatic new heights during World War I. Especially important for the war

Women munition
workers.

effort was the production of munitions. Plants manufacturing airplanes, shells, and ships sprang up across the country. By 1918, 300 000 men and women were employed in Canada in these factories and almost one-third of the shells fired by the armies of the British Empire were being made in Canada.

The munitions industry brought the war dramatically close to home for the citizens of Halifax. Halifax was the Canadian port from which all North American convoys left. On the morning of 6 December 1917 a terrible explosion rocked the city of Halifax. The *Mont Blanc*, a French munitions ship carrying a cargo of time-bomb explosives, collided with the Belgian vessel *Imo* in the harbour. The blast levelled large sections of Halifax, killed 2000, and was heard all over the province. It was even felt in Sydney, over 320 kilometres away. It was one of the worst disasters in Canadian history. All that was ever found of the *Mont Blanc* was a cannon and part of an anchor that landed over 3 kilometres away. A frantic search for people buried in the rubble began. Halifax newspapers carried advertisements seeking information about missing persons:

Private Hilton is searching the city for his wife who is missing since the disaster. She lived at 1373 Barrington Street. Any person having information of her whereabouts, please communicate with this office.

Information required regarding Mrs. Thomas Stockall, 8 Veith Street, and her three children, Allen 7, Doherty 5, and Tommy, 3 years old.

A relief agency was quickly set up by the government to aid the victims of the Halifax disaster.

The Role of Women

World War I brought about great changes in the lives of Canadian women. The war deprived many thousands of women of their husbands, sons, fathers, and brothers. But the war also demanded a much greater involvement by women outside the home. With the general shortage of manpower in Canada, the number of women who were employed in industry rose dramatically. In many cases women started to work in occupations that would have been considered unsuitable for women before 1914. Examine these pictures and documents on the role of women and answer these questions:

1. What do these pictures and documents tell you about women's activities during the war at home and overseas?
2. What problems might women encounter doing these jobs?
3. What changes might occur in the lives of women as a result of these new responsibilities outside the home?

I had a very hard job. It had to be that you run a machine of weights into the shell, and the weight had to be just exact. Quite a few of them didn't have the patience. Well, my father brought us up that when we went on a job, we did it and did it the best we could. So the foreman was very glad. He came about four or five times a day to make sure that the weights in the shells were right. It was interesting work but very hard on your nerves. There was a machine went on fire. This friend from Beaverton was on the machine that blew up, and I run to her and we had to go down on our hands and knees and crawl out of the place. So we had a little experience of what it was to be right in a war.

We decided to become farmerettes when we read in the paper that there was a big crop and they needed people to come, and there were no men. So this friend and I said that we would go. We volunteered. Masses of young people went out and brought that all in.

I wanted to help do my share, and I joined the Red Cross and helped roll bandages and knit socks. My first ones were big enough to fit an elephant, and after that, I became very proficient – *so* proficient that I knit a pair of socks a day without any trouble.

We rolled bandages, and we distributed wool for knitting, and we would go and deliver it to older people that could do it. There were a thousand-and-one things. We made pneumonia jackets and all sorts of things.

You see, *everybody* felt they had to do something. You just couldn't sit there. There was such a thing as just doing nothing but going to afternoon teas and dances and parties, which we had done. That was *out!*

There was a phrase, 'Doing your bit.' Well, that was pretty well the keynote feeling all through that First World War. Everybody was extremely patriotic, and everybody wanted to 'do his bit'.

That was the stock phrase. I don't know who started that. It came out in some speech or other, and everybody took it up. You must 'do your bit'. And we all felt the same way. If there's anything we could do to help, we must do it.

Women, of course, all took to knitting. Every woman was knitting socks and so on for the troops overseas. And there were Bairnsfather cartoons ... he was drawing very humorous cartoons. I remember one that showed a soldier holding up a pair of socks, and the caption was:

Your parcel of socks received. Some fit!
I wear one for a helmet and one for a mitt.
I'll see you after I've done my bit,
In the meantime, where did you learn to knit?

Well, there was some pretty weird knitting done, I suppose, but also some very competent knitting.

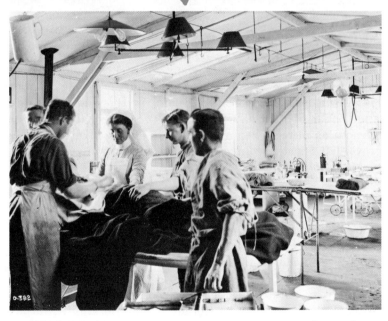

Wartime hospital.

It was during World War I that an important step forward was taken in Canada for women's rights. At the beginning of the 20th century, women in many countries had begun to organize themselves to gain the vote for women. Members of this movement were called suffragettes in Britain, and suffragists in Canada. Their purpose, however, was the same: to win the rights and opportunities that men enjoyed. Getting the vote was just the first step.

Nellie McClung was a suffragist and one of Canada's great social reformers. Born in Ontario in 1873, McClung moved west

Women haying.

as a small girl, living in both Winnipeg and Edmonton. She had tremendous ability as a speaker and a writer, and through her books and articles, she became well known across the country. She wrote, 'Certainly women belong in the home, but not twenty-four hours a day. They should have exactly the same freedom as men.' When World War I broke out, it helped to prove that Nellie McClung was right. Women were called upon to do the jobs formerly performed only by men. They did these same jobs, and they did them as well as men. They proved that women were every bit as capable of working as men. Therefore, women should have exactly the same freedom as men. The war brought women together in volunteer organizations and employment, and once together, they began to talk and dream of political equality with men.

Suffragists campaigned enthusiastically for women's suffrage (the right to vote). Their leaders included Dorothy Davis in British Columbia, Margaret Gordon in Ontario, Emily Murphy and Alice Jamieson in Alberta, and the dynamic Nellie McClung in Manitoba. The first breakthrough for women's suffrage came in Manitoba when, in 1916, women were given the right to vote in that province. Within a few months Saskatchewan, Alberta, British Columbia, and Ontario followed. The main goal of women's suffrage, of course, was to gain the right to vote in federal elections. In the election of December 1917, the government granted the vote to the mothers, sisters, and wives of the men in the Armed Forces, and Canadian nurses serving in the Canadian Armed Forces. By the time the war had ended, the right to vote in federal elections had been extended to all women in Canada over the age of twenty-one.

Conscription

The beginning of the war was welcomed with great enthusiasm in all parts of Canada. Britain was at war, and therefore Canada was at war. Canadians, especially those who were born in Britain, rushed out to volunteer for service. The country was flooded with patriotic appeals. Volunteers marched behind brass bands to the enlistment offices. Men in civilian clothes were sometimes given white feathers as a symbol of cowardice by girls in the street. This unfortunate incident happened once to a winner of the Victoria Cross who had been sent home to recover from an injury. By the end of 1916, as the war dragged on and the death list mounted, the number of volunteers began to dwindle. Obviously the war was not going to be short and glorious as Canadians had first thought.

Early in 1917 Prime Minister Robert Borden left to attend an Imperial Conference in England and to visit the Canadian soldiers at the front. Borden was shocked by the information he was given in Britain. Britain was on the brink of disaster because of the German U-boat menace. Casualties were mounting daily on the Western Front. British military officials urged Borden to send even more Canadian troops to Europe. Meanwhile in Canada volunteer enlistments were not keeping up with the number of men killed or wounded.

ENLISTMENT / CASUALTY RATE FOR 1917

MONTH	ENLISTMENTS	CASUALTIES
January	9 194	4 396
February	6 809	1 250
March	6 640	6 161
April	5 530	13 477
May	6 407	13 457
June	6 348	7 931
July	3 882	7 906
August	3 117	13 232
September	3 588	10 990
October	4 884	5 929
November	4 019	30 741
December	3 921	7 476

Borden returned home and asked Parliament to pass a conscription bill. Conscription means compulsory enlistment in the Armed Forces for all able-bodied men in Canada.

The mention of conscription brought a storm of protest in

some parts of Canada, especially in French Canada. Many English-speaking Canadians believed that the reason why the number of volunteers had fallen was simply that the province of Quebec was not doing its part. Newspapers in English Canada had pointed out that Ontario had provided 63% of the volunteers in proportion to its population, Manitoba and Saskatchewan 81%, Alberta 92%, British Columbia 104%, Maritime provinces 38%, while Quebec had only provided 20% in proportion to its population.

French Canadians simply did not share the enthusiasm that English-speaking Canadians felt for Britain's war. Nor did they feel any real tie to their country of origin, France. The French Canadians had been conquered by British forces in 1760, and deserted by France. Since that time many French Canadians felt they were being treated like second-class citizens in Canada. Louis Riel, they believed, had been hanged by the English-dominated government in Ottawa. Riel had led a rebellion of Métis and Indians against the increasing white settlement in the West. More recently, Ontario's Department of Education had limited the teaching of French in Ontario schools by a bill known as Regulation 17. French Canadians felt they were not being treated as equal partners in Confederation.

Sir Sam Hughes, Minister of Militia, also annoyed the people of Quebec. Hughes made the mistake of appointing a Protestant clergyman to supervise recruiting in Roman Catholic Quebec. He insisted on using English to train French-Canadian volunteers who often did not know the language. Very few French-speaking officers received any important army posts. Only one French-speaking regiment – the 22nd, the famous 'Vandoos' – had been sent to the Western Front to fight. At Courcelette the 22nd regiment served with outstanding distinction. However, it did seem to many French Canadians as though Hughes and his policies were doing nothing to encourage greater French-Canadian participation in the war. Eventually, in 1916, Hughes was dismissed by Borden, but not before he had done long-term damage in Quebec.

Borden knew that conscription was a dangerous idea. It could divide the French and English in Canada. Still he realized that the shortage of manpower was so severe that he had no other choice. The Military Service Bill was passed in the summer of 1917. Military service became compulsory for all males between the ages of twenty and forty-five. Men in vital wartime production jobs, the sick, or conscientious objectors were exempt from fighting. Conscientious objectors were those people who refused to fight on the grounds that war went against their moral and religious beliefs.

Those in Quebec who strongly opposed conscription were led

Wounded soldiers.

by Henri Bourassa and were known as nationalists. Bourassa was the brilliant editor of the Montreal newspaper *Le Devoir* and one of the most powerful speakers in Canadian history. Bourassa was a Canadian who believed that Canada should be independent from Britain. Just because Britain was at war, he argued, there was no reason for Canada to go to war. Bourassa summarized his opposition to conscription in a pamphlet published on 4 July 1917.

We are opposed to further enlistments for the war in Europe, whether by conscription or otherwise, for the following reasons:

1) Canada has already made a military display, in men and money, proportionately superior to that of any nation engaged in the war;
2) any further weakening of the manpower of the country would seriously handicap agricultural production and other essential industries;
3) an increase in the war budget of Canada spells national bankruptcy;
4) it threatens the economic life of the nation and, eventually, its political independence;
5) conscription means national disunion and strife, and would thereby hurt the cause of the Allies to a much greater extent than the addition of a few thousand soldiers to their fighting forces could bring them help and comfort.

More moderate French-Canadian opinion was represented by Sir Wilfrid Laurier, the leader of the Liberal Party. Laurier had struggled all his life to keep Canada united. He could not support conscription because he realized it was an issue that could tear the country apart. Laurier was heart-broken when twenty-two Liberals from Ontario, the West and Atlantic Canada voted with the government for conscription. Only the Liberals in Quebec and a handful of English-speaking Liberals stood with Laurier against conscription.

With a general election coming in December 1917, the government passed two further bills. They were both meant to strengthen Borden's position on conscription. The Military Voters Act provided for the taking of the soldiers' votes overseas. More important was the Wartime Elections Act. It gave the vote to female relatives of soldiers. These women could be expected to vote for conscription and a government that promised to support their loved ones overseas. This act also took the right to vote away from immigrants from enemy countries who had become Canadian citizens since 1902. Since many of these immigrants had fled from Europe to get away from compulsory military service, Borden's party feared they might vote against conscription.

Robert Borden and his chauffeur.

The Conservatives were now joined by the Liberals who had deserted Laurier. Conservatives and Liberals who believed in conscription formed a Union government. The election of 1917 was particularly bitter. Voters were asked by the Union government 'Who would the Germans vote for?' The Liberals were accused of letting down the boys at the front. The results of the voting saw Borden and the Union government returned with an overwhelming majority in English-speaking Canada, and with only three seats in Quebec.

1917 ELECTION RESULTS

NUMBER OF SEATS IN HOUSE OF COMMONS

	Liberal	Union (Conservatives plus some Liberals)
P.E.I.	2	2
N.S.	4	12
N.B.	4	7
Quebec	62	3
Ontario	8	74
Manitoba	1	14
Saskatchewan	0	16
Alberta	1	11
B.C.	0	13
Yukon	0	1
	82	153

The split in Canada that Laurier had feared for so long had finally occurred. There were riots in Montreal and Quebec City against the conscription act. Troops had to be sent in with rifles and machine-guns to restore order. Farmers from both English Canada and Quebec marched to Ottawa in protest in May 1918. They were objecting that their sons – who were needed on the farms – were not being excused from military service. Many immigrants were bitter that their votes had been taken away. When war ended in November 1918, Canada was an unhappy and divided nation.

Did conscription work? The call-up for conscripts did not begin until the new year, 1918. Thousands of men, both French and English Canadians, claimed exemption from service. A man could be excused from military service if he had an essential occupation like farmer, clergyman, or because of physical handicap. By the time the war ended in November 1918, only about 45 000 conscripts had reached the battlefield.

Was conscription a success in Canada? Most historians would agree that conscription was a failure. National unity had been destroyed. English Canadians were lined up against French Canadians, Protestants against Roman Catholics, majority against minority. There was widespread disagreement about conscription between farmers and city dwellers, and between civilians and soldiers. National unity was a high price to pay for 45 000 men.

CASUALTIES OF WORLD WAR I

THE ALLIES (British figures include Canada)	MILITARY DEATHS	WOUNDED	CIVILIAN DEAD
France	1 357 800	4 266 000	40 000
British Empire	908 371	2 090 212	30 633
Russia	1 700 000	4 950 000	2 000 000
Italy	462 391	953 886	not available
United States	50 385	205 690	not available
THE CENTRAL POWERS			
Germany	1 808 545	4 247 143	760 000
Austria-Hungary	922 500	3 620 000	300 000
Turkey	325 000	400 000	2 150 000

DIRECT COSTS OF WAR

U.S.	$22 625 253 000	includes all
Britain	35 334 012 000	expenditures in
Canada	1 665 576 000	carrying on
France	24 265 583 000	hostilities
Russia	22 593 950 000	
Germany	37 775 000 000	
Austria-Hungary	20 622 960 000	
Turkey	1 430 000 000	

PROPERTY LOSSES

Belgium	$ 7 000 000 000	estimates
France	10 000 000 000	land and
Russia	1 250 000 000	sea
Italy	2 710 000 000	
British Empire	1 750 000 000	
Germany	1 750 000 000	

Questions:
1. Which country had the largest number of military dead as a result of the war? Which country had the most wounded?
2. Which of the Central Powers lost the greatest number of men? Suggest possible reasons for this.
3. Which of the Allies suffered the smallest losses? Suggest reasons for this.
4. Which country on the Allied side lost most civilians? Suggest reasons for this.
5. Why would Canadian casualties be included with the figures for the British Empire?

The Cost of the War to Canada

The first item on the balance sheet for the war was written in the red of blood. A total of 60 661 Canadians lost their lives, and another 173 000 were wounded or gassed. Many thousands of this latter group lived on for years in veterans' hospitals. For these men the suffering of war never ended. They were victims who had lost their limbs, their minds, or whose lungs had been destroyed by gas attacks.

The second disastrous effect of the war on Canadian life was the deepening French-English differences over conscription. The gulf between Quebec and the rest of the country steadily widened. The hurt, pain, and distrust lingered on into the peacetime after the war.

On the other hand, Canada emerged from World War I as a more independent nation than it had been when it entered the war. Canada's war effort had helped it to earn a position of prestige among other countries of the world. The outstanding contribution of Canada's soldiers won respect and a separate seat for Canada at the peace conference following the war. Previously, Great Britain would have signed the peace treaty on behalf of all the British Empire. Now Canada signed the treaty as a separate nation. There was no doubt that Canada had achieved the status of an independent nation.

The war had produced a great economic boom in industry in Canada. Steel and munitions production and manufacturing had grown fantastically. During the war almost everyone who could work had a job. Then the demand for wartime goods suddenly stopped. Large numbers of employees were laid off. The problem was further complicated by hundreds of thousands of soldiers coming back into the Canadian labour force. Many returning heroes were disillusioned to find that there were no jobs for them in Canada.

Returning veterans were surprised by a number of other changes. One was the dramatic change in the role of women. The war had given women the chance to use their abilities. Women as wage-earners had won much greater freedom for themselves. Some women actually smoked cigarettes now in public, which would have been unheard of in pre-war society. More important, women had obtained the right to vote as full and equal citizens of Canada.

Another change that surprised the boys who came home was that in most parts of Canada their favourite bars and saloons had disappeared. This was due to prohibition. Closely connected with the campaign for women's suffrage had been the campaign against the evils of drinking alcohol. Many women who fought for the right to vote also joined the Women's Christian Temperance Union. This organization was committed to stamping out the use of all intoxicating liquor. Women like Nellie McClung spoke out strongly against the use of alcohol. Drinkers were urged to sign the pledge to 'abstain from the use of all intoxicating liquor'. Supported by farm, church, lodge, and merchant associations, the women persuaded provincial governments to introduce prohibition. It was argued that it was patriotic to use grain to feed soldiers and civilians rather than to make alcohol. One by one the provinces prohibited the sale of alcohol, with the exception of Quebec. The fact that Quebec was the only province that did not have prohibition was just another factor isolating that province and separating Quebec from the rest of Canada.

By the time the war was over, if a person wanted a drink, it was necessary to have a doctor's prescription or to visit a bootlegger.

As the decade drew to a close, three of the most important Canadian leaders were leaving the spotlight of politics. On 19 February 1919 the great French-Canadian statesman, Sir Wilfrid Laurier, ended his long and illustrious career. After suffering two strokes, he died of a fatal third stroke. With Laurier gone, Henri Bourassa retired from the political scene. Sir Robert Borden, exhausted from leadership during wartime, resigned as leader of the Conservative party in 1920. Three new leaders in Canada were about to emerge – William Lyon Mackenzie King, Arthur Meighen, and J.S. Woodsworth.

Digging Deeper

1 Explain why these statements are true or false.
   a) British-born Canadians volunteered more promptly than Canadian-born citizens.
   b) Only French Canadians opposed conscription.
   c) The conscription issue caused a serious split in Canada.

2 Why did a spirit of excitement and confidence exist in Canada at the outbreak of the war in 1914?

3 What attitude did Borden and Laurier take in 1914 towards the war? What were their reasons for feeling this way?

Explain why Canadians were considered to be part of the British army. What does this suggest about the relationship between Britain and Canada?

4

Which provinces might be expected to support the war most strongly? Suggest reasons why this would be so. Of the first 36 267 Canadian troops to go overseas, 10 800 were born in Canada. More than 23 000 were born in the British Isles. How do you account for the large number of British-born people in the first group going overseas? Among Canadian-born volunteers, what sort of person would be most enthusiastic about enlisting to fight in Europe?

5

Stage a mock parliament to debate the conscription issue, 1917.
Participants: Sir Robert Borden
                     Sir Wilfrid Laurier
                     English-speaking Conservatives
                     Liberals who refuse to support Laurier
                     French-speaking Conservatives and Liberals

6

Debate: 'The first duty of the citizen is to defend the country in which he or she lives.'

7

Taking a Stand

In 1917, Borden took away the right to vote from Canadian immigrants from Germany, Austria, and other countries with whom we were at war. Find out what other measures were taken against these people. Were such actions justified? The individual rights that were taken away are called 'civil liberties'. List some examples in which peoples' civil liberties are taken away today. Is it ever right to take away an individual's civil rights? How can we prevent our civil liberties from being eroded? For more information, you could contact the Canadian Civil Liberties Association, 229 Yonge St., Suite 403, Toronto, Ontario, M5B 1N9.

Poster Project

During World War I the Canadian government found that colourful posters were an effective way of reaching a widely-scattered public. Examine the selection of posters.
1. List four different purposes for which posters were used by the government.
2. What sorts of reasons do the posters suggest for supporting the war effort?
3. To which emotions do the posters appeal?

4. How successful do you think these posters would be? Why?

5. What methods would the government use today to achieve the same purpose?

Divide the class into four groups. On large sheets of paper let the groups design and produce posters which will be used to

- recruit soldiers;
- encourage the purchase of war bonds;
- help reduce food consumption;
- recruit children to work in the war effort.

10

THE PEACE SETTLEMENT

THE TREATY OF VERSAILLES

Almost five years after the murder at Sarajevo, government leaders met at Versailles, near Paris, to sign the peace treaty. Thirty-two victorious countries were represented, including Canada. Canada was not content just to be part of the British delegation. Borden had demanded and received the right for Canada to be represented as a separate nation at the meetings and at the official signing of the treaty. He argued that Canada deserved an independent voice in the peace talks because of its support for the war effort. Most of the important decisions, however, were made by the leaders of the three strongest winning powers. They were Georges Clemenceau, Premier of France, David Lloyd George, Prime Minister of Great Britain, and Woodrow Wilson, President of the United States.

These three world leaders, or the 'Big Three' as they were known, had very different views on what should be done with defeated Germany. Clemenceau wanted to crush Germany once and for all. Twice in his lifetime he had seen Germans invade his homeland. Much of the war had been fought on French territory. Clemenceau wanted to punish Germany and see that it was left too weak ever to attack France again.

On the other hand, President Wilson wanted a fair peace. He argued that the defeated nations should be treated justly so that they would not want a war of revenge in the future. Wilson's view was natural since the United States had suffered less than any nation involved in the war. He also thought that this was a good opportunity to make a better world for the future. Wilson suggested 'Fourteen Points' that included complete disarmament and free trade among nations. He also suggested that a League of Nations be set up. He wanted each nation to send representatives to a permanent world parliament that could settle future disputes between countries.

Prime Minister Lloyd George held a middle position. His country had lost many lives in the war and Lloyd George promised his people that he would make Germany pay. However, he

PEACE

Our Warehouse Closed All Day Monday In Honor of Our Victorious Armies and Allies

T. EATON C°.LIMITED
REGINA.   CANADA

helped to work out many of the compromises that made the peace treaty possible. The major terms of the Treaty of Versailles are given below:

Article 42.

Germany is forbidden to build any military fortifications on the left bank of the Rhine River. It may not build any fortifications on the right bank for a distance of fifty kilometres.

Article 45.

To pay for the destruction of the coal mines in the north of France, Germany turns over to France its coal mines in the Saar Basin for fifteen years.

Article 51.

The territories of Alsace and Lorraine taken from France in 1871 are restored to it.

Article 80.

Germany must accept the complete independence of Austria.

Article 81.

Germany must accept the complete independence of Czechoslovakia.

Article 87.

Germany must accept the complete independence of Poland.

Article 89.

Poland will allow persons, goods, vessels, carriages, wagons, and mails to pass freely between East Prussia and the rest of Germany over Polish territory. (This was necessary because Poland was given a strip of German territory in order to provide it with access to the sea at the city of Danzig. This was called the 'Polish Corridor'. It separated East Prussia from the rest of Germany).

Article 119.

Germany must give up all its rights and titles to its overseas possessions (colonies in Africa and the Far East).

Article 160.

After 31 March 1920, the German army must not exceed 100 000 men. The army shall be used only to maintain order within Germany and to control the frontiers.

Article 181.

German naval forces must not exceed 6 battleships, 6 light cruisers, 12 destroyers, and 12 torpedo boats. Germans are forbidden to have any submarines.

Article 198.

The armed forces of Germany must not include any military air force.

Article 231.

Germany must accept the responsibility for causing all the loss and damage that the Allies and their citizens have suffered. (This is known as the 'War Guilt Clause'.)

Article 232.

The Allied governments require Germany to pay for all wartime damages to the civilian population and the property of Allied powers. (These payments are known as reparations.)

Article 233.

The amount of the above damage will be determined by an Allied Commission.

Article 428.

A guarantee is needed to make sure the treaty will be carried out by Germany. Therefore, the German territory west of the Rhine River will be occupied by Allied troops for fifteen years.

Questions: The Peace Settlement

1. In a chart, summarize the terms of the Treaty of Versailles. Use these headings in your chart:
   - i) military terms;
   - ii) territorial terms in Europe;
   - iii) territorial terms outside Europe;
   - iv) economic terms;
   - v) other terms.

2. Compare the attitudes of the 'Big Three' towards defeated Germany. Examine the terms and decide whose views had more influence on the treaty. Why?

3. Which of the following terms of the Treaty of Versailles do you consider fair treatment for Germany? Why?
   a) The Allies took away all Germany's colonies.
   b) Germany's army was limited to 100 000 men.
   c) Germany was held responsible for causing World War I.
   d) Germany was required to pay $33 000 000 000 as reparations for the war damage.
   e) Germany would not be allowed to place troops in the Rhineland for fifteen years.

4a) Examine the maps of Europe in 1914 and 1919. Locate the countries that received German territory after the war.

4b) Explain what the Polish Corridor was and what happened to the Germany city of Danzig.

5. What possible objections might Germany raise to the terms of the Treaty of Versailles?

6. It has been said that the Treaty of Versailles contained within it the seeds of another war. What do you think this statement means? Do you think this statement is correct? Why?

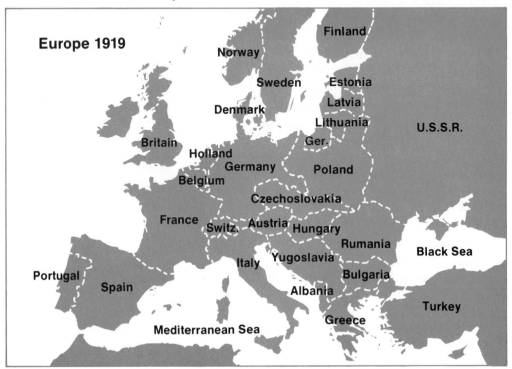

Europe 1919

Other Peace Treaties

Peace treaties with the other Central Powers also brought about major territorial changes in Europe. Four new independent nations were created out of the old Austro-Hungarian empire. These were Czechoslovakia, Poland, Hungary, and Yugoslavia. Austria itself was reduced to a small nation. The peacemakers justified changing the boundaries of nations by the principle of self-determination. This means that people of similar language and nationality have the right to rule themselves.

The Russian empire was also broken up as a result of World War I. Finland, Estonia, Latvia, and Lithuania were given independence as new nations. Russia also lost large regions to Poland, Czechoslovakia, and Rumania. It may seem strange that one of the Allies – Russia – lost so much territory after the war. This happened because Russia had come under communist rule in 1917. A revolution had overthrown the Russian Czar (King), and Russia became the first communist state. This meant its leaders and many of its people believed the government should own all property. They also felt the people should share equally all the things they needed to live. The new Russian government had withdrawn from the war at that time and made peace with Germany. Russia was so busy establishing a new government at home that it did not have the time and energy to continue fighting with Germany. The delegates to the peace conference hoped that these new nations in the centre of Europe would keep communism from spreading westwards from Russia.

Digging Deeper

Compare the maps of Europe in 1914 and 1919.

1

Name and locate the new countries created in Europe, and the empires from which they came.

2

Many small independent countries were created by the peace treaties. People have said this was an unwise decision. Can you suggest any possible problems that might develop as a result of their size and location?

3

What do you think are the lessons to be learned from the study of World War I? Has the world gained anything from the lessons of the War? Give your reasons.

4

Refer back to the summary chart of themes at the end of Unit One (page 54). Using the model below, make a chart for Unit Two. On the chart trace the development of those themes through this unit.

5

IMPORTANT THEMES
IN THIS UNIT

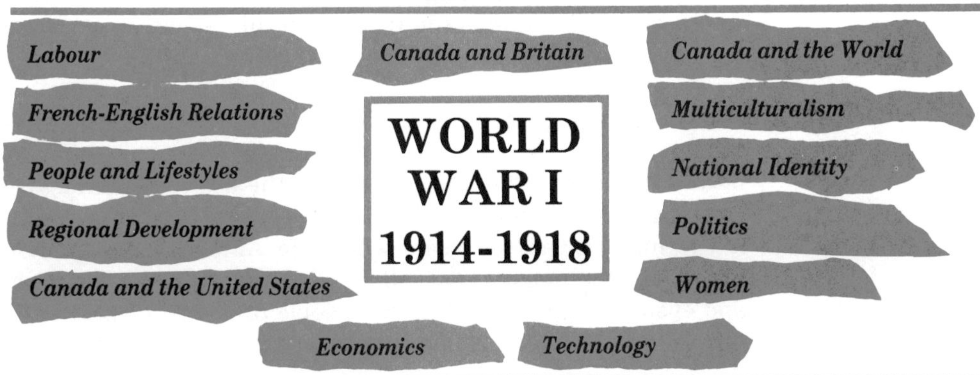

Labour

Canada and Britain

Canada and the World

French-English Relations

**WORLD
WAR I
1914-1918**

Multiculturalism

People and Lifestyles

National Identity

Regional Development

Politics

Canada and the United States

Women

Economics

Technology

11
MOVING INTO THE TWENTIES

Al Capone.

Al Capone rode around Chicago in an armour-plated limousine, accompanied by a bodyguard who sat with a machine-gun on his lap. A flashy dresser, he always wore a priceless diamond ring and carried $50 000 cash in his wallet. He received fan mail from all parts of the world. Some letters asked for the gangster's help in 'rubbing out' irritating neighbours. No one had a more unpleasant reputation in the 1920s than this American gangster. Capone was almost as well known to Canadians as to Americans.

Born to immigrant parents in Brooklyn, New York in 1899, Capone was drawn into violent street gangs as a boy. Later he moved to Chicago and quickly became the head of a crime syndicate that made and sold illegal liquor during prohibition. This is the name given the years when the American government prohibited the making and selling of all liquor – whiskey, beer, and even wine. As a result, some people produced illegal liquor, known as bootleg booze. So vast were the profits from bootleg liquor that even police, politicians, and judges were drawn into Capone's network of crime. He crushed all rival gangs by ruthless tortures and threats and was said to have been involved in more than 400 murders. Capone was known in the press as 'Public Enemy Number One', but no charges of murder were ever brought against him. Eventually he was jailed for tax evasion and sent to Alcatraz prison for eleven years. After his release from prison, Capone lived on a Pennsylvania farm until his death in 1947.

When he was at the height of his power as a leader of organized crime, Capone was only twenty-nine years old. The newspaper headlines and stories of his criminal activities fascinated Canadians and Americans. Al Capone seemed to represent the wild and lawless 1920s.

No wonder people called this decade the 'Roaring Twenties'. It was a time of glamour and prosperity, and yet at the same time an era of enormous crime and corruption. This was the age of 'hot' jazz and the dance called the Charleston. Women finally dared to wear short skirts, lipstick, and rouge. New forms of entertainment became available for almost everyone – movies, radio, dance halls, and cars. During the 1920s it looked as if people were making up for the misery of war by enjoying themselves as much as possible.

The prohibition era in Canada started in 1916 and 1917 during World War I. Many Canadians agreed that it was unpatriotic to enjoy oneself at home while soldiers were suffering hardships at the front. As a result, the manufacture and sale of alcohol became illegal.

Total prohibition never really took place. People could always find a drink if they had the money. 'Speakeasies', which were elegant private clubs, sprang up. Patrons were approved through a peep-hole in the front door, and then entered fashionable surroundings where they could drink to their heart's content. They bought inferior, homemade spirits from bootleggers. It was still possible to buy alcohol legally from a drug store if it was to be used for medicinal purposes. Some druggists did a roaring business by filling prescriptions of alcohol for a tonic.

The United States was also officially 'dry' during this period, and some Canadians made fortunes smuggling Canadian liquor south of the border. By every means possible, 'rumrunners' smuggled their cargo across the line. Under the cover of dense woods, Quebeckers using horse-drawn sleighs and snowshoes smuggled booze into Maine, New Hampshire, and Vermont. From ports along the shores of Lake Ontario and Lake Erie fast boats ran cargoes of rum to the American shores. Estimates suggest that almost one million dollars of booze crossed from Windsor to Detroit each month. On the Atlantic coast schooners from

Raid on bootleggers.

Halifax, Charlottetown, St. John, and other maritime ports took cases of liquor to Americans in chartered boats at meeting points along the American seaboard. A small fleet of World War I planes was used by 'rumrunners' to fly illicit cargo to obscure landing fields in the United States near the Canadian border.

Beyond a doubt prohibition brought some real benefits to society. The crime rate dropped, and arrests for drunkenness decreased dramatically. Workingmen took their pay cheques home instead of to the tavern. Industrial efficiency improved because fewer work days were missed. However, it became obvious during the 1920s that prohibition was impossible to enforce. Underworld characters were making fortunes in illegal liquor. Provincial governments realized that they were losing millions of dollars of potential tax revenue. It became clear that prohibition was unpopular with many citizens. Pressure was brought to bear on governments for a more moderate liquor policy. People argued that legalizing liquor under strict government controls would be easier to enforce than total prohibition. Gradually individual provinces dropped prohibition throughout the 1920s, though Prince Edward Island held out until 1948. In the United States prohibition was finally repealed in 1933.

Were the 'Roaring Twenties' as carefree and exciting as many television programs and movies lead us to believe? Did everyone have money and spend it freely, or were there Canadians who did not share in the prosperity? What were the important changes in the 1920s that affected the lives of all people?

Workers and the Winnipeg Strike

War veterans protesting lack of work.

As World War I ended in November 1918, wartime industries – such as munitions factories – closed down. Women, who played such an important role in the wartime factories, now found they were under pressure to return to household duties so that men could have jobs. Thousands of soldiers were returning home to Canada and looking for work. But jobs were hard to find and many war veterans were unemployed and bitter. Many veterans looked at their medals and wondered why there were no jobs for them in the country they had fought to defend. They also resented the fact that the businessmen at home had become enormously rich by producing goods for the war. Businessmen had made huge profits while the soldiers had been risking their lives in Europe. Now veterans felt that the country owed them something – at least a job and a chance to make an honest living.

People who did have jobs in Canada in 1919 were not much better off than the unemployed veterans. The problem was the rapid rise of inflation. This meant that prices of basic things like food and clothing had increased greatly, while wages had not. The cost of living had gone up between 75% and 80% from 1914 to 1919, but wages had risen by only 18% during the same period. Housing was scarce and costly. Building had failed to keep pace with need, and rents were very high.

The growing unrest and discontent in Canada can be seen in the increase of strikes and lockouts. In 1917 there were 160; in 1918 the number rose to 230; and in 1919 to 326. Most Canadian labour leaders began to feel that the only way to improve conditions for workers would be for them to join together in unions.

Knowing the Terms

Craft Union:
Workers of the same trade or craft join together in an organization to better themselves and their working conditions. The members work for many different employers, but all share the same skill. The Painters' and Decorators' Union is an example.

Industrial Union:
All the workers of an industry join the same organization to improve their working conditions. They may work for different employers, but they all work in the same industry. The United Autoworkers of America is an example.

Company Union:
All the workers of a local company join together to improve their working conditions. The office clerks, drivers, and plant workers of a local dairy would be an example of a company union.

Collective Bargaining:
Representatives of the workers and the employer meet together to discuss their problems. They try to reach an agreement on such items as wages, hours, and conditions of work.

Strike:
Employees refuse to work until the employer reaches an agreement with them on wages and conditions of work.

Lockout:
The employer refuses to allow the employees to work until a settlement is reached.

Blacklist:
The names of union leaders and workers are given by management to other employers so that none will be hired.

Practising the Historian's Skills: Research

Historians have to read many sources in order to study the past. Some possible sources of information are newspaper reports, official documents, eyewitness accounts, and books by other historians. Most of these will be found in libraries.

Researching the Winnipeg General Strike is a good place for you to begin learning the skills of research. *Flashback Canada*, for example, has a whole chapter on the Winnipeg General Strike.

Some of the terms you will need to know are on page 106. You may also want to re-read the section 'Learning to Make Useful Notes' on page 18.

Be sure you find out the following:
- how and why the strike began;
- the opposing sides;

- the major events of the strike;
- 'Bloody Saturday';
- how the strike was broken;
- results of the strike;
- findings of the Royal Commission.

Digging Deeper

Explain how the war helped to bring about prohibition in Canada. What other factors contributed to the spread of the prohibition movement?

1

Suggest some arguments that might be used by supporters of prohibition.
Suggest arguments that could be put forward by those opposed to prohibition.
Who has the stronger arguments? Why?

2

Describe the ways in which Canadians profited from prohibition in the United States after the war. Locate on a map of Canada those areas where it would be easy to run liquor into the United States.

3

Do you think the prohibition 'experiment' worked? Why or why not? What lessons do you think we can learn from the experiment?

4

Someone remarked about the prohibition experiment that 'the cure was worse than the disease'. What do you think he meant?

5

Debate: Since alcohol can be injurious to individuals and society, the government should have the right to restrict its use.

6

Working in small groups, find out what it was like to work in a factory in 1919. Present an illustrated report of your findings to the class. Compare working conditions then with those in factories today. How have things improved? In what ways is there still room for improvement? Try to visit a factory or interview people who work in different kinds of factories. Include information for both 1919 and today on the following:

7

- the number of hours per day and days per week worked;
- the safety, cleanliness, and general appearance of the working environment;
- the compensation available for anyone injured on the job;
- rates of pay and fringe benefits;
- rates of pay for men and women doing the same jobs;
- the amount and kinds of machinery available;
- the strength and activities of labour unions.

12

ECONOMY ON THE UPSWING

THE INDUSTRIAL BOOM

As the 1920s continued, life eventually got better for most Canadians. By the middle of the decade, the economy was on the upswing. At last, prosperity arrived for a generation who had waited so long.

The prairie provinces enjoyed huge wheat crops from 1925 to 1928. War-torn Europe was hungry for Canadian wheat, and the world price of wheat moved steadily upwards. In 1924 Ottawa lowered the tax on imported farm machinery. More and more farmers began to buy trucks and mechanical harvesters, and replace their horses with tractors. Railway branch lines were extended and settlers now moved into the region around Peace River in northern Alberta. The development of early-maturing strains of wheat, such as 'Granite' and 'Reward', meant that wheat could be grown in more northerly regions. More and more farmers organized themselves into wheat pools and co-operatives. Their goal was to loan money to other farmers at lower interest rates than eastern Canadian bankers charged. Farmers hoped that the co-operatives would be able to find customers for their grain, cattle, and dairy products. In this way they could skip the 'middlemen' by marketing their own products. By 1928, Canada had a record wheat crop and a major share of the world market. Though every available grain elevator was bursting at the seams, prices of wheat remained at an all-time high through the first half of 1929.

In the 1920s the production of newsprint became Canada's second largest industry, following agriculture, the first. From Nova Scotia to British Columbia there were vast forests of softwoods such as spruce, pine, and poplar, which are used to make newsprint. Most of the American sources of pulpwood had been used up. Giant American newspapers, such as *The New York Times*, provided a ready market for Canadian pulpwood. By 1929 exports of Canadian pulpwood equalled the total exports of the rest of the world.

Not everyone in Canada thought this was a good situation. Canada's forests were being destroyed. So much newsprint was shipped across the border that the Canadian government finally had to urge Canadian producers to save some of the supply for our own newspapers. Some people thought that a new problem was developing, caused by the fact that our nation's exports were primarily raw materials. Thousands of Canadians were following these raw materials to the United States and finding jobs in American industries.

Quebec and Ontario saw a dramatic increase in the production of hydro-electric power in the 1920s. Niagara Falls had been first used for power in 1895. Soon after that, private companies and governments invested heavily in the production of electricity. Rivers such as the Saguenay and the St. Maurice were developed as resources for water power in the 1920s. The rapidly growing pulp-and-paper industry used huge amounts of electricity. Other industries were also beginning to use methods of production that required hydro-electric power instead of coal. In this same period, people were demanding electricity for their homes in order to use the new electrical appliances coming onto the market. As a result, electricity was installed for the first time in seven out of every ten homes in the nation. Canada's output of hydro-electric power became the second largest in the world.

At the time some people called the 1920s the 'Oil Age'. As more and more Canadians took to the road in automobiles, the demand for gasoline and lubricating oils soared. Also, the increasing use of oil and gas for heating and cooking led to an all-out search for new sources of this 'black gold'. Excitement grew in Alberta about the potential development of oil and natural gas of the Turner Valley south of Calgary. The first major oil find on the prairies – the Dingman Well – had been producing since 1914. However, it was not until the mid 1920s that an oil craze swept through Alberta. In October 1924, oil speculators struck it rich. A drilling in the Turner Valley (known as Royalite #4) came in. The well exploded into flames and burned out of control for several weeks. Eventually the well was tamed and became a great money-maker. It produced a million barrels of oil and large quantities of natural gas. After that the confidence and optimism of the Alberta oil speculators grew. They continued to pour their investment dollars into exploration and development of their oil resources.

Exciting new mining discoveries were made in the 1920s in the Canadian Shield. Large deposits of copper were found near Noranda along the Ontario-Quebec border. By 1929 Canada was producing almost eighty per cent of the world's supply of nickel at Sudbury. In northern Manitoba, the city of Flin Flon was built after the discovery of copper and zinc in large quantities. Kimberley, in British Columbia, developed the world's largest lead and zinc mines. Many of these rich mining deposits were developed with American capital (money).

At the beginning of the twentieth century, the biggest foreign investors in Canada were the British. Bankers from Britain had invested largely in Canadian government bonds and railroads. Very little British capital went into industrial enterprises because of the greater uncertainty of making a profit. The outbreak of a world war in 1914 slowed down British investment in Canada. The British had practically the same amount invested in Canada in 1920 as in 1914.

As British investment in Canada fell off, American investment increased. Americans preferred to put money into the rapidly expanding areas of the Canadian economy – mining, pulp and paper, and hydro-electric power. Another difference between American and British investors was in the amount of control they took. British investors usually left Canadian businessmen alone to run their businesses in their own way. Americans, on the other hand, usually introduced the 'branch plant system'. American investors saw advantages and profits that could be made by opening branch plants for the Canadian market. These branch industries were copies of the American parent company. The branch plant produced the same product as the parent company in the United States. Because the manufactured products could be marked 'Made in Canada', the parent company avoided high tariff (tax) barriers. In return for the foreign capital and the jobs it provided, Canadians had to accept the increasing 'Americanization' of the economy. Many important decisions concerning Canadian branches were made in the United States. Top management jobs frequently were held by Americans. Profits earned by the Canadian branch plant were often drained away from Canada and found their way back to the United States.

BRANCH PLANTS IN CANADA

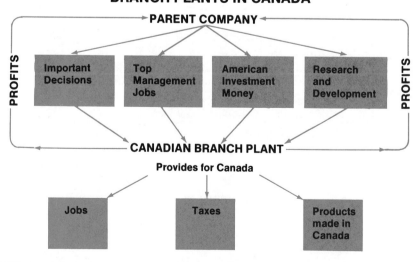

FOREIGN CAPITAL INVESTED IN CANADA 1900-1930

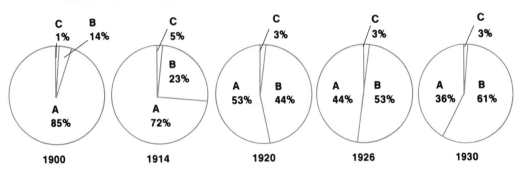

A = Britain
B = U.S.A.
C = Other

Canadian opinions about American investment differed widely. Some people thought that American investment was greatly to be feared. They saw the possibility of a complete economic takeover of Canada by the United States. Others argued that it was a good thing. American capital would help develop Canada into a powerful nation.

One of the important results of the industrial boom of the 1920s was that more and more Canadians gradually started to believe in their own country again. People grew more optimistic about Canada. Riches seemed to be within the reach of anyone. They could see others around them who had struck it rich.

Tycoon and family.

Probably the most powerful business tycoon of the time was Sir Herbert Holt. Holt arrived in Canada from Ireland as a nineteen-year-old during the depression of 1875. One of his first jobs was working as an assistant engineer on railroad construction. Eventually Holt built up a multi-million-dollar empire which included railroads, banks, mines, hotels, utilities, and the Famous Players theatres. He was the president of twenty-seven major business enterprises. Montrealers in the late 1920s complained. 'We get up in the morning and switch on one of Holt's lights, cook breakfast on Holt's gas, smoke one of Holt's cigarettes, read the morning news printed on Holt's paper, ride to work on one of Holt's streetcars, sit in an office heated by Holt's coal, then at night go to a film in one of Holt's theatres.' Holt had no hobbies and few close friends. Although he was the richest man in Canada, few people really knew him well. When he died in 1941 at the age of eighty-five, his coffin was followed by eight cars filled with flowers. However, few mourners bothered to attend his funeral.

Most of the rich tycoons had a lifestyle that matched their enormous wealth. They lived in thirty- or forty-room mansions filled with fine furniture and priceless paintings. John McMartin, a millionaire goldminer, spent $70 000 decorating the dining-room ceiling of his summer home in Cornwall, Ontario. It had real bullrushes glued to the plaster, and stuffed flying ducks suspended by invisible wires. James Ross of Montreal owned as many as eight Rolls-Royces and seven yachts. Many wealthy tycoons owned private railway cars that carried pianos, bathtubs with gold-plated taps, fireplaces, Tiffany lamps, and wine cellars stocked with rare and expensive vintages. The wife of a Canadian tycoon once engaged a whole suite on a train to bring her dog from Montreal to New York. She left careful instructions that the animal was to sleep only on a lower berth.

Financial success stories inspired ordinary citizens to believe that they too could dream of riches and prosperity. Two dollar bets on horses, investing in stocks and bonds, and hockey pools were all seen as ways for the ordinary working man and woman to get rich quick. The 1920s was a take-a-chance time in Canada!

Digging Deeper

Give reasons why Americans invested in Canada in the 1920s.

1

Use the following terms related to the branch-plant economy correctly in a sentence –
branch plant
tariff barrier
parent company

2

Today Canadian economic nationalists oppose American investment in this country. Do some research to find out what they consider are the harmful effects of a branch plant economy.

3

The defenders of the U.S. investment in Canada claim that American capital is vital to the Canadian economy. Do some research to find out the advantages of American investment in this country.

4

Research. Using the text and other sources, do some further research on the economic boom of the 1920s in at least one of these regions. Summarize your findings in chart form.

5

	Atlantic Canada	Central Canada (Quebec and Ontario)	Western Canada	Northern Canada
Exported Products				
New Industries				
Newly Developed Resources				
Growing Cities				
Transportation				
Population Changes				

13
INVENTIONS BRING CHANGE

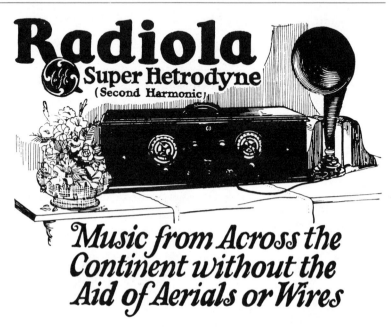

Radiola
Super Hetrodyne
(Second Harmonic)

Music from Across the Continent without the Aid of Aerials or Wires

Radio was the great invention of the 1920s. The sending of messages by dots and dashes (Morse code) had been known for years. However, by 1920 it became possible to broadcast voices, news, and music through the airwaves by using radio signals. It was the invention of the radio that helped to shrink the vastness of Canada's size. People living in isolated rural parts of the country were brought in touch with the cities of the nation. It became possible for a farmer living far from the city to twist the dials on his battery set and listen to a hockey game from Montreal or a music program from New York. Radio provided cheap entertainment in people's homes.

The first scheduled radio broadcast in North America took place in May 1920 over Montreal's station XWA (later CFCF). Other Canadian cities quickly followed, and by 1922 there were more than thirty Canadian radio stations. The earliest home sets had no tubes but used a crystal (a thin piece of quartz). Listeners tuned in a signal by moving a fine wire 'whisker' over the surface of the crystal. Sounds from crystal sets were never very loud, so earphones were often needed. Several pairs of earphones were provided when neighbours came to visit and to 'listen in'. As the craze for crystal sets swept the country, demand far exceeded supply. Many sets were home-made, and newspapers carried articles telling how to build a do-it-yourself set for under $3.00. A person could take a crystal set on a picnic, hang the antenna on a tree, and sit back and listen through the headphones. In the 1950s, when transistorized portable radios with earphones were introduced, people thought they were a great

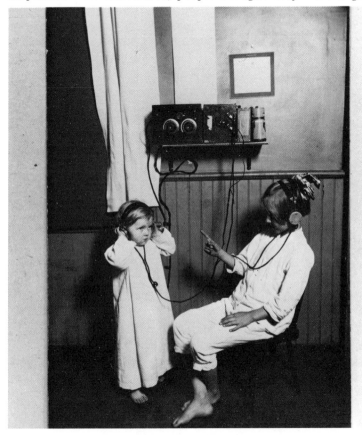

A crystal set.

invention. They had forgotten the crystal sets of the 1920s which pre-dated the transistorized radios by thirty years.

Before long, much more improved and expensive radio sets were sold. These were built in elaborate wooden cabinets. Tubes replaced the crystal and whisker, and speakers replaced earphones. The radios operated by large batteries that had to be recharged frequently. In 1925, a brilliant young Toronto inventor, Edward (Ted) S. Rogers, discovered a way of plugging the radio directly into household electric current. His invention was the world's first battery-less radio, which sold for approximately $150. The company formed to manufacture his product was Rogers-Majestic. In February 1927 Ted Rogers set up his own radio station in Toronto. His station's call letters – CFRB – continue today to stand for his invention (R for Rogers and B for battery-less).

The Automobile

MOTOR VEHICLE REGISTRATION IN CANADA	
1903	220
1911	22 000
1921	465 000
1931	1 201 000

One of the most obvious signs of the prosperity of the 1920s was the growth of the automobile industry. Fewer than 22 000 cars and trucks were registered in Canada in 1911, but by 1930 there were 201 000 vehicles registered to Canadian owners. The idea for a 'horseless carriage' began in France and England shortly after the invention of the railroad. Horseless carriages were driven by steam engines. Because their engines required too much fuel to make steam, they were unmanageable. The invention of the gasoline engine made it possible to produce a horseless carriage that could be run by a smaller and lighter engine. These were called automobiles, meaning 'moving by themselves'. During the 1890s, Americans such as Henry Ford built horseless carriages. The early models took a long time to build and only the very rich could afford to buy them.

Ford dreamed of making an inexpensive car that almost anyone could afford to buy. But if this was to be done, the cost of making cars had to be lowered. Ford decided to apply to car manufacturing a method of mass production that was beginning to be used in some other industries. This method made use of an assembly line, a division of labour, and standardized parts. How did the mass production of automobiles work? Ford set up a line or belt running from one end of the building to another. At the beginning of the line were the frames of the cars. At first the line did not move and workers walked along it adding parts to the automobiles. Later the line itself moved like a conveyor belt. As the line moved, new parts were added to the frame by workers who remained in one place. By the time a car reached the end of this line, it had been assembled and was ready to be driven. Each worker on the assembly line had a separate job to do. Some added parts, while others secured the parts in place and tightened them. This is called division of labour. Ford used standard parts for his cars, which meant that wheels, engines, and bodies were exactly alike for each car. As a result Ford was able

to produce the famous, practical 'Model T' at a price that average North Americans could afford. The 'Tin Lizzy', as the Model
T was affectionately called, had a hideous design. But in 1924 it
could be purchased for around $395. In Canada alone 750 000
Model Ts were sold!

Twenty-nine different companies attempted to manufacture
cars in Canada in those early days. A group of businessmen in
Windsor established Ford of Canada in 1904. Three years later,
in Oshawa, the McLaughlin family began to manufacture the
Buick car. Next they secured the rights to Chevrolet, but in 1918
sold out to General Motors. William Stansell produced a Canadian luxury car known as the London Six. It was powered by a
firetruck engine and roared along on wooden wheels. Stansell
used to give the Toronto-Windsor train a ten-minute headstart,
and then race it to Toronto. In 1924 Stansell ran out of money
and the firm folded. Already the three largest American companies – Ford, General Motors, and Chrysler – had begun to dominate the automobile industry in Canada.

The automobile has probably done more than any other
machine to change our way of living. It put North Americans on
wheels. It brought all parts of the country together. It put the
word 'neighbouring' into the language of rural and city people
alike. On Sunday, after church, a family with a car could call on
relatives fifteen or twenty kilometres away, and still be home for
supper and evening chores. New industries sprang to life because of the car: gasoline, rubber, glass, and paint. New jobs
were created in service stations, parking lots, and repair shops.
Traffic police and street lights appeared on streetcorners. The
family car made it possible to have a summer cottage and to
travel longer distances for summer vacations. Along the major
roads, tourist cabins and hotels popped up to house the increasing number of travellers. More and more trucks were used for
hauling freight and food from factories and farms. Governments
began to spend increased amounts of money on highways. Main
roads were paved and even country roads were given a surface of
gravel. A crank and a tow rope were standard equipment. The
crank was needed to get the engine started. A tow rope was
required because motorists never knew when they might
become stuck in mud or snow. More than one pleasant Sunday
drive was spoiled when the family car became mired in a muddy
road. As in the days of the old stagecoach, everyone climbed out
of the car and tried to free it by using nearby fence poles as
levers. Most people did not attempt to drive in the winter at all.
They put their car up on blocks because the engines tended to
seize up with the cold. Few municipalities had invested in any
snow removal equipment. The car made it possible for people to
live farther from their place of work. People sought open and

green spaces for their houses, so suburbs started to sprawl on the outskirts of many cities. It became increasingly difficult to sell a house without a garage and a driveway.

Nevertheless, engineering advances continued to be made throughout the 1920s. By the end of the 1920s accelerator pedals replaced buttons, in-car heaters replaced hot water bottles, and the electric starter button replaced the crank. Windshield wipers and brake lights were added to make driving safer. Cars were no longer available only in black, but in almost all colours of the rainbow. Big six-cylinder models boasted maximum speeds of 100 kilometres per hour. But by now even a low-cost car was $900, or the equivalent of a person's annual salary. If you were a millionaire you might pay $14 000 for a Packard.

However, the automobile has created problems too. No one knew that this great invention would pollute the air, cause incredible traffic jams, and bring death to thousands of people each year. Criminals also made use of the automobile. In 1919 the Vancouver police were reporting at least six robberies a night in which the thieves made their 'getaway' in a car. Police departments were soon forced to buy automobiles themselves.

Sam McLaughlin

In 1971, R. Samuel McLaughlin celebrated his one-hundredth birthday. As Chairman of the Board of General Motors of Canada, this famous business leader looked back at the phenomenal growth of the automobile industry. His father had established a thriving industry by building a better horse-drawn carriage. McLaughlin carriages were known far and wide for their expert craftsmanship, and the company quickly outgrew its beginnings in country shops in Tyrone and Enniskillen, Ontario. Soon McLaughlin carriages had to be manufactured in a larger factory in Oshawa. Not long after Sam joined his father in business, he persuaded him to start making automobiles as well as carriages. The well-made McLaughlin body would remain, but the horse would be replaced by a Buick engine. Everything except the engine was made in Oshawa. In 1907 the first McLaughlin Buick could be marked 'Made in Canada'.

In 1915, R.S. McLaughlin was offered the opportunity to make the Chevrolet automobile in Oshawa also. Louis Chevrolet, a daring racing driver and an excellent mechanic, had designed an exciting model which was winning popularity in the United States. However, Sam knew that if Chevrolets were built in large volume in Oshawa, it would mean the end of the carriage company. Reluctantly he went to his father and suggested that production be stopped on his father's beloved carriages. Carriage sales were declining steadily while automobile sales were skyrocketing. Sam's father sadly agreed, though he never totally accepted the automobile that bore the family name.

A final big decision was made by the McLaughlins in 1918 when they decided to sell out to the American-owned General Motors. As a condition of the deal, Sam agreed to stay on as president of the Canadian operation in Oshawa. In the years that followed he saw the manufacturing of automobiles and parts grow to be one of the most important industries in the country.

Sam McLaughlin always loved horses and racing, and had a large stable of thoroughbreds. During World War II, when gasoline was rationed, the president of General Motors put his car up on blocks and drove to his office in a carriage pulled by one of his horses. McLaughlin's racehorses won distinction throughout North America. His trophies included a collection of sold gold cups and saucers. Even though he owned gold teacups, Sam McLaughlin said he preferred to drink tea from ten-cent china cups.

Digging Deeper

1   Imagine that you are living on a homestead in Alberta during the early 1920s. Your farm is a long way from urban centres. Your nearest neighbours are located a few kilometres away. What difference would a radio make to your family's life?

2   Make a list of ten jobs that came into being with the invention of the automobile.

3   Draw a chart of the benefits and problems that have resulted from the invention of the automobile.

4   How has the car contributed to the quality of Canadian life? Would we be suffering from urban sprawl today if the car had not been invented?

5   Cars create large amounts of pollutants. Yet anti-pollution devices use more fuel and give fewer kilometres per litre. Suggest ways of combating this double problem.

14
POLITICS OF THE 1920s

Arthur Meighen.

As the 1920s began two new politicians moved into the spotlight as leaders of Canadian political parties. Both the Liberals and Conservatives had new leaders. The Liberals chose William Lyon Mackenzie King to succeed Sir Wilfrid Laurier, and the Conservatives selected Arthur Meighen to replace Sir Robert Borden.

In July 1920 Arthur Meighen was sworn in as prime minister of Canada. Sir Robert Borden had been worn down by the strain and stress of leadership during the war years. He stepped down to make way for his right-hand man. Born and educated in Ontario, Meighen went to Manitoba as a young man to practise law. He became widely known as a successful trial lawyer, and in 1908 was elected to Parliament. Meighen had many of the qualities of a successful politician. He was brilliant in debate, using razor-sharp words to shred the ideas and arguments of his political opponents. But for all of his talents, Meighen was never able to win the affection of the Canadian voters. His reserved manner and his gaunt appearance earned him the reputation of being a 'figure of ice'. While Meighen was respected, he was never loved.

The Canada that Meighen inherited was restless and torn apart by regional interests. French Canada was still seething over the conscription crisis of 1917. The Maritimes were demanding more jobs, increased recognition, and better treatment for Atlantic Canada. Prairie farmers, suffering from a postwar slump, opposed tariffs. They claimed these only increased their costs of operation. Farmers also demanded that railways be taken over by the government and freight rates reduced. Organized labour in Winnipeg saw Meighen as a friend of big business and an enemy of the worker. During the Winnipeg General Strike in 1919, he had declared, 'There is absolutely no justification for a general strike.' With so many groups opposed to them, Meighen and the Conservatives lost the federal election in 1921.

The man who became prime minister in 1921 was destined to be the most successful Canadian political leader of his age. For almost thirty years, until his death in 1950, William Lyon Mackenzie King dominated political life in Canada. King established a record of being prime minister longer than any other leader. He served 7825 days, during which time he won six general elections.

Grandson of William Lyon Mackenzie, the rebel leader of 1837, King dreamed of entering politics. After a brilliant academic career at university, he became a newspaper reporter and an expert on labour relations. When he entered Parliament in 1908, King was soon invited by Laurier to become Minister of Labour.

William Lyon Mackenzie King and his parents.

On the surface King seemed to possess few qualities that would attract large numbers of voters. He was not attractive. He was a pudgy little man, dumpy in appearance. He was cautious and careful, and extremely shrewd. King was in many ways a lonely and unhappy man who was friendless except for his pet dog and a couple of associates with whom he corresponded freely. His beloved mother, who died in 1917, was the most important person in his life, and King never fully recovered from her death. His desire to make contact with her led to an interest in spiritualism. Like many other Canadians of the day, he tried through mediums and seances to contact the dead. There were times when King believed he had received political advice from important figures of the past, including Laurier.

King's political genius lay in his realization that without national unity, there was no hope for Canada. King knew that he would have to form policies that would be acceptable to various groups and sections of the nation. He had the uncanny knack of being able to do this. His secret was that he listened to what various regions of Canada wanted, and waited for a long time before reaching a decision. Then he worked out compromises and bargains among the diverse interests in the country. As a result King was often able to maintain unity among Canadians.

The twenties was a good time to be prime minister in Canada. There was prosperity, almost full employment, and general contentment throughout the country. King moved Canada slowly and cautiously towards a more independent policy in foreign affairs. He recognized that foreign affairs was an area in which French and English Canadians were potentially divided. Following World War I, King tried to keep Canada outside of European military involvement. He expressed this attitude in 1922 when Britain asked for Canada's military support during the Chanak crisis with Turkey. As part of the peace treaty with Turkey, some British troops were left to guard the straits between the Mediterranean and the Black Sea. In 1922 Turkey threatened to move a large army back into this area. For some weeks there seemed to be every possibility of a war between Britain and Turkey. Some Canadians objected to helping Britain with the Turks. It seemed that Britain was taking Canada's support for granted. As some said, 'Who in Canada has ever heard of Chanak until this moment?' King sensed this national feeling and insisted that the whole matter had to be discussed with the Canadian Parliament before troops could be sent. Fortunately, Britain and Turkey resolved their differences and the crisis passed. However, Canada had taken an important step towards having an independent foreign policy.

In 1926 the relations between Britain and its colonies were

redefined. A meeting of all the members of the British Empire was held that year. At the Imperial Conference, King demanded to know the powers of the dominions, and the nature of their relationships to each other and to Britain. It was decided that Canada and the other dominions were a self-governing, independent, 'commonwealth of nations'. Members of this commonwealth were equal in status and united by a common allegiance to the king or queen. The Commonwealth was a voluntary family of nations scattered throughout the world.

By the Statute of Westminster, in 1931, Canada had become fully independent in all but two minor legal details. Appeals could still be carried from the Supreme Court of Canada to the Judicial Committee of the Privy Council in Britain. Also, it was still necessary for Canada to ask the British Parliament to amend the Canadian constitution (B.N.A. Act). However, it was understood that both of these legal arrangements would be ended when Canadians agreed on powers to be held by the provincial and federal governments. Except for these two minor details, Canada had achieved full independence.

One of the most controversial episodes in the history of Canada's Parliament happened in 1926. It has come to be known as 'the Constitutional Crisis'. In the general election of October 1925, the Conservatives won 117 seats to the Liberals' 101 seats. King, who was prime minister before the election, refused to turn over power to his hated rival, Arthur Meighen. King remained in office, despite his defeat at the polls. He was confident that he could govern with the support of twenty-four members of the Progressive party. With Progressive support, King managed to hold on until 28 June 1926. At that time scandal rocked King's shaky government. Customs officials had been accused of smuggling illegal liquor into the United States and the Liberal party was accused of receiving 'kickbacks' from the smugglers. Knowing that he would be defeated in the House of Commons, King asked the Governor-General to dissolve Parliament and call another federal election.

Normally a governor-general accepts the advice of the prime minister on the matter of dissolving Parliament and calling an election. However, Governor-General Lord Byng, who had commanded British and Canadian troops at Vimy, refused to do this. Lord Byng thought that Meighen, leader of the largest group in the House of Commons, should first be given an opportunity to form an alternative government. Meighen and the Conservatives were delighted. However, the Meighen government lasted only until 2 July 1926, when they were defeated in the House of Commons. It was then necessary to hold an election. One of the chief issues for the Liberals was whether a governor-general had the right to reject the advice of his prime minister. Liberals had not forgiven Lord Byng for refusing to dissolve Parliament on Mackenzie King's request. Recalling his grandfather's struggle in 1837 against a governor who would not listen to the elected representatives of the people, Mackenzie King argued that the same problem existed in 1926. He complained that a British governor-general seemed to be telling Canadians who their prime minister should be, and when elections should come. He claimed that the governor-general's actions threatened Canada's independence. Canada was being reduced to the status of a British colony. Confused by the constitutional issue, Canadian voters forgot the customs scandal and returned the Liberals to government. Mackenzie King was again prime minister, and Arthur Meighen was all but finished as the national Conservative leader.

Digging Deeper

Who was the prime minister during most of the 1920s? What was his attitude towards relations with Britain?

1

Name the two ways in which Canada did not become fully independent under the Statute of Westminster in 1931. Try to suggest possible reasons why full independence was not asked for by Canada.

2

Do some research on the Commonwealth today. Begin by marking the members of the Commonwealth on a world map. Individual students can investigate a single Commonwealth country with a view to representing it during a discussion of such topics as

3

* the role of the Queen in the Commonwealth;
* the possibilities of a central Parliament for the Commonwealth;
* the multicultural aspect of the Commonwealth.

Research 'Women of the Commonwealth'. Possible subjects could include: Queen Elizabeth, Margaret Thatcher, Mother Teresa of Calcutta.

4

15

FADS, FASHIONS, AND ENTERTAINMENT

Fads swept the country during the Roaring Twenties. No one can explain how fads 'catch on', but suddenly many people get interested in something and take it up with great enthusiasm. Before you know it, everyone is doing it. Usually the craze does not last long and fads are dropped as quickly as they are taken up.

From the gambling parlours of China came one of the first fads of the twenties. It was the ancient Chinese game of mah-jongg. The game is a combination of dice and dominoes. It is played with tiles made from the shinbones of calves. The game caught on quickly in North America, and in 1923, 1 500 000 sets were being imported. In homes across the land people were shouting 'pung!' and 'chow!' and other Oriental words connected with the game. Mah-jongg parties became the rage and people even imported Chinese robes, furniture, and decorative objects to make their parties perfect. But by 1927 the novelty had worn off. The mah-jongg set that had cost $25 in 1923 could be purchased then for $1.69. It was time for a new fad.

The novelty that replaced mah-jongg was the crossword puzzle. Two young American publishers, Simon and Schuster, brought out a book of crossword puzzles with a pencil attached. Suddenly everyone was crazy about crosswords! Dictionary sales soared. Some railways even provided dictionaries to help travellers solve crossword puzzles.

Every kind of long race or contest became the rage of the twenties. Non-stop talking, kissing, eating, drinking, flagpole sitting, and rocking chair marathons were some of the contests in which people tried to establish records. Of all of the marathons, dancing was the most popular. Dancers sometimes competed for prizes of thousands of dollars. Couples dragged themselves around the dance floor with blistered feet and backs aching with fatigue. One man dropped dead on the dance floor after eighty-seven hours of continuous dancing. Some contestants kept themselves awake with smelling salts and ice packs and a few desperate dancers slipped sleeping pills into the drinks of their rivals. Mary (Hercules) Promitis of Pittsburgh took a tip from

Flappers, 1928.

bare-knuckle prizefighters and soaked her feet in vinegar and brine for three weeks before a 1928 marathon. Her feet were so pickled that she felt no pain at all!

Fads also filled the world of fashion. For young women the flapper look was the new rage. A flapper was a rather wild young girl who dressed outrageously in order to attract attention. In winter she wore galoshes with buckles unfastened to create the greatest possible flap. Hemlines rose above the knees, silk stockings were rolled down, and the flat-chested look became popular. Long hair was cut off and set in a short – 'bobbed' – boyish style. Fashions for a young man were often as outrageous. He sported baggy pants or knickers, a bright snappy hat, and a bow tie. His hair was greased down and often parted in the middle to imitate the popular movie idols of the day.

For flappers only one kind of music would do, and that was jazz. Jazz moved north from New Orleans and was made popular by such musicians as Duke Ellington and Louis Armstrong. Out of the black culture also emerged the dance of the decade – the Charleston. Its fast and wild pace quickly caught on with the high-spirited younger generation. Members of the Boston city council tried to have the dance banned, but the Charleston

The Charleston.

was here to stay, and it became the emblem of the roaring Jazz Age.

Stunt flyers and air travel were also part of this high-stepping decade. Canadian aces, who returned from the First World War, bought up war surplus biplanes and barnstormed across the country. For 'two bucks a flip' they would take up the more adventuresome for an airplane ride. These aces would perform daring stunts over country fairs. As onlookers below gasped in horror, they would dive and loop-the-loop, and even hang from the wings of their flimsy craft. Eventually the public and government began to see the possibilities of air travel. Bush pilots helped to open up the northern frontiers of Canada by flying prospectors and supplies into mineral-rich areas of the Canadian Shield. In 1927, the Post Office hired other pilots to fly mail into remote communities within Canada. In the same year a young American air-mail pilot, Charles A. Lindbergh, completed the first non-stop solo trans-Atlantic flight from New York to Paris. This important event signalled the possibility of long distance air travel. Suddenly the world seemed smaller!

Slang of the Twenties

EXPRESSION	MEANING
all wet	wrong, mistaken
baloney	nonsense
bee's knees	compliment meaning a wonderful person or thing
big cheese	very important person
bump off	to murder
bunk	nonsense
carry a torch	to be hopelessly in love
cat's meow	superb, wonderful
cheaters	eyeglasses
crush	falling in love
dogs	human feet
drugstore cowboy	a fashionably dressed young man who hangs around public places trying to pick up girls
dumb dora	stupid girl
flapper	typical girl of the 1920s with bobbed hair, short skirt, and rolled-down stockings
flat tire	boring person
gate crasher	an uninvited guest
giggle water	alcohol
gyp	cheat
hep	up-to-date
high hat	snobbish
hooch	bootleg liquor
hoofer	chorus girl
kiddo	friendly form of address
kisser	lips
a line	insincere flattery
ossified	drunk

ritzy, swanky	elegant
real McCoy	genuine article
runaround	delaying action
scram	to leave quickly
Sheba	a young woman with sex appeal
sheik	a young man with sex appeal
speakeasy	a bar selling illegal liquor
spiffy	fashionable
struggle buggy	a car in which boys try to seduce girls
swell	marvellous
whoopee	a wild time

Things To Do

Make up a conversation between two students using the slang of the twenties.

Make a list of current slang expressions that are used to express the same meanings.

Since crossword puzzles were a great fad of the twenties, try making some. Use a sheet of graph paper. The answers should all be slang words of the twenties. Include clues to help your classmates solve the crosswords.

Silver Screen

Talking films were one of the greatest inventions of the twenties. But 'talkies' did not arrive in Canada until 1927. For most of the decade, films were silent. They used subtitles on the screen and sound effects were provided by a piano or an orchestra. The stars of the silent screen were idolized by the Canadian and American public alike. The gods and goddesses of Hollywood provided all the excitement that ordinary people lacked in their daily lives. Charlie Chaplin, affectionately called the 'Little Tramp', needed no words to get across his hilarious comic routines. Douglas Fairbanks Sr. played exciting roles as a swashbuckling adventurer in such films as *The Thief of Bagdad*. Women swooned when they saw Rudolph Valentino in the film *The Sheik*. When Valentino died in 1926, police had to be called in to control the screaming mob that surrounded the chapel during his funeral. One American girl, pictures of Valentino clutched in her hand, shot herself. Two Japanese girls flung

A sound-effects man.

themselves into a volcano. The Italian leader Mussolini had to appeal to the grieving women of his country to stay calm.

Among actresses, the Canadian-born star, Mary Pickford, was often called 'America's Sweetheart'. Born in Toronto in 1893, she started on the stage at the age of five. She was paid $10 a day for her first film but at the height of her career was earning $10 000 a week.

As her popularity soared, Mary Pickford came to represent the luxury and wealth the film industry brought to its stars. When she retired from the screen, 'America's Sweetheart' bought the rights to all of her old silent movies and refused to release them. Most Canadians have no memory of Mary Pickford because she was the only one who had access to the films that made her one of Hollywood's most famous actresses. Not until after her death in 1979 were her films re-released. Greta Garbo, Gloria Swanson, Theda Bara, and Clara Bow (known as the 'It' girl) were other glamorous beauties of the silent screen.

The silent screen era ended abruptly in 1927. *The Jazz Singer*, starring Al Jolson, started talking films. The arrival of the talkies was a great technological advance, but some of the silent screen stars could not make the transition successfully. Although Clara Bow had 'It' for several years, the talkies revealed her thick Brooklyn accent, and she soon fell from stardom. Because of the talking pictures, a new era of Hollywood films with much more natural acting began. Gone were the days of the exaggerated gestures used so much in silent films.

The talkies made movie-going a way of life for most people. By the end of the decade there were more than 900 movie

Mary Pickford.

houses across Canada. Many of them were huge ornate palaces with carpeted aisles, sweeping staircases, and theatre organs used to entertain the audience at intermission. Movies were here to stay. Every kid wanted to spend Saturday afternoon at the show, and for many adults Hollywood movies were the most popular entertainment.

Sports

The twenties was Canada's 'Golden Age' of sport. Hockey, football, and baseball were becoming professional. The real sports heroes of the decade were amateurs. They were often unknowns who came out of nowhere to grab the headlines and establish world records. Percy Williams is an outstanding example. This twenty-year-old sprinter, almost unknown in Canada, stunned onlookers at the 1928 Amsterdam Olympics. In both the 100- and 200-metre sprints he won a sensational double gold victory. Even competing athletes acknowledged him as 'the greatest sprinter the world has ever seen'.

George Young was another complete unknown who came out of Toronto in 1927 to score a triumph in long-distance swimming. Only seventeen years old, Young and a friend hitchhiked to California to join in the thirty-two-kilometre swim from the mainland to Catalina Island. Young was the only one of the 102 starters to finish the race, and the first to complete the crossing. For his victory Young proudly picked up the prize money – $25 000.

Lionel Conacher.

Canada's most famous male athlete of the first half-century was Lionel Conacher. He piled up trophies and medals in wrestling, boxing, lacrosse, hockey, football, and baseball. One day in 1922 Conacher starred in championship games in two different sports. He hit a triple in the last inning to give Toronto Hillcrest the city baseball championship. Then he drove across town to play for Maitland in the Ontario Lacrosse Championship. In this game he scored four times and Maitland won 5-3. In football Conacher also excelled. In the 1922 Grey Cup game, he scored fifteen points leading the Toronto Argonauts to a 23-0 win over the Edmonton Eskimos.

The twenties was also a 'Golden Age' of sport for women. Before World War I, the sports activities open to women were still very much in keeping with the traditional concept of femininity – croquet, skating, fencing, cycling, and lawn tennis. These were sports that could be performed gracefully without the kind of movement that caused sweating. By the 1920s, though, there was a greater social acceptability of body-contact sports. Women began to compete in a more rough and aggressive style. Many people still feared that competitive sports for women would lead to a loss of femininity.

In the early part of the 20th century basketball became popular and was one of the first team sports played by women at a competitive level. The Edmonton Grads dominated the world of women's basketball for over twenty years. Coached by Percy Page, they were a team made up of students or graduates of

The Edmonton Grads in 1935.

McDougall Commercial High School in Edmonton. From 1915 to 1940 the team played 522 games and lost only 20. They were winners of regional, provincial, national, and international matches. The Edmonton Grads represented Canada at four Olympics (1924-1936), and won twenty-seven consecutive Olympic games. Their conditioning and quick-passing teamwork made the Grads the undisputed world champions of women's basketball. Dr. James Naismith, the Canadian-born inventor of basketball, proclaimed the Edmonton Grads the greatest basketball team that ever stepped out on a floor.

Among individual Canadian female athletes, no one surpassed a Russian-Jewish immigrant girl from Ontario – Fanny Rosenfeld. 'Bobbie', as she was known to sports fans, excelled in so many sports during her athletic career that she was called the 'best woman athlete of the half-century'. She was a star at basketball, hockey, softball, and tennis, but her greatest triumphs came in track and field. In the 1925 Ontario Ladies' Track and Field Championships, she was first in discus, long jump, low hurdles, and the 200-metre sprint, and second in the javelin and 90-metre dash. During the Amsterdam Olympics of 1928, Rosenfeld won a silver medal in the 100-metre dash and a gold medal in the women's 400-metre relay team. In the 800-metre race Rosenfeld settled for fifth place, rather than pass a younger, less experienced team-mate. The career of Canada's best woman athlete of the half-century ended sadly in 1933. Arthritis forced Bobbie Rosenfeld to retire from active sports and take up a career as a journalist.

Another Canadian woman excelled at Amsterdam in 1928. Ethel Catherwood jumped 1.6 metres – a height no other jumper could match. Catherwood was widely praised as a superb athlete and a strikingly beautiful woman. Sports writers nick-named her the 'Saskatoon Lily' because of her beautiful face and her tall slim body.

The list of outstanding women athletes of this decade could be continued at length. Unfortunately the 'Golden Age' of women's sports did not last. By the mid-1930s many educators and medi-cal doctors argued that girls and women were biologically unfit for athletics. It was feared that aggressive and highly-competi-tive sports activities would lead to dangers in child-bearing. Not until the 1960s did Canadian women regain the glory they won in the 1920s in a wide range of sports.

Digging Deeper

Bring some records to class and listen to the music of the 1920s. Try to get someone to demonstrate the Charleston and other dances of the twenties.

1

In your opinion who is the best male athlete in Canada today? Who is the best female athlete in Canada today? Give reasons for your opinions.

2

Research a Canadian woman athlete who has made a significant contribution to sport. Or, compare a female athlete of the 1920s with one who has distinguished herself in the same sport in the 1970s or 1980s. What effects did the social and political climate of the times have on the athletes? Suggested names might include the following:

3

Then
Ethel Catherwood – Track and Field
Bobbie Rosenfeld – Track and Field
Ada Mackenzie – Golf
Jean Wilson – Speedskating
Gladys Robinson – Speedskating
Myrtle Cook – Track and Field
Florence Bell – Track and Field

Now
Marlene Stewart Streit – Golf
Jocelynne Bourassa – Golf
Diane Jones Konihowski – Track and Field

Abby Hoffman – Track and Field
Sylvia Burka – Speedskating
Karen Magnussen – Figure Skating
Nancy Garapick – Swimming
Cindy Nicholas – Swimming

4

Do some additional research on other sports heroes of the 1920s:

U.S.A.
Babe Ruth – Baseball
'Red' Grange – Football
Jack Dempsey – Boxing
Bob Jones – Golf
Johnny Weissmuller – Swimming
Gene Tunney – Boxing
Knute Rockne – Football
Bill Tilden – Tennis

Canada
Howie Morenz – Hockey
Georges Vezina – Hockey

5

'There is cause for concern among our male coaching staff over the pressure for girls' sports. Facilities are a problem. We've got a boys' gym and girls' gym. Before, we could use the girls' gym for wrestling and B-team basketball and a lot more than we can now. I think girls have a right to participate but to a lesser degree than boys. If they go too far with the competitive stuff they lose their femininity. I guess if I had my choice, I'd like to keep boys' teams going up in importance and let the girls stay about where they are now.'

Using your school or community as a model and the quotation above, debate recreation and sports opportunities for women. Are women forbidden or discouraged from playing certain sports? Does *your* school or community centre offer equal facilities and opportunities for both sexes?

16
LEAVING THEIR MARK

Emily Murphy.

Women

Women in Canada had won the right to vote in federal elections by 1918, but still did not enjoy all the privileges men had.

An event took place that pointed out this lack of equality. Emily Murphy was the first woman judge appointed in Edmonton to a court to hear cases involving women. A lawyer in her courtroom challenged her right to judge any case because she was a woman. He said that no woman was a 'person' in the eyes of the law. Emily Murphy was supported by the Supreme Court of Alberta which said that a woman had every right to be a judge. This should have settled the matter, but it did not.

During the 1920s women's groups asked the Prime Minister of

Canada to appoint a woman to the Senate. The British North America Act outlined the qualifications required for an appointment to the Senate. It said that qualified 'persons' could be appointed to the Senate. Again, the old question of 'persons' showed its ugly head. Was a woman a 'person' in the eyes of the law?

In August 1927, Emily Murphy and four of her friends decided to petition the Prime Minister. The group of women included Nellie McClung, Louise McKinney, Henrietta Edwards, Irene Parlby, and Judge Murphy. They asked, 'Does the word "persons" in Section 24 of the British North America Act include female "persons"?' In April 1928, the Supreme Court of Canada decided that women were not 'persons' qualified for appointment to the Senate in Canada.

Judge Murphy and her supporters, nicknamed the Famous Five, were discouraged but not defeated. They decided that they would appeal their case to the Privy Council in Britain. The Privy Council was the highest court of appeal in the British Empire.

After three months of consideration and four days of debate, the judges of the Privy Council announced their decision. They declared that the word 'persons' included members of the male and female sex. Women were indeed qualified to sit in the Senate of Canada. Emily Murphy won her fight.

Many of her friends thought that Emily Murphy deserved to be the first woman appointed to the Senate. However, it was two more years before the first woman was named to a Senate seat. When it did happen it was not Emily Murphy, but Cairine Wilson, who received this honour. Senator Wilson of Montreal had worked as an organizer and president of the National Federation of Liberal Women.

The Group of Seven

For three weeks in May 1920 an exhibition by seven young artists covered the walls of the Toronto Art Museum. The theme of the show was the Algonquin landscape – rocks, lakes, and jack pines. Toronto had never seen anything like it. One of the artists, A.Y. Jackson, described the reaction:

Our first exhibition had a very poor reception ... Some of the people who saw the exhibition were amused, and some indignant. Some members threatened to resign from the Art Gallery ... There was plenty of adverse criticism, little of it intelligent. A great deal of it was mere abuse, much of it from people who had not even seen the exhibition ... "Products of a deranged mind," "art gone mad," "the cult of ugliness," these were some of the words used to describe the paintings.

Why did the Canadian public find this collection of paintings so startling? For one thing, the themes of the works were different. No longer were these artists content to paint scenes of meadows, windmills, and pastures. Instead they had lugged their easels and pallets into the forests of the Canadian Shield. Here they painted bold canvases of the wild country around Georgian Bay and Lake Superior. The Group of Seven, as they were called, created a new image of Canada. They found inspiration for their art in the north where others were making fortunes in mines, lumber camps, and paper mills. In strong, bold colours, these artists presented the ruggedness and endless variety of the Canadian landscape.

The Group of Seven, around 1921.

Seven artists formed the famous Group: A.Y. Jackson, J.E.H. MacDonald, Lawren Harris, Arthur Lismer, Frederick Varley, Frank Carmichael, and Frank Johnston. They were trained mostly as commercial artists. They spent most of their free time in the north painting the landscapes that characterized their style. The original seven were not the only artists in the country. Tom Thomson, a close friend of the Group, had drowned in 1917. A.J. Casson, Emily Carr, and L.L. Fitzgerald were among those greatly inspired and influenced by the works of Thomson and the Group.

Though their work was first rejected by the public, gradually it won praise and acceptance. As often happens with Canadian artists, they had to be accepted abroad before they were honoured at home. At an exhibition in London, England, in 1925, paintings of the Group of Seven were warmly received. A British art critic said of the landscapes:

Canada reveals herself in colours all her own, colours in which the environment of Nature plays no insignificant part. She has mixed her colours with her restless unrestrained energy, her uncontrolled forces. We feel, as we look at these pictures, the rush of the mighty winds as they sweep the prairies, the swirl and roar of the swollen river torrents, and the awful silent majesty of her snows.

The success of Thomson and the Group of Seven was one of the high points of this decade. These young artists had decided to paint 'Canada', and developed a new approach many felt appropriate to the Canadian scene. When most people think about Canadian painting in the 1920s, the landscapes of the Group of Seven come vividly to mind.

Emily Carr

In the summer of 1928, Emily Carr lived in an isolated Indian village in British Columbia. Often she lived in the homes of the Indians, whom she admired and respected. She spent her days sketching the weathered old totem poles, the houses and the villages, later recording these in the brilliant colours of her paintings. The Indians were actually her first exhibitors, hanging her paintings proudly in their homes.

Emily Carr was born in Victoria, British Columbia in December 1871. Her childhood was unhappy and lonely. As a young girl she often took refuge in the woods, where she developed a deep love of nature. Her fondness for bird and animal life lasted throughout her life and greatly influenced her artistic work in later years. Some people said that Emily Carr preferred animals to people. Her collection of companions included dogs, cats, a parrot and a rat, and even a pet monkey named Woo. Her respectable neighbours were shocked when she wheeled her animals around in a baby carriage while shopping in Victoria. Many people considered Emily Carr at best a bit strange, if not eccentric. Unable to earn a living by painting, she was forced to run a boarding house and take in tenants. For a long period of time she even gave up painting altogether.

Emily Carr did return to painting after meeting Lawren Harris, one of the Group of Seven painters. He encouraged her to paint the British Columbia forests that were so much a part of her life. As a result she returned to the lush, dense overgrown forests of British Columbia. She painted deep in the quiet forests, where the sun's rays

Emily Carr and her pet monkey, Woo.

hardly came through the thick branches. The trees she portrayed on her canvas looked like soldiers guarding the secrets of the forest. Emily Carr used sweeping strokes of paint to illustrate the feeling and power of the forests. She painted only the essentials of her landscape and left out smaller details, which she found distracting. When she was in her fifties Emily Carr saw her work begin to gain gradual acceptance. Some of her canvases were accepted for display in the National Art Gallery at Ottawa. But then came a series of heart attacks that prevented her from continuing her trips into the wilds of British Columbia. So Emily Carr turned her talents to writing. She wrote of her childhood, of her life in the woods, and of her paintings. She called her book *Klee Wyck*, 'the laughing one', a nickname the Indians of the Pacific coast had given her. To her great surprise, *Klee Wyck* won the Governor-General's Award for non-fiction. Her success as a writer drew renewed public interest in her paintings.

In 1941 the city of Victoria finally recognized Emily Carr by giving her a seventieth birthday party. She died in 1945, but today her paintings are exhibited in every major Canadian collection, and Emily Carr is recognized as one of Canada's best known painters.

KKK

One of the most undesirable elements of American life that crept into Canadian society was the Ku Klux Klan. The Klan was a secret organization, originally founded in 1866 in the southern United States. Its aims were to terrorize former negro slaves and to stop them from voting. Secret rituals, midnight rides, and ceremonies where crosses were burned attracted attention. Klan members wore white robes and hoods to disguise themselves as they tarred and feathered negroes or whipped their victims into unconsciousness. By 1923 Klan membership in the United States reached a high of 9 000 000.

During the 1920s the Ku Klux Klan spread to Canada and grew on the prairies and in Ontario. Anyone considered to be 'different' was called an enemy by the Klan. Their hatred was directed against Jews, Roman Catholics, foreigners, immigrants, and communists. On 1 July 1927, when other Canadians were celebrating the 60th anniversary of Confederation, the Klan gathered in Kingston, Ontario. They planned 'to awaken the conscience of Canada against foreigners, immigrants and members of non-Protestant religions.' Just a month earlier the largest Ku Klux Klan 'konclave' ever held in Canada took place in Moose Jaw. Almost 10 000 people from all parts of Saskatchewan heard Klan organizers demand that the city get rid of bootleggers, gamblers, and all foreigners involved in illegal activities. After two hours of spellbinding speeches, the crowd went out and burned a twenty-metre cross at the foot of Caribou Street.

A terrible incident took place in Oakville, Ontario in February 1930. The Klan objected when they heard a marriage was about to take place between a white and a black. They marched boldly along the main street in Oakville and burned a cross in protest. Four Klan members were charged under an old law that said masks could not be worn at night. One Klan member was found guilty and sentenced to three months in jail.

Interest in the Klan eventually dwindled in Canada and public opinion turned against it. In 1979 the F.B.I. estimated that there were 8000 Klan members in the United States and a few hundred in Canada.

Digging Deeper

1

Research the background of the 'Famous Five'. Each of the other four women was chosen by Emily Murphy to join her in signing the petition requesting the Supreme Court to declare that women are 'persons'. Try to decide why Murphy chose each one.

2

Write a dialogue for three people in which a modern feminist explains to Emily Murphy and Nellie McClung the problems facing women in Canada today. Include information on what gains you think Canadian women have made since the time of Murphy and McClung. What would the suffragists' reaction be to the changes in the position of Canadian women?

Name some Canadian women of today that you think should be appointed to the Senate. Give your reasons.

3

Stage an art exhibition for your class of the work of the Group of Seven. Collect reproductions of pictures or slides. Try to select paintings which illustrate the features of Canadian art which were outlined by J.M. Millman, the British critic quoted earlier. Explain which paintings are your favourites and why.

4

Discuss how the Group of Seven contributed to Canada's national identity.

5

Look carefully at as many copies of the work of Emily Carr as you can find. What do you think the artist was trying to say through her paintings? Do you like the paintings? Why or why not?

6

Lawren Harris was one member of the Group of Seven. Who were the others and what was the purpose of the Group? Choose an artist from the Group of Seven and do some research on his life. Did he face the same problems as Emily Carr faced?

7

Which of the following do you consider to be the greatest hero – a doctor conducting medical research, a sports celebrity, a rock star, a political leader, or an artist who portrays Canada in his or her paintings? Explain your opinion.

8

Choose one name from the list below.
> Mary Pickford
> Emily Carr
> Al Capone
> Doctors Banting and Best
> Tom Thomson

a) Discuss the ways in which this person has made history.
b) Who would you add to this list of history-makers of the twenties? Why?

9

Class Project –
A Decade in a Box

In a large cardboard box collect all the information you can find to show what life was like in the 1920s. Imagine the box will be a kind of time capsule to be opened by a future generation. Besides written work, try to include some or all of the following: records, articles of clothing, pictures, tapes of recorded interviews, drawings, models, and charts and graphs. Organize the material so that it tells a complete story of life in Canada during the 1920s.

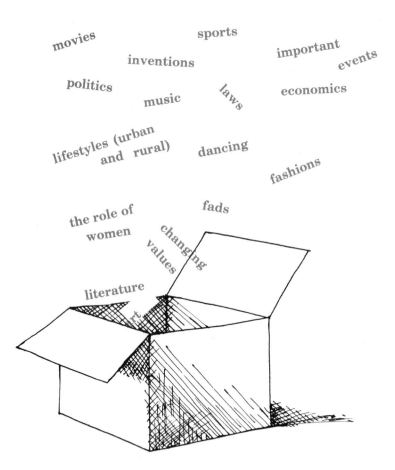

You could try out your time capsule on another class in your school. Later, in groups, you could make time capsules for each of the decades after the 1920s.

Refer back to the summary chart of themes at the end of Unit One (page 54). Using it as a model, make a chart for Unit Three. On the chart trace the development of those themes through this unit.

17

THE GREAT CRASH

'I was always sick two Fridays of every school year, that is when I was in grades 10 and 11 at Kelvin High School in Winnipeg. The first Friday was in early October and the second was late in June. I guess you can figure that one out.

'Those two days were when the school had its big dances, the two of the year. Sure, I got asked. I'd get two or three invitations a couple of weeks ahead, and it is pretty hard to tell a fellow you like that you are going to have the flu two weeks ahead. But I managed it. I always had the flu, which translated means I didn't have any clothes. At school we wore a sort of black uniform, all the girls, so that's how I got by there, but at a dance, no way.

'Kinda sad, isn't it? I might have met my one true love at one of those affairs.'

Your parents probably cannot remember much about the Depression. They were too young. You can scarcely imagine it.

What was it really like in the 'Dirty Thirties'? Look at the following pictures in this unit to get an idea of what the conditions were like.

What caused the Great Depression? Many people would answer this question by saying the stock market crash of 1929. However, the stock market crash was not the cause – it was only a symptom that the economy of North America was very sick. In order to understand the Depression you have to understand how the stock market worked and what was happening in the 1920s.

Suppose you were living then. You and a group of friends want to form a new company to produce racoon coats (which were very fashionable). You will need to buy furs, rent a building, pay workers (furriers), hire salesmen, and pay for advertising. You estimate that you will need $100 000 to start your company. How could you raise the money? You could use all your savings, or you could borrow the money from the bank, or you could raise money by selling stocks in your company. In this last case you get people to invest in your company by buying stocks. If you sold 10 000 stocks at $10, you would have the $100 000 necessary to start your company. Each stock represents a piece of the business. The stockholder owns a share of the business and shares the company's successes and failures. To show his or her investment in the business, the stockholder is given a piece of paper called a stock certificate.

A Stock Exchange.

Most people would like to know how to make a fortune on the stock market. The answer is simple: buy plenty of stocks when the price is low and sell those stocks when their price is high. That sounds easy, but a great deal of knowledge, skill, and good luck are needed to make a fortune! Suppose that you would like to try. This is what you would do.

First, you would visit a stockbroker whose job it is to buy and sell stocks in a kind of marketplace known as the stock exchange. (Buying and selling stocks, and the place in which this is done, are both called the stock market.) The stockbroker will place your order for you and carry out the details of your transaction.

Let us suppose that you decide to buy some shares in a company called Canuck Racoon Coat Company. The stocks themselves represent a share in the ownership of that company. If there are 10 000 shares in the Canuck Racoon Coat Company and you own 100 of them, you own 1/100 of the company's shares.

People buy shares in companies in order to make money. Suppose you buy your 100 shares of Canuck Racoon Coat Company. You pay $25 per share. Your total investment is $2500. A few months later the value of the stocks has risen to $35 per share. This has happened because business has been booming and racoon coats have become a very popular item of clothing. At this point you sell your 100 stocks at $35 per share. You paid out $2500 but got back $3500. The difference of $1000 is called a profit or capital gain. In both buying and selling transactions you will have to pay your stockbroker a small fee for handling the business for you.

There is another way to make money from your stocks. Companies will usually divide up some of the profits among the shareholders. These payments to shareholders are called dividends. Since you own 1/100 of the stocks in the Canuck Racoon Coat Company, you are entitled to receive 1/100 of the amount the company pays out in dividends.

The prices of stocks go up and down almost every day. There are many complicated reasons for this. One of the most important reasons is that if people wish to buy a certain stock, prices will go up because they are willing to pay the price. If nobody wants a particular stock, or if several people wish to sell it, the price on the market will probably fall.

Exercise:
Explain in your own words the meaning of each of the following:

stocks	stock exchange	capital gain
stockbroker	investor	dividend

The Stock Market Game

1. Pick three or four class members to be stockbrokers. The brokers set up their offices in the corners of the classroom. Brokers are given a supply of stock certificates and a stock record page.

2. The rest of the class are investors. Each investor makes up an expense sheet.

3. The purpose of the Stock Market Game is to gain experience in playing the stock market. Your aim is to make as much money as possible. You start with $5000 that has been left to you as an inheritance in your grandmother's will. You may invest any amount of money in one company or all three. For the purpose of the game, you cannot sell your stock during the first three cycles. The investor must carefully record each purchase on the expense sheet.

Cycle 1   Year 1925
Stocks for the following three companies are for sale:

Consolidated Mining and Smelting of Canada at $50 a stock
Winnipeg Electric Light   at $30 a stock
International Nickel   at $25 a stock

Investors are given time to visit the stockbrokers and record their investments. ⟫⟶

Cycle 2   Year 1927

Two years have passed. The economy of the country has been strong and the stocks have increased in value. Each investor calculates the profits made on these stocks if these stocks had been sold in 1927. Your teacher will tell you the amount of the increase.

Cycle 3   September 1929

Each investor calculates the profits made on these stocks.

Debriefing

Class discusses:
a) If this were real life, how would you feel?
b) What would investors do with their profits?
c) What would companies do with their profits?

Cycle 4   29 October 1929 – 'Black Tuesday'

Each investor calculates the losses on these stocks. Investors should be given an opportunity to sell stocks to the teacher if they wish.

Debriefing

Class discusses:
a) How do you feel about your losses?
b) What would you do if this were real life?
c) How would your actions affect the economy of the country?
d) How would companies suffer?

Cycle 5   Year 1932

Investors who have held onto their stock must calculate their losses.

Debriefing

Class discusses:
a) What alternatives are open to investors?
b) Who would be buying stocks in 1932?
Teachers may, if they wish, develop new steps of stock prices to illustrate future upswings in the business cycle.

The Business Cycle

Economic conditions are generally subject to constant change. There are good times when the economy is on the upswing, and there are bad times when business declines. Economists who chart the upswings and downswings of the economy over a period of years call these ups and downs the 'business cycle'. They identify four stages:

1) prosperity;
2) recession;
3) depression;
4) recovery.

The economy of North America in the 1920s is a good example of the prosperity stage in the business cycle. Prices and wages are high. Few people are unemployed. Business profits and production are high. When a recession sets in, business begins to slow down. Companies that have produced too many goods begin to realize they cannot sell everything they produce. Therefore they begin to lay off some workers and cut back production. Unemployment rises. Workers who have been laid off have less money to spend. Others who still have jobs are more careful about how they spend or invest their money. Sales begin to fall. If the recession becomes very serious and widespread, it is known as a time of depression. Now many businesses are forced to lay off employees; some may go bankrupt. Unemployment reaches high levels. Eventually a shortage of consumer goods develops because of the cutbacks in production. To meet the demand businesses begin to increase production and to call back workers. Wage earners now have more money to spend and to put into the economy. The recovery stage of the business cycle commences. Eventually prosperity returns.

'A RECESSION is when a neighbour has to tighten his belt. A DEPRESSION is when you have to tighten your own belt. And a PANIC is when you have no belt to tighten and your pants fall down.'

T.C. Douglas,
first leader of the N.D.P.

THE BUSINESS CYCLE

DEPRESSION

Sales—LOW Wages—LOW
Prices—LOW
Production—LOW Business Profits—LOW
Business Failures—HIGH
Demand for goods—LOW
Labour Unrest—FEW STRIKES
Unemployment—VERY HIGH

RECESSION

Sales—DECLINING Wages—FALLING
Prices—FALLING
Production—DECLINING Business
Profits—DECREASING
Business Failures—INCREASING
Demand for Goods—DECLINING
(Buyers' Market)
Labour Unrest—HIGH
(Many Strikes)
Unemployment—INCREASING

RECOVERY

Sales—RISING
Prices—RISING
Production—INCREASING Wages—RISING
Profits—INCREASING Business
Business Failures—DECREASING
Demand for goods—FEW STRIKES
Labour Unrest—FEW STRIKES
Unemployment—FALLING

PROSPERITY

Sales—HIGH Wages—HIGH
Prices—HIGH
Production—HIGH Business Profits—HIGH
Business Failures—LOW
Demand for goods—HIGH
(Sellers' Market)
Labour Unrest—MANY STRIKES
Unemployment—LOW

18
CAUSES OF THE GREAT DEPRESSION

The stock market crash of 1929 did not cause the Depression. Rather, it was a symptom that the economy of North America was very, very sick. What had happened to the once strong and healthy North American economy? What were the causes of this sickness? What remedies could be prescribed to make it well again?

There seem to be as many explanations for the Depression as there are experts to diagnose the illness. However, some of the major causes are as follows:

Fruit Store, around 1930.

1. Over-production and over-expansion

During the prosperous 1920s Canadian and American agriculture and industry reached high levels of production. Almost every industry was expanding. They spent large amounts of their profits adding to their factories or building new ones. Huge supplies of food, newsprint, minerals, and manufactured goods were being produced in Canada and simply stockpiled. Automobile centres such as Oshawa and Windsor produced 400 000 cars in 1930. To do this made little sense because Canadians already owned over a million cars and in the best year ever had purchased only 260 000. The Canadian market could absorb only so many goods. Even in the general prosperity of the 1920s many Canadians could still not afford to buy everything they wanted. As a result, large stocks of newsprint, radios, shirts, shoes, and cars began to pile up unsold in warehouses. Soon factory owners began to panic and slowed down their production until some of these surplus goods could be sold. Workers were laid off. This meant that fewer and fewer families had money to spend on goods already produced. This in turn slowed down sales even more.

Industrialists seemed to have forgotten a basic lesson in economics: you should only produce as many items as you can sell. In the 1920s wages were simply not high enough for people to buy everything being turned out in the factories.

Questions:
1. Name some products that were stockpiled.
2. Why were Canadian families not buying these products?
3. Explain how over-production led to factory slow-downs.
4. Explain: 'You should only produce as many items as you can sell.'

2. Canada's dependence on a few primary products

Canada depended too much for its wealth on a few primary or basic products. These included wheat, fish, minerals, and pulp and paper. Canada's most important exports were these goods. They are known as staples. As long as there was a heavy demand in the world for these products, Canada would prosper. However, if there was a surplus of these goods on the world market, or if foreign countries stopped buying from Canada, our economy would be in serious trouble.

In the depression, certain areas of Canada, which depended largely on one primary product, found themselves in deep economic trouble. The Maritimes and the West were especially hard hit.

Secondary industries involve the processing or manufacturing of primary products. These would also suffer from any slow-down in production. A good example is wheat. In the late 1920s Canada faced growing competition from Argentina and Australia which were also wheat-exporting countries. The price of wheat on the world market began to fall. To add to the problem,

western farmers were faced with terrible droughts in the summers of 1929, 1931, and 1933-37. Without adequate rainfall, no crops grew. With little income, farmers could not purchase machinery and manufactured goods from eastern Canada. Many could not afford to pay the mortgages on their farms. With no wheat to be shipped and no flour to be ground, railways and flour mills began to feel the pinch. The farmers' problems had caused a chain reaction on many parts of Canadian society.

A drought near Swift Current.

Questions:
1. Name examples of primary industries.
2. Name four industries that would also suffer if the farmer could not sell his wheat or had no wheat to sell.
3. What would the economic consequences of a decline in the world sales of wheat be for Canada? What would the chain reaction be?

3. Canada's dependence on the United States

The economy of Canada in the 1920s was closely linked with that of the United States. This is still true today. In those years we bought sixty-five per cent of our imports from the Americans. Forty per cent of our exports were sent to the U.S.A. The Americans were our most important trading partner. The U.S.A. had replaced Britain as the largest buyer of Canadian products and the largest supplier of investment funds for our industries. Even then we were in danger of what today is called a 'branch-plant economy'. It was not surprising that when the American economy got sick, Canada also suffered. One comedian said, 'When the United States sneezed, the rest of the world got pneumonia.'

When the Depression hit the United States, banks closed, industries collapsed, and people were out of work as factories shut down. No longer did Americans need our lumber, paper, wheat, and minerals. It was inevitable that Canada's economy would suffer too.

Questions:
1. How much did Canada export to and import from the U.S.A.?
2. Why did a depression in the U.S.A. have such serious repercussions in Canada?
3. What do you think is meant by a 'branch-plant economy'? Give examples.

4. High tariffs choked off international trade

In the 1920s European nations were recovering from a devastating war. They needed many of the surplus manufactured goods that the U.S. and Canada produced. Unfortunately they were heavily in debt from the war and often could not afford to buy them.

At the same time, many countries adopted a policy known as protective tariffs. In order to protect their home industries from foreign competition, they placed high tariffs (taxes) on foreign imports. Country X found that its goods were being kept out of country Y by high tariffs. Soon country X placed high tariffs on imports from country Y. Thus world trade began to slow down. Surplus goods in one country were kept out of another country that needed them. While high tariffs were used to protect home industries, they choked off international trade.

Questions
1. Why do countries put high tariffs on foreign goods? Who benefits from high tariffs? Who suffers?
2. Why was international trade important to Canada?
3. How did high tariffs between countries choke off international trade and contribute to the Depression?

5. Too much credit buying

All through the twenties Canadians were encouraged by advertising to 'buy now, pay later'. A famous comedian, Will Rogers, said that the way to solve the traffic problem was to remove from highways all cars that hadn't been paid for. He meant that so many cars were bought on credit that very few cars would actually remain on the road. Will Rogers was only joking but his remark points up the fact that by 1929 credit buying was a well-established custom. Why wait to buy a washing machine or a phonograph or a tractor or a piano when you could have it now with a small down payment?

Many families got themselves hopelessly into debt with credit buying. The piano that cost $445 cash was purchased with $15 down and $12 a month for the next four or five years. It ended up costing far more than it was worth. Sometimes by the time the purchases were paid for, they were ready for the junk pile. One radio comedian joked that he had said to his wife, 'One more payment and the furniture is ours.' To this she replied, 'Good, then we can throw it out and get some new stuff!'

If the wage-earner took sick or was laid off work it was often impossible to keep up the payments. As the Depression worsened, many people lost everything. Their refrigerators, stoves, washing machines, cars, and even their homes were repossessed by their creditors (the people they owed money to).

Eviction in Montreal.

Questions:
1. How did too much credit buying lead to problems for many people during the Depression?
2. Is it ever wiser to buy on credit rather than with cash? If so, when?
3. Why do many people prefer to pay cash while others use credit? Which way seems best to you?

6. Too much credit buying of stocks

For many people in the 1920s, the stock market seemed an easy way to get rich quickly. People in all walks of life gambled on the stock market. Rich business tycoons invested in shares but so did their chauffeurs and the typists in their offices. Feelings of confidence were at an all time high. People expected that prosperity would last forever.

It was not even necessary to have a lot of money to play the stock market. You could buy stocks on credit just as you could a phonograph or a washing machine. The only thing needed was a small cash down payment, usually about ten per cent. The broker loaned you the rest of the money (at a high interest rate of course!). But to buy a thousand dollars worth of stock you needed only a hundred dollars cash. The idea was that as soon as your stocks went up in value you could sell them. Then you paid back your loan to your broker and pocketed the profits. This risky process was called 'buying on margin'.

Buying stocks on margin was not too expensive if stocks kept rising quickly in value. But what if your stocks didn't go up? Or, worse still, what if they went down? How would you pay back your loans? You would have to sell your stocks or risk financial ruin.

This is exactly what happened in October 1929. When the value of stocks started to drop, people panicked. They started to sell. Prices fell even lower as more and more stocks were dumped onto the market. The market was like a giant roller-coaster racing downhill. Nothing could stop it. In a few hours the value of most stocks nosedived by more than fifty per cent. Shareholders lost millions. Big and small investors were wiped out in a few hours. Slowly it began to dawn on people that hard times were here. The Great Depression had begun.

Questions:
1. How does a person gamble when playing the stock market?
2. Explain 'buying on margin'. Use an example to show that you understand how it works.
3. Why did investors panic in October 1929? As more and more investors tried to sell out, why did prices decline even more rapidly?

Digging Deeper

To help understand the effects of the Depression, identify a major industry in your area and assume it goes out of business. List all the secondary industries related to that industry. How will they be affected by the shut-down?

1

What could governments have done in the 1920s to prevent a depression?

2

Invite a local stockbroker to visit your classroom. Ask questions you may have about how the stock market works. You should ask him to explain the changes in regulations that would prevent the stock market from crashing today as it did in 1929.

3

Compare the economic conditions of the late 1920s with those of today. Speculate about the possibility of a depression occurring again.

4

Write an article to accompany the following headline from the *Toronto Star*, 29 October 1929:

5

STOCK PRICES CRASH EARLY; SLIGHT RALLY LATER

This unit is full of new vocabulary about the stock market. Make a dictionary in your notebook of all the new words you encounter.

6

19

WHAT WAS IT LIKE?

In the memory of living Canadians, nothing like the Great Depression had ever happened before. It had a devastating effect on most people. To get an understanding of what social conditions were like in Canada in the 1930s, examine the material that follows. There are pictures, letters written to Prime Minister Bennett from suffering citizens, facts and figures, and memories collected through interviews with Canadians who remember those days.

Many unemployed men drifted from town to town across Canada looking for jobs. They rode 'free' on the railways by hiding in boxcars, perching on their roofs, or riding the rods underneath the trains.

In 1935 Winnipeg brought the Grey Cup west for the first time. In 1936, the western champions, the Regina Roughriders, could not raise $5000 for the trip to Toronto to play the deciding game. The Grey Cup went back to the east by default.

Mother Nature added to the problems of the West by turning off the tap. The resulting drought meant that large sections of the prairie topsoil just blew away during the 'Dirty Thirties'. Black blizzards of dust buried fences and drifted up to eaves of houses. In some places the dust drifts were so deep that highways had to be closed.

Railway crews used steam shovels to clear dust from the tracks near Grainger, Alberta.

Another disaster to hit the West was grasshopper plagues. The insects ate the crops as soon as they popped out of the ground. They even ate clothes hung out to dry on the line.

In the 1930s the Saskatchewan government paid children a penny for each gopher tail they turned in. It was an attempt to save the parched wheat from the hungry rodents.

Steam shovel clearing track in Alberta.

There was no unemployment insurance, no family allowance, and no government medical care. The only help available was government relief. Relief was emergency financial assistance to the unemployed to keep them from starving. There was no uniform system of relief across the country. The federal government gave large sums of money to local municipalities who administered the relief in their own way. The unemployed were never given cash, but only vouchers. The vouchers could be exchanged for food, rent, and other necessities.

Poor family returning to Saskatoon.

Many penniless prairie families simply gave up in despair and abandoned their farms. The desperation and poverty can be seen on the faces of this family who are heading for the Peace River country. Between 1931 and 1937, 66 000 people left Saskatchewan, 34 000 left Manitoba, and 21 000 left Alberta.

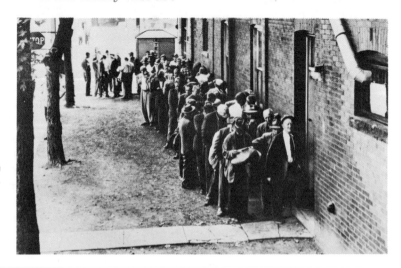

Soup kitchen line-up in Toronto.

At that time of this country's existence there was no money, there were no jobs, and yet everybody who had a job really looked down his nose at the poor guy who didn't. I've never been able to understand this. I wouldn't say there was no compassion, but people seemed to take the attitude that if you didn't have a job you were just a bum.

'Pogey' was hobo slang for food, clothing, and shelter provided by public relief agencies.

A Manitoba judge, George Stubbs, observed of relief, 'It's not quite enough to live on, and a little too much to die on.'

A family of seven in Toronto in 1934 received $6.93 each week for food.

You asked me what a Bennett Buggy was? There were hundreds of them, and I wonder if there is even one now in some museum, some farm exhibit somewhere. In the twenties, farmers bought automobiles, Chevs, Fords, Overlands, Reos, the Hupmobile, oh, ... a lot that they don't even make any more. Then came the crash and the drought and nobody had

A Bennett Buggy.

any money for gasoline, let alone repairs, and they'd thrown out all those fine old buggies every farm used to have, so what was left? A car that wouldn't run.

Somebody got the idea of lifting out the engine and taking out the windshield and sticking a tongue onto the chassis with double trees and that's where

old Dobbin and Dolly got back to work again. Two horsepower. Eight kilometres an hour, but those oat burners got you there. Then somebody got the idea, the country was full of wits, to call these contraptions Bennett Buggies. Poor old R.B. Bennett. All over Saskatchewan and Alberta there were these carved up cars,

named after him, and a constant reminder that he'd been prime minister when the disaster struck.

Of course, it was wonderful advertising for the Liberals too. Bennett Buggies – there goes the guy who got us into this fix.

Applying for relief was the most humiliating thing a man had to do. When you were on relief, the fact was clearly advertised to the world. Merchandise acquired by voucher was seldom wrapped. Merchants did not feel obliged to wrap shoe boxes or clothing when the customer was in no position to complain about it.

In Ontario, relief applicants had to turn in their liquor permits before any aid was given. At that time citizens had to have a government permit to buy alcohol. Telephones had to be disconnected and the driver's licence handed in. This was done to guarantee that taxpayers' money was not used to finance any kind of luxury. Accepting a job or refusing to accept a job meant the immediate end of relief.

In 1932 the federal government began to finance a system of relief camps for single unemployed men. Many of the camps were in isolated areas of British Columbia. The men worked eight hours a day cutting brush, moving rocks, and building roads. In return they were fed and sheltered and paid 20¢ a day. The camps, however, became a source of great discontent. The

Inside a Relief Camp.

The On-To-Ottawa Trek.

wage of 20¢ a day was considered little better than slave labour. In June 1935 thousands of men, fed up with life in the B.C. relief camps, boarded freight trains bound for Ottawa to protest the government. This was known as the On-to-Ottawa Trek. The men got as far as Regina, where they were stopped by the Mounted Police. In the riot that followed one man was shot dead and fifty were wounded. Many of the strike leaders were arrested and the protest was put down. Eventually most of the strikers were persuaded to return home or back to the camps on special trains, and they were promised wage increases to 40¢ an hour.

Sample Prices of the 1930s

Toronto relief officials gave a family of seven $6.93 a week for food. Use the following shopping list to plan a menu for a family of seven, spending no more than 99¢ a day.

Milk	10¢ / quart	Cheap cut	
Eggs	15¢ / dozen	of roast beef	12¢ / pound
Potatoes	25¢ / 25 pounds	Butter	25¢ / pound
Rolled oats	5¢ / pound	Sugar	16¢ / pound

Peanut butter	16¢ / pound	Cabbage	4¢ / pound
Carrots	4¢ / pound	Flour	5¢ / pound
Onions	4¢ / pound	Dried beans	4¢ / pound
Prunes	12¢ / pound	Molasses	13¢ / pint
Bread	5¢ / loaf	Turnips	4¢ / pound

Analyse the menus that have been prepared. Do you consider them appetizing and nutritionally balanced? Why or why not? What problems could develop with a steady diet of these kinds of meals?

'Did you have a job during the Depression?'

'– No, but my brothers in Kingston worked for 15¢ a day by driving tractors. I was on relief. They gave us prunes [to eat] and a pair of boots once a year. We got pants but no suits – just salvage, surplus clothes. I once asked Mayor Kaiser for food but he said no. That guy [the mayor] had butter on his table. Everyone else had fatty, lardy margarine. To get my relief, I killed rats in the dump on Gibb Street and dug sewers and ditches.'

'What was life like for you during the Depression? Did your husband have a job?'

'– I remember my husband was very sick for the first few years of the Depression. That started things off badly for us. He worked for a farmer and got $19 a month. We had to try to get by on it, but if his parents hadn't helped us, I don't know what we would have done. The doctor in Beaverton was really good and I remember he operated on my husband right on our kitchen table. He was really sick for a while there but the doctor had us pay him only $100. We owed him well over $500 but he told us he would wipe his books clean of what we owed him.'

'Can you think of ways you used to get extra money?'

'– We couldn't take in boarders because we couldn't afford to pay for food for them. I never drew a dime of welfare or relief and I'm darned proud of it. I was in World War I and I got a little pension.'

'– People just couldn't earn money – there was none available. Because I was on relief I lost my driver's licence. I remember we used to get coal from the trains that passed by. Some of the engineers [the men who fed the coal into the train's engine] would throw some coal out for us as the train went by.'

'Where did you get your clothes from?'

'– Mother made all the clothes for us from old clothes that had been given to us. I remember she knitted wool stockings because it was so cold. Mother's relatives in the States would send us old clothes and many of these had moth holes in them. I was embarrassed to wear the old clothes. It seemed mine were the worst of all the kids in the school. A few times my aunt from Toronto brought us kids some brand new clothes. She also would bring us some of her home-made muffins and scones.'

Boiling up lunch by the C.N.R. tracks.

'How did you feel about the railroad riders?'

'– They were terrible. I was never one of them myself. They used to ask me for food and I would tell them to stay in one place. But they said when you start to go you must go; you can't stop – like a rolling ball.'

'– I guess they had nothing else to do since they had no jobs and couldn't afford to pay the train fares. A lot of them came to our place asking for food. We gave them meals but we made sure they washed first because they were all so dirty. We couldn't turn away these hobos since we had something to eat ourselves.'

'What was Christmas like?'

'– Mother and Papa always made sure we would get something for Christmas. Once they bought us a box of chocolates and that was a real treat. In our stockings we would get some apples, an orange, and some candies. For a Christmas tree, Papa would cut down a tree from the farm and we would decorate it with the ornaments Mother had saved from our old home in Toronto.'

'– It was sort of grim and we had to make the best of it. We always had our own fowl for Christmas dinner but we couldn't afford to spend a lot on gifts. I remember giving a towel to my mother-in-law one Christmas. We gave little things like that. For the children we bought clothes and the odd toy – a top, ball. They always got a big kick out of helping me make the Christmas decorations out of tissue paper.'

'What did you do for entertainment?'

'– There were parties held every second Saturday for those who didn't work. A great interest was shown in sports by everybody. Playing softball and flying kites were especially popular.'

'– We had a radio and went to the movies a few times. The kids would go swimming in the lake and creeks.'

'– There were plenty of house parties. Everybody from around town would get together and we all had a good time. The music was provided by anyone who could play an instrument.'

'How did your family make a living? What was life like for you during the Depression?'

'All during the twenties my father was a bricklayer in Toronto, but by mid-1930 he no longer had a job. There was just no longer any work available for him. We believed that the only people who had jobs in Toronto were those who worked in offices and businesses. My parents figured that the only solution was to go and live on a farm where we could get enough to eat. As a result, my family sold our home in Toronto and moved to a farm near Ashburn, Ontario in the fall of 1930. Not having enough money, we bought the farm on a mortgage basis. There was an apple orchard and we raised various farm animals such as cows, chickens, and pigs. To earn money for our family, my parents travelled to Toronto in their old Durant [a make of car] and sold the farm goods there. We only had the car for a few years because it broke down and we could not afford to have it repaired. During their trips to Toronto, my parents went from
≫→

house to house trying to sell apples and eggs. They did not make much money selling their farm produce because few people would buy, or could afford to buy, the goods.'

'– The reason people wouldn't admit poverty was because they were too proud. I remember people brought coal sacks uptown to get relief. It was very humiliating for people to be seen with these. Not everyone got relief though, because there wasn't enough to go around.'

Southwark, Alberta, 13 May 1931

Gentlemen:

I am a married man, with three children dependant upon me. I am a returned soldier, having served in the Canadian Expeditionary Forces as a VOLUNTEER, and not as a conscript, in the front line trenches in 1915, and was finally discharged in April 1919 as medically unfit. I do not receive an army pension. I hold the Mons Medal, The Canadian General Service and The Victory Medals of the last war, also the Class 'A' France button and the Class 'B' (England) button. At present there is in my house the following NECESSITIES, (and NO LUXURIES)

Bread 2 home-made loaves
Flour NONE
Yeast NONE
Dried raisins ½ a packet
Sugar NONE for past 3 days
Butter NONE
Fat, Dripping, Lard, etc. NONE
Meat None, have had 40¢ worth in past six weeks.
Vegetables, About half bag, potatoes, None of any other kind.

Tea 2 ounces
Coffee, cocoa, etc. NONE
Soap NONE OF ANY KIND. Neither toilet nor laundrey.
Milk About 2 quarts
Oatmeal about 3 lbs.
Salt 5 cents worth
Wheat about 3 lbs.
Syrup, Honey, Jam, Peanut Butter or other 'Spreads for bread' NONE
Eggs ONE DOZEN.

Note: On Sunday evening May 3rd we had 164 eggs showing that we have eaten 152 eggs in past 9 days or over 3 eggs each per day. Yesterday noon my wife and children arrived at the point where they could no longer eat the eggs and keep them down. It is more than a week since any of my family had butter on their bread, the previous week they had one pound, kindly GIVEN by a local friend.

As you are aware, I have received 'relief' from the village during the past winter amounting to about 39 dollars, of which I have 'Worked-off' about 24 dollars, the remainder of which I am willing and anxious to work off at any time, or to repay when I am able. Tomorrow I am withdrawing my 8 year old son from school attendance, as he is not getting enough nourishment to permit of his being able to study, and furthermore we have no soap to wash him or ourselves, or any of our clothes.

Thanking you for your kind assistance in the past, and assuring you that I would prefer remunerative work to charity, I am,

Gentlemen,
Very truly yours,
Richard J. O'Hearn

Passman Sask.
16 Oct 1933

Dear Sir

I am a girl thirteen years old and I have to go to school every day its very cold now already and I haven't got a coat to put on. My parents can't afford to buy me anything for this winter. I have to walk to school four and a half mile every morning and night and I'm awfully cold every day. Would you be so kind to sent me enough money to so that I could get one.
My name is

Edwina Abbott
[Reply: $5.00]

May 20/31

Mr. Bennette

Since you have been elected, work has been impossible to get. We have decided that in a month from this date, if thing's are the same, We'll skin you alive, the first chance we get

Sudbury Starving Unemployed

Craven Alberta
Feb 11-1935

Dear Sir

Please don't think Im crazy for writing you this letter, but I've got three little children, and they are all in need of shoes as well as underwear but shoe's are the most neaded as two of them go to school and its cold, my husband has not had a crop for 8 years only enough for seed and some food, and I don't know what to do. I hate to ask for help. I never have before and we are staying off relief if possible. What I wanted was $3.00 if I could possible get it or even some old cloths to make over but if you don't want to do this please don't mention it over radios as every one knows me around here and I'm well liked, so I beg of you not to mention my name. I've never asked anyone around here for help or cloths as I know them to well.

Yours Sincerly
Mrs. P.E. Bottle
[Reply: $5.00]

Ottawa
Marth the 4th 1932

Dear Sir,

I am just writing a few lines to you to see what can be done for us young men of Canada. We are the growing generation of Canada, but with no hopes of a future. Please tell me why is it a single man always gets a refusal when he looks for a job. A married man gets work, & if he does not get work, he gets relief. Yesterday I got a glimpse of a lot of the unemployed. It just made me feel down-hearted, to think there is no work for them, or in the future, & also no work for myself. Last year I was out of work three months. I received work with a local farm. I was told in the fall I could have the job for the winter; I was then a stable man. Now I am slacked off on account of no snow this winter. Now I am wandering the streets like a beggar, with no future ahead. There are lots of single men in Ottawa, who would rather walk the streets, & starve, than work on a farm. That is a true statement. Myself I work wherever I can get work, & get a good name wherever I go. There are plenty of young men like myself, who are in the same plight. I say again whats to be done for us single men? do we have to starve? or do we have to go round with our faces full of shame, to beg at the doors of the well to do citizen. I suppose you will say the married men come first; I certainly agree with you there. But have you a word or two to cheer us single men up a bit? The married man got word he was ⟫→

169

going to get relief. That took the weight of worry off his mind quite a bit. Did the single man here anything, how he was going to pull through? Did you ever feel the pangs of hunger? My Idea is we shall all starve. I suppose you will say I cant help it, or I cant make things better. You have the power to make things better or worse. When you entered as Premier you promised a lot of things, you was going to do for the country. I am waiting patiently to see the results. Will look for my answer in the paper.

Yours Truly R.D. Ottawa

Murray Harbour·P.E.I.
March 24 1935

Premier Bennett:
Dear Sir:

I am writing you to see if their is any help I could get.
As I have a baby thirteen days old that only weighs One Pound and I have to keep it in Cotton Wool & Olive Oil, and I havent the money to buy it, the people bought it so far and fed me when I was in Bed. if their is any help I could get I would like to get it as soon as possible.
their is five of a family, Counting the baby.
their will be two votes for you next Election
Hoping too hear from you soon
Yours Truly.
Mrs. Jack O'Hannon
[Reply: $5.00]

Grimsby, Ontario
Nov. 3rd, 1933.

Dear Sir
Why not put some of these foreigners and Indians in their own country and give a white man some show, as they are taking the work away from the Canadian men and I would think the Government could do something to prevent all of this. And the people wonder in Canada why so much robbing is carried on. Now why is it? If we have any government at all, why not look into it as our country is overrun by foreigners.

Ardath, Sask.
Aug. 24/35

Dear Mr. Bennett,
I have heard mamma and daddy talk about you so much, and what a good man you are. I am a little boy eight years old and I'm in Grade III at school. I've wanted a little red wagon to hich my dog to for so many years, but daddy has no money. Please, Mr. Bennett would you send me enuff money to buy my wagon. Thank you so much.

Your very good friend,
Horace Gardiner

Ardath, Sask.
Aug. 31/35

Dear Mr. Bennett,

Thanks very much for the money. I'm going to get the wagon. Mamma said I could.

Your friend,
Horace Gardiner

P.S. I am going to vote for you when I get to a big boy.

Your friend,
Horace Gardiner

Questions: Letters to Prime Minister Bennett

1. What sort of personal problems did people write about to Prime Minister Bennett? What could he do for them?
2. What were the special problems faced by the growing number of young single men? Was it right that married men got work or relief while single men did not? Why did the government give special preference to married men?
3. Why would a woman who wrote to Bennett beg him not to mention her name?
4. What help would be available today for a woman who gave birth to a one pound (450 grams) baby? What help was available to her in 1935? Do you think it was the duty of the government to help her? Why?
5. Explain what you think one writer meant when he said, 'I would prefer remunerative work to charity.'
6. Why would the veterans of World War I think the government ought to give them special help? Were they justified?
7. Why would some citizens express bitterness against foreigners during the Depression?

Digging Deeper

Which regions of Canada were hardest hit by the Depression? Suggest reasons why this was so.

1

Why were relief vouchers for food and rent given out during the Depression instead of cash? Do you think vouchers were a good or bad idea? Why? We sometimes hear of people today abusing the welfare system. Should vouchers rather than cash be given to welfare recipients today?

2

3 Imagine that your family's income dropped suddenly because the wage-earner was unemployed. Make a list of the possessions you would sell in order to raise money. Rank these things in order from those you would be most willing to sell to those you would be least willing to sell.

4 Write a human-interest story based on a photograph in this unit.

5 Debate: Any able-bodied man who is unemployed and receiving relief should be required to work at some project, such as sweeping the streets, in order to earn his relief money.

6 During the Depression many people in Canada suffered a great deal. The wealthy, however, noticed very few changes in the way they lived. Do some research to gather information on how the rich lived in Canada during the 1930s. Include facts on automobiles, holidays, clothing styles etc. Write an essay on 'How the Other Half Lived'.

Depression Interview

Interview people old enough to remember the Depression. Take notes or tape-record their impressions. Use the following questionnaire or make up one of your own. Share with your class what you discover in your interviews.

Suggestions for Conducting Good Interviews:
1. Know what information you are after – have a definite reason for the interview.
2. Prepare well in advance by researching the topic to be talked about.
3. Write out your questions beforehand. The right question is the only way to get the right information.
4. Think of secondary or follow-up questions to get deeper explanations.
5. Write down as much of the information as you can in notes or take along a tape recorder.
6. Expand your notes as soon as possible after the interview.

≫→

Subject's Name

Approximate Age During the Depression

Place of Residence During this Period

1. When someone mentions the Depression, what kind of thoughts come into your mind?
2. Why was there a depression?
3. Did you have a job during the Depression?

If YES
a) How much did you earn?
b) Did you try to add to it in any way?
c) What was your attitude toward the unemployed?

If NO
a) How did you survive?
b) Were you in debt?
c) How did you pay your rent?
d) What help could you get on relief?
e) Were you ever hungry?

4. What were the prices of goods that you remember?
5. What did you do for entertainment?
   What did teenagers do on Saturday nights?
   What was Christmas like during the Depression?
6. What was your happiest experience of those years?
   What was your most unhappy experience?
7. How did you feel about the people running the government? Did you think they were doing all they could?
8. Could there be another Depression? Why? Why not?

20
THE SEARCH
FOR SOLUTIONS

When the stock market crashed in 1929, the prime minister of Canada was the Liberal, William Lyon Mackenzie King. King did not seem to know what to do about the Depression other than to wait it out and hope things would get better. Then in 1930 King made the biggest political mistake of his entire career. Providing relief was the responsibility of the provinces and King, a Liberal, said that he would not give a 'five-cent piece' to any province that did not have a Liberal government. In the election of 1930, those words kept coming back to haunt King. The voters refused to forget King's 'five-cent piece' speech. The Liberals were voted out of office, and the Conservative party came into power.

The prime minister who replaced Mackenzie King was Richard Bedford Bennett. Bennett was a multi-millionaire lawyer from Calgary. He was a stern, dignified, and very prosperous looking gentleman.

During the election campaign Bennett had promised, 'I will end unemployment or perish in the attempt.' When he came to power, however, Bennett seemed to have no new ideas for handling any economic crisis. His policies were to give emergency funds to the provinces for relief. Military-style relief camps were set up for jobless single men in isolated parts of the country. The highest tariff in Canadian history was introduced to protect Canadian business from foreign competition. Unfortunately none of these acts had any great impact on the Depression. These measures were like first-aid treatment and did not cure the Depression. As times became more difficult, more and more people began to blame Bennett for their problems. Cars that could not run for lack of gas were hitched up to farm animals and called 'Bennett buggies'. The collections of shacks where the unemployed camped around cities were called 'Bennett boroughs'. 'Bennett coffee' was a cheap substitute for coffee made from roasted wheat or barley. Newspapers used as covers to keep warm on park benches were known as 'Bennett blankets'. A 'Bennett barnyard' was an abandoned farm.

R.B. Bennett knew that the people of Canada were growing increasingly angry with the government. Finally, in 1935, just before an election, Bennett startled the nation by starting a pro-

R.B. Bennett.

gram of radical reforms. The people called this 'Bennett's New Deal'. The program was copied to a large extent from a similar one introduced in the United States. In 1933 President Roosevelt had introduced a 'New Deal' to end the Depression. Roosevelt's idea was to use the government's resources to get the economy going. He reasoned that if people could afford things, more things would be manufactured and more workers would be employed who, in turn, would purchase more goods. Therefore Roosevelt's New Deal gave farmers government money and began many large federal projects to increase employment for many people.

In 1935 Bennett decided to take action. He called for legislation to establish unemployment and social insurance, set minimum wages so workers could not be paid less than a specific wage, limit the hours of work, guarantee the fair treatment of employees, and control prices so that businessmen could not make unfair profits.

Most people were startled by Bennett's radical new ideas. His political opponents suggested that the New Deal was nothing more than a plot to win votes in the forthcoming election. J.S. Woodsworth dismissed the whole New Deal as a 'death-bed conversion' of R.B. Bennett. Most Canadian voters were also suspicious. They felt that Bennett had left his reforms too late to do any good. In the election of 1935, King and the Liberals swept back to power in a landslide victory. The Liberals took 171 seats to the 39 seats taken by the Conservatives. R.B. Bennett left Canada and went to England. He accepted a title from the king and spent the rest of his days in a mansion in the south of England.

NEW POLITICAL PARTIES

As the 'Dirty Thirties' dragged on, more and more people became dissatisfied with the two main political parties, the Liberals and the Conservatives. The old parties seemed to have no new and fresh ideas for solving the economic troubles. Several new political parties were formed which promised to take more drastic action to eliminate the problems of the Depression. Three of the more important parties formed in the 1930s were the Co-operative Commonwealth Federation (C.C.F.), the Social Credit, and the Union Nationale. The first two have since achieved success at both federal and provincial levels. The Union Nationale, however, has always been a provincial party restricted to the province of Quebec.

The Co-operative Commonwealth Federation (C.C.F.)

The Co-operative Commonwealth Federation was born in the province of Saskatchewan. That province was probably the most severely hit by the Depression and the drought. A group of farmers, workers, teachers, and preachers came together under the leadership of a former Methodist minister, J.S. Woodsworth. In Regina in 1933 the C.C.F. outlined its program in a statement of policy that is known as the Regina Manifesto. The C.C.F. was a socialist party. It wanted the government to own the production and distribution of all key industries. It suggested that the income and business profits of the very rich be taxed heavily in order to provide social benefits for everybody.

Some of the main policies of the C.C.F. were as follows:

1. Vital industries and public services such as hydro-electric power, water supply, and transportation and communication should be taken over by the government.
2. Banks and insurance companies should be run by the government in order to control their profits.
3. There should be legislation to establish decent living standards and economic security for all workers (unemployment insurance, old age pensions, family allowances, sickness and accident insurance, and a limitation of the hours of work).
4. Health services, including hospital and medical costs, should be made available free to everybody.

5. Banks and mortgage companies should no longer be able to take over a farmer's land (foreclose on the mortgage) if he is unable to keep up the mortgage payment.
6. There should also be insurance for the farmer against unavoidable crop failure.
7. Large-scale public works projects should begin immediately to provide work for thousands of unemployed. These programs, including improvements such as housing and slum clearance, would greatly improve social conditions.

The C.C.F. won considerable success in the West. It became the government of Saskatchewan for many years under the leadership of T.C. Douglas. It changed its name to the New Democratic Party in 1961. More recently there have been N.D.P. governments in Manitoba and British Columbia as well. In national politics the C.C.F.-N.D.P. has not won enough support to be elected to govern. However, policies of the C.C.F.-N.D.P. have been very influential on both the Liberal and Conservative parties. A number of policies first suggested by the C.C.F. – for example unemployment insurance and old age pensions – were taken over by the other two parties in later years.

Social Credit

The farmers of Alberta, suffering the severe hardships of the Depression, turned to the Social Credit party as an answer to their problems. The first leader of the Social Credit in Alberta was William Aberhart, a radio preacher. 'Bible Bill', as Aberhart was known, had a vast radio audience and used his program to spread his idea of religion and politics.

W.J. Aberhart making a speech.

The program of Social Credit was built on the theories of a Scottish engineer, Major Douglas. Douglas pointed out that there was never enough money to buy the goods available. If there was more money in circulation for people to spend, sales would boom and industries would thrive. Aberhart seized on this idea and suggested that all citizens of the province should own its natural resources and share in its prosperity. His plan was to credit every man and woman each year with enough money to feed, shelter, and clothe themselves. Each citizen would be issued a certificate known as the Basic Dividend that was as good as money. The Dividend could be used to buy food, shelter, and clothing, and was given above any salary the citizen might be earning. Adults over the age of twenty-one would receive $25 a month. Young people from seventeen to twenty would receive between $10 and $20 depending on their age, and children under sixteen would receive $5 a month.

Aberhart's other extreme ideas about the control of banking and currency were never permitted. Banking and currency in Canada are federal matters and Aberhart's legislation was not allowed by the federal government. Instead, Social Credit became a party that defended the rights of business and a free, uncontrolled economy – the very opposite of the C.C.F. However, to most Albertan families, many of whom had little or no cash, the idea of the Dividend was highly attractive. The Social Credit party won office in Alberta and continued to hold power until long after the Depression ended. Social Credit governments have also been formed in the province of British Columbia.

Union Nationale

The Union Nationale party was founded in Quebec in 1935. It began as a protest against the high unemployment and the severe economic hardships of the Depression. Within a year the Union Nationale was able to win an important victory and become the government of the province of Quebec. Its leader was Maurice Duplessis.

The Union Nationale was a party of French Canadians. To them, the Depression emphasized the great economic gulf between the French and English in Canada. As the Depression dragged on, it seemed that the Quebec poor were generally French-speaking workers and farmers, while the rich were generally English-speaking people. Duplessis appealed to French-Canadian feelings of exploitation by the English minority. The party stood for the defence of the French language and culture and the Roman Catholic faith. Duplessis promised to protect his people from the English, the federal government, and communism. The Union Nationale was defeated in the election of 1939, but was returned to power in 1944. Duplessis maintained absolute control over the politics of Quebec until his death in 1959.

While these three new political parties had an impact in their provinces, politics in the 1930s had a limited effect in ending the Depression. What really helped to bring about the end of the Great Depression was the Second World War. As this war became inevitable, hundreds of unemployed men headed for the recruitment offices. Jobs in the armed forces meant the chance to work again. Factories that had been silent for years suddenly sprang to life. The Great Depression was about to end, and a greater evil ready to begin.

Digging Deeper

What could governments have done in the 1930s to reduce the horrible effects of poverty and unemployment?

1

Evaluate the effectiveness of R.B. Bennett in solving the problems created by the Depression.

2

Compare the solutions to the Depression which R.B. Bennett used with those employed by J.S. Woodsworth, William Aberhart, and Mackenzie King.

3

The Social Credit party in Alberta distributed money to Alberta citizens in order to encourage them to spend freely and thus increase industrial production. Some critics of this policy ridiculed it as 'funny money'. How does the government distribute money today in order to reduce poverty and increase purchasing power? How does this policy compare with Aberhart's 'funny money'?

4

The Depression was a critical turning-point in Canadian history. Make a list of present government agencies and services that were not available in 1930 for Canadians.

5

In the spring of 1935 thousands of men left relief camps in the West and started on a protest demonstration headed for Ottawa. Do some research on this On-To-Ottawa Trek. What were the demands of the protesters? Find out what happened when the marchers confronted the police in Regina. What was the outcome of the Trek?

6

21

THE GREAT ESCAPE

Atop the Empire State Building, King Kong swats away at attacking planes just before they shoot him down. Kong fights heroically for his life and his love. The screaming girl in his hairy paw is the Alberta-born leading lady, Fay Wray. When Miss Wray was first asked to play the role, she was told she would co-star with the tallest and darkest hero of Hollywood. Naturally she thought this would be the Hollywood heart-throb, Clark Gable. Instead, the hero turned out to be an enormous gorilla.

This was the golden age of Hollywood. People went to the movies seeking romance and adventure. For the price of a 25¢ ticket people could forget the dust storms and relief vouchers and enter the make-believe world of the Hollywood stars. The films, radio shows, songs, and magazines of those days provided a brief escape from reality. In the movies all the women were beautiful and all the men handsome. Crime did not pay and true love always triumphed in the end. Great film extravaganzas such as *Gone With the Wind* and Walt Disney's Mickey Mouse were popular box office attractions. Though all the films came from Hollywood, at least a dozen stars were Canadians. These included Beatrice Lillie, Marie Dressler, Norma Shearer, Deanna Durbin, Raymond Massey, and Walter Huston, who became famous international stars.

Of all the Hollywood child stars, none was loved more than Shirley Temple. She made her first film in 1934 at the age of four, and for the next four years was Hollywood's top box-office attraction. Her golden ringlets endeared her to millions as she sang and danced. Miss Temple's $300 000 yearly salary was boosted by the sale of Shirley Temple dolls, doll clothes, soaps, books, and ribbons. Many parents in the 1930s named their daughters after her and also did their daughters' hair in ringlets like those worn by the famous child star.

The one possession every family tried to keep during the dark days of the Depression was their radio. A floor model Philco, a Rogers Batteryless, or even an old battery-powered Atwater-Kent – any radio provided a vital escape from the dreariness of ordinary life. In the 1930s the radio was the gathering spot in the home. Since these were the days before television broadcasting, families depended on the radio for home entertainment.

Shirley Temple dolls.

Like the movies, the most popular radio shows came from the United States. They included 'Jack Benny', 'George Burns and Gracie Allen', 'The Lone Ranger', 'The Inner Sanctum', and of course 'Amos 'n' Andy'.

At the height of its popularity in the early years of the Depression, 'Amos 'n' Andy' had a larger audience than any other program in the history of broadcasting. 'Amos 'n' Andy' had to do with the comic misadventures of a pair of young black men who came north to Harlem, New York from rural Georgia to make a fortune in the taxi cab business. In New York they got mixed up with a 'con man' known as the Kingfish who was always trying to swindle them with get-rich-quick schemes. Listening to the hilarious adventures of Amos 'n' Andy each evening amounted to a national craze in both the United States and Canada. Restaurants and bars had to put in radios so that their

Amos 'n' Andy.

customers could listen to the program between 7:00 and 7:15 p.m., or else they would not have any customers. Incredible as it seems, some movie theatres stopped the film in mid-reel and at 7:00 p.m. wheeled in a radio and tuned in 'Amos 'n' Andy'. Moviegoers would have stayed at home otherwise. The Bell Telephone Company recorded a dramatic drop in the number of phone calls made between 7:00 and 7:15 each evening. Probably no one benefited more from the 'Amos 'n' Andy' craze than their sponsors, the makers of Pepsodent toothpaste. In the depths of the Depression, when many companies were going broke, Pepsodent saw its sales triple. Until this time most of the sponsors of network radio programs had been the manufacturers of radio sets. So, for better or worse, 'Amos 'n' Andy' proved that sponsoring a popular radio show could lead to the sale of vast quantities of such goods as toothpaste, soaps, cigarettes, coffee, and laxatives.

Because Canadian airwaves were being filled with American radio shows, Prime Minister Bennett felt something had to be done. The Canadian Radio Broadcasting Commission was started in 1933 to counteract American influence. Three years later the Canadian Broadcasting Corporation (C.B.C.) was on the air. Money was made available by the government to build more stations across the country and to improve the quality of Canadian broadcasting. In spite of the best efforts of the C.B.C., American programs were still more popular.

Probably no other radio broadcast affected Canadians more deeply than the one heard on 11 December 1936. It began with the words, 'At long last I am able to say a few words of my own.' It was the voice of King Edward VIII announcing his intention to marry a divorced American woman, Wallis Simpson. Because of that marriage, he was abdicating (leaving) the British throne. He soon became the Duke of Windsor, and his romance became the love story of the decade.

Three years later the C.B.C. covered the royal tour to Canada by the new king, George VI, and Queen Elizabeth. The first visit of a reigning monarch to Canada was carried by radio to even the most remote areas. The C.B.C. was proving that it could be a powerful force in establishing a sense of national unity across Canada and counteracting the American influence.

Like radio programs and movies, the magazines of the 1930s did not concentrate on the events of the Depression. Instead, they tried to reassure and amuse people and were filled with beautiful cover girls urging people to buy various advertised products. Again American magazines were the biggest sellers – *Reader's Digest, Time*, and *Life*. However, popular Canadian magazines included *Liberty, MacLean's, Chatelaine,* and *National Home Monthly*. Women's magazines tended to discuss

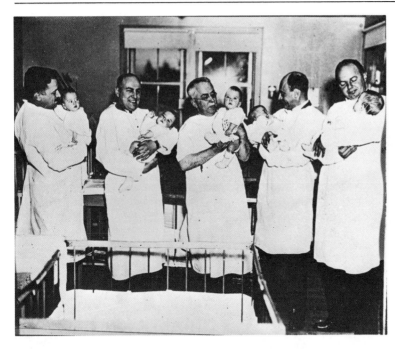

The Dionne quints.

babies, how to look after a husband, recipes, fashion, and caring for the home. Sexual matters and the status of women were considered to be controversial topics and were avoided.

Newspapers also downplayed the harsh conditions of the Depression because people became tired of reading bad news. Instead newspapers gave a great deal of space to human interest stories. One of the most spectacular was the birth of the Dionne quintuplets. Annette, Emilie, Yvonne, Cecile, and Marie, the world's first quintuplets to survive, were born to a poor Ontario family in 1934. Because the family was poor and already had several children, Ontario made the government the guardian of the Quints. A special home was built for the girls and nurses and teachers were provided for them. The Dionnes became a major tourist attraction, and millions of Canadians flocked to Callander, Ontario to look at the babies through a special one-way screen. The girls became an overnight sensation. Before long they were being used to sell many commercial products, including canned milk, syrup, dolls, breakfast foods, and soap. There were movie contracts to make a film called 'The Country Doctor' starring the Quints. Their earnings from all sources were estimated to be over one million dollars. Eventually the parents entered a court case to win back their five children. The Quints rejoined their family. From that time on the girls tended to live more private lives.

Another human interest story that made headlines in the 1930s concerned Wilfred 'Wop' May. He was the former war ace

'Wop' May.

chased by the Red Baron on the day Roy Brown shot the Baron down. Now May was one of a group of courageous bush pilots flying supplies and mail into isolated communities of Canada's northland. In the winter of 1932 May answered the call of the R.C.M.P. for assistance in hunting the 'mad trapper of Rat River'.

Indians along the Rat River had complained to the Mounties that Albert Johnson was robbing their traps. When a Mountie came to investigate, Johnson shot him and disappeared into the arctic wilderness. One of the most sensational manhunts in Canadian history began. For twenty-nine days the Mounties chased the 'mad trapper'. May tracked Johnson's movements from the air and reported to the Mounties on the ground. Eventually Johnson was brought down in a barrage of gunfire, but not before he had managed to wound another Mountie. May saved the life of the wounded policeman by flying him out to the hospital at Aklavik. Thanks to May and a growing number of other bush pilots, the Northwest Territories and the Yukon were opened up to development by the end of the 1930s.

Baseball was the sports rage of the Depression. Because most people had a lot of time on their hands and no money to spend, baseball was a favourite pastime. Every town had at least one team. People travelled great distances to play ball or watch the game.

Every fad that struck the United States was quickly copied in Canada. Card games such as bridge, begun in the United States, became Canadian favourites too. The game Monopoly started a craze because players could buy, sell, invest, borrow, and accumulate a fortune without risking a cent of real money.

Throughout the 1930s daily life in Canada was growing more and more like daily life in the United States. People were so preoccupied worrying about money and trying to escape from the Depression that there was not much concern about this situation. The influence of the United States on Canada through films, radio, magazines, and fads did not become an important political issue until the 1960s.

SOME RESULTS OF THE DEPRESSION

A famous author, Caroline Bird, has said that everybody who lived through the Depression carried an invisible scar on their minds that would be there permanently. The Depression would affect their thinking for the rest of their lives. What she probably meant is illustrated in the following comment of a person who was a teenager in the 1930s. 'I would never again like to live through a depression. It makes a person want to cry remembering how horrible life was back then. My parents had to work so hard and they suffered a great deal. Me, I never buy a thing on credit. I always wait until I can afford to pay for everything in cash. We hang on to our money because in 1929 everyone was in the stock market and everybody lost. I want to have some money put away for a rainy day.'

To such a person, the free spending and extravagance of her children and grandchildren seem unreasonable. She will never be able to get over the fear of having to face another depression.

At the same time, many survivors of the Depression are determined that their children will be spared the hardships and poverty they lived through. Therefore, they tend to give their children luxuries they could never afford when they were young.

It was during the Depression that the idea of the welfare state took root in Canada. This was the belief that society should support its citizens to prevent extreme economic hardships. Today parents receive family allowance cheques to help them raise their children. During the 1930s this kind of a monthly cheque would have seemed like a small fortune to many starving families. Today there is also unemployment insurance so that no one is allowed to starve because a job is not available. Senior citizens are provided with money by old age pensions. The ideas for the government helping its citizens originated during the Depression. In federal politics the C.C.F. and N.D.P. have helped to persuade the Liberal and Conservative governments to provide social services for Canadian citizens.

Digging Deeper

1 A major element of the entertainment of the 1930s was escapism. Define escapism. Why do you think people found it enjoyable during the Depression?

2 Make a list of popular forms of entertainment today. How does your list compare with the entertainment of the 1930s? How do you think people will rate this decade fifty years from now?

3 Art and music can tell you a great deal about the people and the problems of the thirties. Assemble a collection of slides or pictures of Canadian art in this period. Include artists such as: Emily Carr, Paraskeva Clark, Andre Bieler, and Jean-Paul Lemieux. Bring some records of the 1930s to class and play the sounds of the big bands of that era. Listen to Benny Goodman, Paul Whiteman, Jimmy Dorsey, Mart Kenney, Trump Davidson and Artie Shaw. What sort of things were people singing about in the thirties?

4 Debate: The government is expected to provide too many services for Canadians today. People should not expect the government to look after them from the cradle to the grave. People should care for themselves.

5 Debate: Kids today have got it too easy. If they had lived through the Depression they would have known hard times but would be better for it.

6 The jobless rate in Canada in 1979 was higher than at any time since the Great Depression. What are the causes of unemployment? Who suffers the most? How does it differ from earlier unemployment? Are there any cures in sight?

22
CANADIANS IN THE NEWS

J.S. Woodsworth

Pastor, social reformer, pacifist, labour leader, and parliamentarian – James Shaver Woodsworth played all of these roles in his lifetime. Woodsworth was born not far from Toronto in 1874. After his education at Manitoba, Toronto, and Oxford Universities, he worked for many years as a pastor among the immigrants in the terrible slums of north Winnipeg.

During World War I Woodsworth became a pacifist. The thought of war and men killing each other turned his stomach. He was appalled that small Canadian boys at home chased and stoned little dachshunds because they thought they were 'German' dogs. He was annoyed when restaurant owners renamed hamburgers 'nips' to make them sound more patriotic. Most of all he was shocked that many clergymen openly tried to recruit young men to fight in the war. Woodsworth's views of the war were very unpopular. This never made him back down from what he considered right. In 1918 he resigned from the Church and took the only job he could get – a longshoreman on the Vancouver docks. Although he was frail and not used to the heavy work, he did have a family with six children to support. This job gave Woodsworth a new understanding of the worker and he became deeply involved with the problems of labour organization. When the Winnipeg General Strike broke out in 1919, Woodsworth was one of the strike leaders fighting for better working conditions for the Winnipeg worker.

It was as a parliamentarian that Woodsworth made his greatest contribution. Elected to Parliament by the voters of Winnipeg Centre in 1921, he served as an M.P. until his death in 1942. Woodsworth's Christian beliefs filled him with great compassion for poor and oppressed people everywhere. Tommy Douglas, one of the early leaders of the C.C.F., recalled an Ottawa winter day in the 1930s. The tiny figure of Woodsworth, wearing his father's old overcoat which had been cut down for him, made his way toward the Parliament buildings. A pathetic crowd of unemployed men raised a cheer as he passed by. Douglas found Woodsworth in the entrance of the building with tears running down his cheeks. Such was the great feeling held by Woodsworth for the poor people of Canada.

J.S. Woodsworth.

When the Co-operative Commonwealth Federation was formed, J.S. Woodsworth became the new party's president. Many Canadians were afraid of supporting a party like the C.C.F. because it sounded too socialist, too radical, and too much like communism. J.S. Woodsworth was a socialist, perhaps the most influential socialist in Canadian history. Once, when his beliefs were challenged, he replied with the following definition of socialism:

I am not afraid of the word Socialism which comes from a perfectly good Latin word which means comradeship, which means that today we as individuals are no longer living isolated lives, that no nation is any longer living an isolated life, but rather that we are living in society in a thousand and one complicated relationships and that we must adapt our political ideals and our political institutions and our political policies to meet the new situation that confronts us.

Woodsworth dedicated his life to a crusade against all sorts of social injustice. With tireless energy, he worked to give ordinary Canadians a chance for a better life. Woodsworth did not live to see many of his ideals achieved. However, many of his dreams have since been made real by later governments of Canada, which makes this Canadian 'a man to remember'.

Dr. Norman Bethune

Norman Bethune was born in Gravenhurst, Ontario in 1890. From early childhood he liked to think and act for himself. When war broke out in 1914, he left medical school and was one of the first to join up. He was wounded when he went to the aid of another soldier during an artillery barrage and was sent back to Canada to recover. There he completed his medical training and became a doctor.

In 1926 an X-ray indicated that Bethune had tuberculosis, for which there was no cure. As the disease spread through his body he read of a new theory of treating tuberculosis. It suggested a surgical procedure that collapsed the diseased lung to prevent the tubercular growth from spreading. He insisted on acting as a guinea pig for the untried theory. Bethune gambled and won. In two months he was out of the hospital and practising medicine again. His operating skill as a lung surgeon and as an inventor of instruments used in chest surgery soon earned him a world-wide reputation.

When a civil war broke out in Spain in 1936, Bethune volunteered to go to the battlefront. In this war forces loyal to the democratic government of Spain were trying to put down a revolution led by General Franco. Franco was getting a great deal of help from the German and Italian dictators, Hitler and Mussolini. Bethune dedicated himself to working as a friend of Spanish democracy. He organized ambulance services and developed the first mobile blood unit to bring emergency blood supplies to injured soldiers in the front lines. Eventually his friends in Spain were defeated and Bethune came home to Canada. But it was during those years in Spain that Bethune became more and more interested in communism and eventually joined the Communist Party.

Nineteen thirty-eight found Norman Bethune in China. His growing communist sympathies and his great desire to help suffering people drew him into the service of Mao Tse-Tung, leader of the Communist Chinese. The communists were fighting the nationalists for control of China in a bloody civil war. In China he was welcomed and appointed medical chief of the Red Army (Communist). Medical facilities were poor and money for them almost non-existent. Bethune had to start from scratch to build a medical corps. He trained hundreds of Chinese and set up field hospitals to perform operations and care for the wounded. In doing so he worked himself to the point of exhaustion. His diary entry for August 1938 records his feelings:

I have operated all day and am tired. Ten cases, five of them serious ... It is true I am tired but I don't think I have been so happy for a long time. I am doing what I want to do.

189

In August 1939, Bethune was operating under terrible conditions. No surgical gloves were available and a small cut from his scalpel allowed an infection to enter his body. His finger began to swell and soon the infection spread throughout his body. By 12 November Bethune was dead of blood poisoning.

All across China the death of Dr. Bethune, whom they called Pai-Chiu-en, was mourned as a great loss. The Chinese remember Bethune with a large statue in Shih-chia Chuang and a hospital named in his memory. Two postage stamps have been issued in China commemorating his life. His contribution and sacrifice for China have been written up in magazines and books and read by millions. It is strange that the name of Dr. Bethune is much better known and revered in the People's Republic of China than in his homeland of Canada.

Digging Deeper

Refer back to the summary chart of themes at the end of Unit One (page 54). Using the chart as a model, make a chart for Unit Four. On the chart trace the development of those themes through this unit.

23
THE RISE
OF THE NAZI
DICTATOR

On 4 August 1944, Nazi soldiers burst into an attic over a ware-house in Amsterdam. An informer had told them that eight Jews were hiding there. The Nazis found the Frank family and four other Jews. They had hidden in these cramped quarters for two years. While searching the attic, the sergeant picked up Mr. Frank's briefcase, and asked if there were any jewels in it. Mr. Frank said that it contained nothing except papers. Disappoint-ed, the Nazi threw the papers onto the floor. The little group that had spent twenty-five months in that attic was sent off to concentration camps.

However, there remained on the floor of the attic the diary of a thirteen year old girl, Anne Frank. All the time she and her family were in hiding, Anne had been describing the isolation and constant fear in which they lived. Though Anne died at the age of fifteen in a concentration camp, her diary was later dis-covered and published. It is the remarkable story of one young Jewish girl and her will to survive the Nazi persecutions. The following two passages from her diary tell part of Anne's ordeal:

20 June 1942

After May 1940 good times rapidly fled; first the war, then the surrender of Holland, followed by the arrival of the Germans which is when the suffering of us Jews really began. Anti-Jewish decrees followed each other in quick succession. Jews must wear a yellow star, Jews must hand in their bicycles, Jews are banned from trains and are forbidden to drive. Jews are only allowed to do their shopping between 3 and 5 o'clock, and then only in shops that bear the placard 'Jewish shop'. Jews must be indoors by eight o'clock and cannot even sit in their own gardens after that hour. Jews are forbidden to enter theaters, cinemas, and other places of entertainment. Jews may not take part in public sports. Swimming baths, tennis courts, hockey fields and other sports grounds were also prohibited to them. Jews must go to Jewish school and many more restrictions of a similar kind.

9 October 1942
Our many Jewish friends are being taken away by the dozen. These people are
treated by the Gestapo [Nazi secret police] without a shred of decency, being loaded
into cattle trucks and sent to Westerbork, the big Jewish camp. Westerbork sounds
terrible: only one washing cubicle for a hundred people and not nearly enough lavato-
ries ... It is impossible to escape; most of the people in the camp are branded by their
shaved heads .... We assume that most of them are murdered. The English radio
speaks of their being gassed.

Anne Frank was just one of the 6 000 000 Jews who died in
the horrible concentration camps of Nazi Germany. Another
24 000 000 soldiers and civilians from all sides – Canadians, British, French, Russians, Dutch, Germans, Italians, Japanese,
Americans, and others – bring the staggering loss to 30 000 000
casualties in World War II. What caused the world to erupt once
again into the second major conflict of this century?

Case Study: Germany After World War I

Why did the German people turn to Hitler from 1918 to 1932?

Economic Problems: Inflation

Instead of taxing its people to finance World War I, Germany
had borrowed the money. Thus it had burdened its citizens with
a huge debt. To pay off this debt after the war, the German government simply printed more paper money. This was done even
though the country's industry, agriculture, and commerce were
not expanding because of the heavy reparations that had to be
paid. Instead of German wealth going back into the economy, it

went to pay off the war debt. The rapid printing of marks (the basic unit of German currency) unsupported by real economic value caused severe inflation.

In the spring of 1922, about 300 marks could buy an American dollar. By early 1923, it took 50 000 marks to buy an American dollar! Soon Germans needed billions of marks to pay for a postage stamp. It took a shopping bag of marks to get on a street car. Men often carried their wages home in wheel barrows full of almost worthless paper money. A life time's savings could become valueless in a matter of weeks. The bartering of goods became the accepted method of trading. Workers were paid daily and spent their pay as soon as possible lest its value should have fallen by the next day. As the paper money dropped in value, the government kept 300 paper mills working twenty-four hours a day to churn out more of the useless currency.

ADVERTISEMENTS FROM A BERLIN PAPER FOR
SCHMIDT'S DELIKATESSEN

	1918 Prices	1923 Prices
Cabbage	2 marks per lb	6 million marks per lb
Dill Pickles	1¼ marks per lb	5¾ million marks per lb
Wieners	3 marks per lb	7 million marks per lb

(1 kg. = 2.2 lbs.)

Questions:
1. Define 'inflation'.
2. What was the major economic problem Germany faced after the war and why did it arise?
3. How did the German government attempt to solve the economic crisis?
4. Who would suffer the most from inflation? Why?
5. Who might benefit from the inflation? Why?

Political Instability

After World War I Germany was split up into more than a dozen major political parties. No party was strong enough to undertake the gigantic task of rebuilding a war-torn country. The main political parties fell into three general groups.

COMMUNISTS	SOCIAL DEMOCRATS	NATIONAL SOCIALISTS (NAZI)
Beliefs: Government should be run by the councils of workers. Industries and agriculture should be owned by the government rather than private individuals. The power of the military should be reduced. Workers should be powerful and protected.	Government should be run by elected representatives from all parties. A few key industries, such as railroads, should be owned by the government. The terms of the Treaty of Versailles, which limited the size of the army to 100 000 should be honoured. The Constitution must guarantee the rights of minority groups and workers.	Government should be be run by the army and the wealthy. Industry should continue to be privately owned. The power of the military should be increased. Democratic government should be outlawed. The activities of Jews and foreigners should be severely restricted (since the Nazis believed that these two groups were responsible for Germany's economic problems).
Supporters often found among: Factory and agricultural workers, some intellectuals (teachers, professors), pacifists (those opposed to any form of fighting).	Some workers, professional people, Roman Catholics, some businessmen.	Army, unemployed, big business, farmers, aristocrats.

Questions:
1. What were the positions of the major political parties in Germany towards:
   a) the military?
   b) industry?
   c) who should run the government?
2. Which party would likely support the Treaty of Versailles?
3. Why would owners of big businesses and the very wealthy be willing to support the National Socialists and Hitler?
4. If you were a Jewish citizen living in Germany, which political party would you support? Why?

The Treaty of Versailles

The people of Germany were humiliated by the harsh terms of the Treaty of Versailles. They considered the new boundaries and reparation payments to be unjust. The 'war guilt clause' was seen as a black stain on the honour of all Germans. On the morning of the signing of the Treaty of Versailles, the *Deutsche Zeitung* (German News) called for

VENGEANCE!

Today in Versailles the disgraceful Treaty is being signed. Do not forget it! The German people will, with unceasing labour, press forward to reconquer the place among the nations to which we are entitled! Then will come vengeance for the shame of 1919!

Questions:
1. Review the main terms of the Treaty of Versailles listed in column A. Decide which of the groups or classes of people in column B would be opposed to each term. Why?

A	B
a) The French took rich prizes of German territory west of the Rhine – the Saar Valley with its coal fields and the provinces of Alsace and Lorraine. b) The German army was limited to 100 000. Germany could have no submarines, aircraft, or heavy artillery. c) Germany was required to pay five billion dollars in reparations. d) Germany's colonies were parcelled out to France, Britain, and Japan. e) Germany had to admit that it was totally to blame for all the losses and damages of the war (war guilt clause).	i) The military. ii) Big business owners. iii) The middle class. iv) The working man. v) The whole German people. vi) The nationalists.

2. To which of the groups in column B above was Hitler appealing when he promised
a) to rearm Germany?
b) to get revenge on Germany's enemies?
c) to cancel the Treaty of Versailles?
d) to expand the army?
e) to restore German honour?
f) to win back by force all German territory?

Depression and Unemployment

In the United States in 1929 the stock market crashed, marking the beginning of a world-wide depression. The shock waves hit Germany full force. Germany depended on money from abroad; Germany exported manufactured goods and borrowed heavily from the United States to pay war reparations. Because of failing businesses everywhere, banks in Germany closed, unable to meet the demands of their depositors.

Unemployment in Germany grew from 2 258 000 in March 1930 to 4 355 000 in October 1931 to 6 031 000 in March 1932. Those Germans who still had jobs saw their scanty wages fall steadily from month to month. Unemployed miners spent the winter in unheated rooms, sometimes breaking through fences at the mine to steal a few lumps of coal. In the woods around Berlin, families pitched tents or lived in packing crates when they couldn't afford to pay rents in the city. In the country, farmers stood with loaded rifles in a futile attempt to keep out the hordes of starving men who came out from the city to steal food for their families. Unemployment insurance lasted for the first three months of joblessness. After that people were reduced to welfare or begging in the streets.

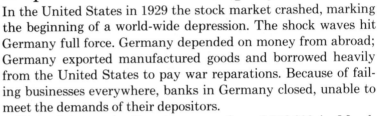

NEWS ITEM: BERLIN 1932
Unemployment has now reached six million, half of Germany's labour force! People are deliberately seeking arrest in order to receive free food in prison.

To workers in the middle class who were bitter about inflation and economic troubles, Hitler and the Nazi party said:

'Believe me, our misery will increase! The government itself is the biggest swindler and crook. People are starving on millions of marks! We will no longer submit! We want a dictatorship.'

Questions:
1. Why would the American Depression have an effect on the German economy?
2. What could Hitler and the Nazis promise the unemployed in order to win them over to the Nazi Party?
3. To the middle classes, ruined by the inflation and depression, what did Hitler say was the cause of their problems? What did Hitler promise to do about the situation?

STEPS TO THE WAR

During the years from 1918 to 1932, Adolf Hitler organized the Nazi party in Germany. Hitler promised the German people he would get back the land lost during World War I and restore Germany to world leadership. He preached to them that the pure German race, called Aryan, was the 'master race' and deserved to rule the world. Hitler guaranteed to rid Germany of communists. He also blamed the Jewish people for Germany's defeat in World War I and for the economic hard times that followed. From the very beginning Hitler had been obsessed by hatred of the Jews (anti-Semitism). As early as the 1920s, when he wrote his book *Mein Kampf*, he was describing Jews as 'deadly poison', 'vermin', and 'leering devils'.

Hitler and the Nazi party gained control of the German Parliament in 1933. Once in power, Hitler became a dictator, depending on force to keep control. Anyone who opposed him was rounded up by his secret police, the Gestapo and the S.S. (schutzstafflen), and thrown into prison or concentration camps. Jews were banned from all government jobs, broadcasting, teaching, working on newspapers, and in entertainment. By the Nuremberg Laws, Jews were not allowed to marry non-Jews. A Nazi campaign was begun to make life thoroughly miserable for the German Jews. Jews were banned from many shops and public buildings. Nazi bullies stood outside Jewish-owned stores and threatened customers who wanted to enter. By 1936 most Jews in Germany found it almost impossible to earn a living. Those who could escaped from Germany in that early period. Among those who left Germany was Albert Einstein, who worked on the atomic bomb.

Just before the war broke out, Hitler had begun a systematic rounding up of the Jews, placing them in concentration camps. When a German embassy official in Paris was shot by a young Jew in November 1938, a savage attack on German Jews followed. A fine of 1 000 000 marks was forced on the Jewish population. Seven thousand Jewish shops were looted, and 20 000 Jews arrested, many of whom were beaten savagely.

With Hitler in power, Germans were allowed to read and hear

Adolf Hitler.

only what their leaders wanted them to know. Newspapers and radio were totally controlled by the Nazi party. Books containing ideas that did not please Hitler were burned in huge public bonfires. Teachers were required to be members of the Nazi party, and students were pressured to join the Hitler Youth Movement. Thus the minds of young Germans were being moulded in the Nazi philosophy. Priests and clergymen who dared to protest Hitler's methods were thrown in prison. Nazi Germany had become a totalitarian state where everything was controlled by the government.

Hitler had promised to make Germany a strong country. One of his first steps was to strengthen the army and the air force. A new German army was created under the slogan, 'Today Germany. Tomorrow the world!' Weapons of war started to pour out of German factories. In a swiftly rearming Germany, the Nazi bullies were wiping out the last remnants of opposition to the new Nazi regime.

In Canada at this time, as almost everywhere, there was massive unemployment. In the United States and Britain millions were unemployed and on relief. In these countries there appeared to be no easy cure to the economic troubles. But in Germany, millions of people had now been persuaded that Hitler was the answer to all their problems. It meant the end of democracy in Germany and unthinking obedience to the dictator (the Fuehrer). Hitler had persuaded the Germans that their problems would be solved if they could get back the territories taken by the Treaty of Versailles.

The Nazi attempt to regain lost territories began in March 1938. Nazi soldiers crossed the frontier into Austria. Hitler argued that Austria had to be a part of Germany because many Germans lived there, and all Germans deserved to live under the German State (the Reich). Hitler rode in triumph at the head of his army through the streets of Vienna, the capital of Austria. He found that through Nazi threats and troublemakers he could win victories without battles. Without firing a shot, Austria came into the German Reich. The other nations of the world did not attempt to stop Hitler from taking Austria because no one wanted to risk another world war.

Czechoslovakia was next on Hitler's list. Hitler demanded a piece of Czechoslovakia known as the Sudetenland. This territory was near the German border and contained a large number of German-speaking people. The brave Czechs were ready to fight Hitler, but France and Britain were not willing to help them. British Prime Minister Neville Chamberlain and Premier Daladier of France met with Hitler in Munich and agreed to allow Germany to have the Sudetenland. They believed this would save the world from war. The Czechs were not consulted. They felt furious about being sold out by their allies, but were helpless to resist. Though Chamberlain said the Munich agreement meant 'peace in our time', many people disagreed. Winston Churchill, who was to follow Chamberlain as the British prime minister, called the agreement 'appeasement', or giving in to the demands of a potential enemy. He argued that Hitler should be stopped now, at all costs.

Though Hitler had promised at Munich that he would make no new demands for territory, he soon broke that pledge. Six months later, in March 1939, Germany occupied all of Czechoslovakia. Then in August of the same year, Germany shocked the world by signing a non-aggression pact with Soviet Russia. The two long-time enemies, Germany and Russia, promised not to fight each other and secretly agreed to divide Poland between them. Hitler was now free to plan his moves against France and Britain in the west since he no longer had to fear an attack from the Russians on the east.

Next Hitler demanded that the Polish corridor, awarded to

Poland by the Treaty of Versailles, be handed back to Germany. Poland refused. On 1 September 1939, the German army drove over the borders into Poland. The Poles were helpless to defend themselves against the German's new style of warfare, called *blitzkrieg* or 'lightning warfare'. *Blitzkrieg* demanded surprise, force, and boldness, and close co-operation among the air force, tanks, artillery, and infantry. In the *blitzkrieg* the German *Luftwaffe* (air force) bombed enemy aircraft on the ground, army barracks, headquarters, bridges, and railways. After the air attacks the Nazis raced ahead in tanks and armoured cars, moving deep into enemy territory. In the face of this concentrated attack the Poles could do nothing. The situation was now so dangerous that Britain and France realized they would now have to rush to the defense of Poland. There could be no more appeasement. Two days later, on 3 September 1939, first Britain and then France officially declared war on Germany.

Digging Deeper

1

In your notebook arrange the steps to the war in the order in which they happened:

Munich Agreement

Treaty of Versailles

Hitler demands Sudetenland

Hitler becomes leader of Germany

Germany invades Poland

Germany begins to rearm

Britain and France declare war on Germany

Hitler invades Austria

Germany signs pact with Russia

2

Decide whether the following are true or false:

a) A dictator depends on force to stay in power.

b) France and Britain gave in to Hitler at Munich because Germany had promised to pay reparations.

c) Britain and France approved of Hitler's actions when he seized other countries.

d) France and Britain declared war on Germany when Austria was taken over.

e) In the Nazi state industrialists received generous contracts to produce weapons of war.

3

Discuss: Should force have been used by nations of the world to stop Germany when it invaded other countries?

24
THE DARK
YEARS

Black headlines on 3 September 1939 announced the grim news: 'Britain and France at war with Germany!' Canadians were shocked yet eager to do what they could to help Britain. However, in September 1939 Canada's entry into the war was not automatic, as it had been in 1914. Canada was no longer a colony of Britain bound to follow the mother country into warfare. In the years following World War I, Canada had become an independent nation.

Prime Minister Mackenzie King quickly summoned the Canadian Parliament to discuss Canada's involvement in the war. Though there was almost total support for the idea of using force to check the spread of Nazism, no one was quite sure how

Montrealers reacting to the war declaration.

to go about declaring war on Germany. Lester Pearson, a Canadian diplomat in London, was sent to inquire discreetly of the British officials how one went about declaring war. On 9 September 1939 the Parliament of Canada advised King George VI that Canada was declaring war on Germany. The next morning the message was received from London that the King had signed Canada's declaration of war. It was a momentous occasion – the first time that Canada had declared war on its own behalf. Though Canada was getting ready to fight, it had only about 10 000 men in its armed forces. The Canadian army possessed only 14 tanks, 29 Bren guns, 23 anti-tank rifles, and 5 small mortar guns. The Canadian navy had exactly 10 operational vessels. It would be some time before Canada's armed forces reached an effective fighting size.

Within the first four weeks of action, Hitler's modern army had outnumbered and crushed the old-fashioned Polish defenses. Next, the powerful German forces overran Denmark, Norway, Belgium, and the Netherlands. Hitler was free now to turn against France. For the second time in twenty-five years German troops poured across the French borders. Nazi forces moved around and above the Maginot line (a chain of forts and traps built to protect the eastern border of France).

Inside a troop transport.

Thousands of British troops had rushed across the English Channel to help defend France. However, during the rapid German advance British forces became trapped and had to retreat to the seaport town of Dunkirk on the French coast. The British hastily collected a fleet of all available boats in order to get their soldiers back home again. Three hundred thousand men were evacuated safely to Britain, but most of the heavy British war equipment had to be abandoned on the beaches of France. It was a terrible defeat for the Allies. France had fallen in six weeks and Paris was now occupied by the Nazis. A new French army known as the 'Free French', led by General Charles de Gaulle, was set up in England. The 'Free French' army vowed to continue its fight against the Nazis.

Mussolini, the Italian dictator, at this moment decided to enter the war on the side of Germany. Almost all of Europe was in the hands of the Axis powers, Germany and Italy. There remained only the island of Britain. The *Luftwaffe* had several thousand bombers ready for heavy action. The German strategy was to knock out Britain by destroying its capital, London. The Germans hoped to paralyze the British government and demoralize the people by heavy bombing. Night after night wave upon wave of bombers attacked London and other important cities. The Nazis called it a war of terror. It was designed to destroy the peoples' will to resist. Though thousands were killed, the British refused to give up. To the amazement of all, the greatly outnumbered Royal Air Force shot almost 3000 Nazi planes out of the skies in two months. Speaking of the Royal Air Force, Prime Minister Churchill said, 'Never was so much owed by so many to so few.' For more than a year the gallant pilots of the Royal Air Force defended Britain in what came to be known as the 'Battle of Britain.' The Battle of Britain proved too costly for the Nazis in terms of men and aircraft. The Germans temporarily gave up the idea of trying to bomb Britain out of the war.

During this testing time for Britain, American help began to arrive. From 1939 to 1941 the United States remained neutral and was not directly involved in the fighting. However, the United States had developed a 'cash and carry' system which allowed any nation to buy arms from them. The Americans expected that the arms would be paid for in cash and the buyers would carry them away in their own ships. This policy benefited Britain and France because they had the ships to transport the equipment, but Germany did not.

After the fall of France, President Roosevelt urged his country to become a great producer of ammunition in order to help protect democracy. Finally in 1941, the Americans adopted a 'lend-lease' policy. By this act, the Allies were not required to pay cash for war supplies from the United States. The reason for the

R.C.A.F. pilots.

American generosity was that the President considered the defence of Britain important to the security of the United States.

In June 1941 Hitler decided he could not defeat Britain from the air, so he turned eastward. He attacked his own ally, Russia. Hitler wanted to seize the natural resources of Russia – grain, coal, iron, and oil. At first German armies scored tremendous successes in Russia. In just three months they reached the outskirts of Moscow and Leningrad, the two most important Russian cities.

By now Hitler's ally in the Pacific, Japan, had become obsessed with the strategy and surprise of *blitzkrieg*. On 7 December 1941, Japanese planes came without warning and bombed the American naval base at Pearl Harbor, Hawaii. The attack, a complete surprise, left half the American fleet crippled or sunk. The next day the United States declared war on Japan. Three days later Germany and Italy, Japan's allies, also declared war on the United States. By 1942 the Japanese had engulfed all of the Philippines. A small Canadian force had been captured at Hong Kong, and the British colonies at Singapore, Malaya, Burma, and South-east Asia were controlled by the Japanese.

It seemed that victory for the Axis powers was close at hand. In Europe, Hitler's troops occupied almost every capital from Oslo in Norway to Athens in Greece. In the Pacific, Japan had a stranglehold on South-east Asia. It appeared just a matter of time before Japan and Germany took control of the remaining areas.

Hitler was now in a position to proclaim to his followers that the Nazi empire in Europe would last for a thousand years. The Germans, according to their Fuehrer, were destined to be the 'master race' and all other people their slaves. The process of making people slaves had already begun in Germany. Nazi leaders were sentencing millions of Europeans, mostly Jewish, to slave labour and concentration camps.

Hitler had strengthened the defences of Nazi-controlled Europe until it was a fortress which it seemed no one could conquer. But soon the tide of war would begin to turn.

25

THE TURN OF THE TIDE

By August 1942 the Allies had a plan. It was to send Canadian and British troops, restless for action, to test the German forces along the French coast at Dieppe. For some time the Russians had been demanding that the Allies launch an invasion in the west. This would relieve some of the German pressure on the Russians in the east. The raid at Dieppe was planned to be a quick punch at the German stronghold. The Allies hoped to worry the Nazis, gather crucial information about their coastal defences, and then return safely to Britain. Dieppe would be a dress rehearsal for the full-scale Allied invasion of Europe, which would follow.

At 4:50 on the morning of 19 August 1942, 5000 Canadians began to land out on the beaches near Dieppe. Boys from such places as Calgary, Saskatoon, Hamilton, Montreal, and Saint John eagerly sought action. However, the German forces were ready for the attack. By early afternoon nearly 900 of the Canadian troops were dead or dying, and over 1000 were wounded. Nineteen hundred prisoners of war were taken by the Germans, and only 2200 of those who landed that morning returned to Britain.

A French Canadian who fought with the Fusiliers Mont-Royal recalled his experience at Dieppe:

... the wounded and dead lay scattered on the beach. Some of the wounded were trying to swim out to the boats [and] many were bleeding heavily, reddening the water around them. [Once ashore,] mortar bombs are bursting on the shingle and making little clouds which seem to punctuate the deafening din ... close to me badly mutilated bodies lie here and there. The wounded scream ... the blood flows from their wounds ... For myself, I am absolutely astounded to have reached the shelter of a building. I was certain that my last hour had arrived.

Typical of the bravery of Canadians at Dieppe was that of chaplain of the Royal Hamilton Light Infantry, John Foote. For his bravery in carrying wounded soldiers from the beaches to safety in boats, he won the Victoria Cross. In the end Foote himself did not leave, but stayed behind to be with the men who were taken prisoner by the Germans. Foote said that these Canadians needed his service more than those who returned safely to Britain.

Wounded Canadians at Dieppe.

In spite of the horrible loss of life at Dieppe, and though it appeared to be a major disaster, important military lessons were learned. When the decisive invasion of Europe finally came two years later, the Allies remembered their Dieppe experience. This time fire support by sea and air would be overwhelming, and a way would be found to land large numbers of troops and equipment on the open beaches of France.

In 1942, despite its great navy, the island of Britain was in deadly danger. The highly industrialized island of 50 000 000 people could not live or fight without food and supplies from outside. In this second World War, as in the first, the Atlantic Ocean played a vital role. Britain depended on the food and war supplies being brought through the life line from North America. Everything depended upon the navy and its air division to make sure the precious cargoes got through safely. This was not an easy task, for German U-boats lurked in the dark waters of the Atlantic Ocean. German U-boats (*Unterseebooten*) were deadly submarines able to pick off helpless merchant ships from the United States and Canada as they steamed towards British ports. Winston Churchill said later, 'The only thing that ever really frightened me during the war was the U-boat peril.' By day the U-boats hid submerged, and at night they surfaced. The merchant ships were sitting ducks for their attacks. Cargo vessels were being sunk at the rate of twenty a week, and the Germans were busy building eight U-boats for every one they lost. Fortunately, the Allies also improved their anti-submarine measures. The use of the convoy system, improvements in radar for underwater detection of submarines, and the protection of patrol aircraft helped drop the rate of Allied losses. By the end of the war nearly 800 German U-boats had been sunk. In total the Canadians made twenty-seven kills.

In 1942 Canada was committed to a policy of 'total war'. Total war means the concentration of all industries, materials, and manpower upon the war effort. The war now affected everybody in Canada. Ration cards became necessary for buying gasoline, butter, sugar, meat, tea, and coffee. Since these goods were in

Rationing.

short supply, the government limited the quantity a person could buy. Without the ration coupon, a person could not obtain these products. At the minimum, a family was restricted to 545 litres of gasoline annually for its family car. Rubber tires, tubes, and antifreeze were very scarce. Many people could not take long trips in the summer. The butter ration was never less than 170 grams per person per week. Each person was allowed 680 grams of choice cuts of meat per week, or 1135 grams of cheaper cuts. Sugar was distributed so that each person got at least 227 grams per week. Liquor and nylon stockings were scarce and became luxury items. Silk stockings were scarce because the silk was needed for parachutes. In Ontario an adult was restricted to one small bottle of liquor per month. For most people, rationing caused little or no real hardship. Most people realized they were lucky not to be in Europe where the real war was being fought. People were encouraged not to hoard food, and to stretch their supplies as far as they would go. One woman recalled how the newspapers were always urging readers to do their bit for the war effort.

The newspapers, they were just propaganda sheets. My goodness, on the front pages, war, war, war, and in the insides, how to cook cheaper, how to do Victory Gardens, why we should have car pools, buy Victory Bonds and tell our friends they were traitors if they didn't load up on them too ...

You remember those Sunday sections, they were jammed with war stuff. How to cook cabbage, make cabbage rolls, and then drink the cabbage juice. Or carrots. Spinach. Did they think we didn't know that stuff, like how to make a dollar do the price of ten? You'd think the idiots in their big offices in Toronto and Ottawa didn't know about the Depression we just went through – ten years of nothing.

In many kitchens bacon fat and bones were saved to provide glycerine for explosives. People gave up buying new aluminum pots and pans and new stoves so that more airplanes could be built. Every child became a scrap gatherer. Scrap metal, rags, paper, rubber, foil, and wire coat hangers, anything that could be salvaged for the war effort was collected. Posters urged the whole family to help win the war.

Before the war Canada was primarily a supplier of raw materials. In three years Canada had become a great industrial power. Now Canadian munitions factories turned out bombs, shells, and bullets for small arms. Shipyards worked full blast building cargo ships, trawlers, mine sweepers, small warships used in anti-submarine attack, and landing craft. Shipbuilding became the second largest employer in the country. Aircraft manufacturers, such as DeHavilland, produced everything from training planes to fighting craft. In 1942 the government decided to stop the production of civilian cars and turn over all automobile plants to the production of war vehicles. The last of the McLaughlin Buicks rolled off the assembly line. Now the plants produced trucks, jeeps, Bren gun carriers, and artillery tractors. It has been calculated that half of the vehicles used by the British in the North Africa campaign were stamped 'Made in Canada'. The Nazi general Rommel gave orders to his troops to try and capture Canadian-made jeeps which did not get stuck in the sand as the German ones did. All kinds of military vehicles, tanks, radar equipment, and the drug penicillin were now produced in large amounts in Canada for the war effort. Steel out-

Canadians building a merchant ship.

put doubled, while aluminum production increased by six times its original amount. Canadian farmers, dairymen, and fishermen provided astonishingly large amounts of wheat, flour, cheese, canned salmon, fish oil, bacon, ham, canned meat, and dried eggs for Britain and the Allies. From eastern Canadian ports, particularly Halifax and Sydney in Nova Scotia, endless convoys of cargo set sail bound for Britain. Despite the heavy losses, the bulk of the much-needed supplies from Canada and the United States began to get through. With tanks and trucks and an adequate supply of food and ammunition, the Allies could face the Nazis on an equal basis. 'There is no doubt now,' said Winston Churchill, 'of the eventual outcome.' The tide had turned in the favour of the Allies. The almost unbroken series of retreats and defeats was over the Allies. British and American soldiers were now on the offensive in the deserts of North Africa. American G.I.s (enlisted men) advanced against the Japanese, island by island in the steaming jungles of the Pacific. Canadian, British, and American troops landed in Sicily and fought their way north into Italy. And on the Russian front the most critical battle of all at Stalingrad approached a climax.

For over five months the Nazis had fought a savage battle to gain control over the city of Stalingrad in southern Russia. Stalingrad, now called Volgograd, was an important industrial city which controlled the rich oil fields of south Russia. The harsh Russian winter took its toll on the German troops. Hitler refused to allow a retreat from Stalingrad, saying, 'Where the German soldier sets foot, there he remains.' By January 1943, two vast Russian armies had completely surrounded and trapped about 250 000 Germans. At least 100 000 Germans were

killed and the remnants of the Nazi army surrendered to the
Russians. An eyewitness described the plight of the beaten Germans:

Completely cut off, the men in field grey slouched on, invariably filthy and invariably
louse-ridden, their weary shoulders sagging, from one defence position to another.
The icy winds of those great white wastes which stretched forever beyond us to the
east lashed a million crystals of razor-like snow into their unshaven faces ... It lashed
tears from the sunken eyes which, from over-fatigue, could scarce be kept open, it
penetrated through all uniforms and rags to the very marrow of our bones.

Many have said that the Russian victory at Stalingrad was the
turning point of the war. This was the farthest point of the Nazi
advance into Russia, and the greatest defeat Germany had yet
suffered. The Russians now started to push the Germans back
towards Berlin.

Meanwhile, the systematic bombing of cities in Germany by
the Allies had begun. At first the bombing was called 'precision

After the bombing.

Before and after photographs of a bombed German city.

bombing'. Its aim was to destroy German industries, railways, highways, bridges, and oil refineries. However in 1942, Allied air chiefs decided to try to destroy the German fighting spirit by mercilessly pounding cities from the air. On the night of 30 May a thousand bombers raided the city of Cologne. From 24 to 31 of July, Hamburg was attacked eight times. Sixty percent of that city was destroyed by fire bombs and 80 000 civilians were killed. Later in the war, cities such as Dresden and Berlin were subjected to wave upon wave of British and American bombers.

D Day – Day of Deliverance 1944

'O.K., we'll go!' With these words General Eisenhower, Commander-in-Chief of Allied Forces, announced the beginning of the long-awaited invasion of Europe. Since the disastrous attempt at invasion at Dieppe, the Allies had been carefully planning. This time they would be ready. The Normandy beaches of northern France were selected as the site of the inva-

sion. Normandy was close to Britain and the invading army, supply ships, and reinforcements would not have far to travel. A huge army gathered in the south of England. American troops numbering 1 250 000 joined a similar number of British and Commonwealth troops. Four thousand landing craft, seven hundred war ships, and eleven thousand planes were ready. Early in April 1944 Allied bombers destroyed rail lines and military trains in northern France. In May they bombed air fields and did serious damage to *Luftwaffe* bases.

The Germans guessed that an invasion was coming because of the troop buildup in Britain. However, the Germans expected the attack to come at Calais and stationed their best forces near there. Sixty Nazi divisions in northern France and the Netherlands were under the command of Field-Marshall Rommel.

D-Day was fixed for 5 June 1944, but had to be postponed because of bad weather. The weather cleared briefly the next day, and Eisenhower gave the order to go. At 2:00 a.m. on the sixth of June, paratroopers were dropped to protect the landing

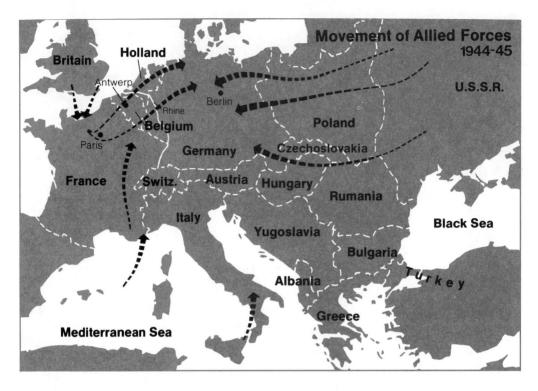

Movement of Allied Forces 1944-45

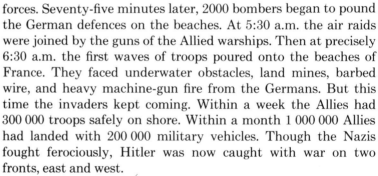

forces. Seventy-five minutes later, 2000 bombers began to pound the German defences on the beaches. At 5:30 a.m. the air raids were joined by the guns of the Allied warships. Then at precisely 6:30 a.m. the first waves of troops poured onto the beaches of France. They faced underwater obstacles, land mines, barbed wire, and heavy machine-gun fire from the Germans. But this time the invaders kept coming. Within a week the Allies had 300 000 troops safely on shore. Within a month 1 000 000 Allies had landed with 200 000 military vehicles. Though the Nazis fought ferociously, Hitler was now caught with war on two fronts, east and west.

In August 1944 another Allied force invaded the southern part of France on the Riviera. These troops marched north to join those who landed at Normandy. Hitler struck back by unleashing his secret weapons, the flying bomb V-1 and the deadly, faster-than-sound rocket V-2, at war-weary Britain. These missiles were launched from Europe and aimed at British cities. Fortunately, as the Allied invading forces swept north through Belgium, they overran the rocket launching sites. As the Nazis retreated from Holland, they mercilessly flooded the low lands. As often happens in war, the innocent civilian population were the ones who suffered the most – homes were destroyed and children suffered malnutrition. Until the Allies could bring in food supplies, some of the Dutch were reduced to eating tulip bulbs.

The troops were not the only ones fighting the war. Thousands of people in Europe joined in the fight against the Axis powers. They fought as civilians or 'underground'. These bands of partisans, as they were known, struck at the Nazis in any way

Canadian soldiers surrounded by Dutch civilians.

they could. They blew up railroads, factories, and bridges. They reported on Nazi troop movements and often helped to rescue Allied airmen shot down in German-occupied territory. Without the contribution and aid of these undercover agents, the liberation of Europe probably would have taken much longer.

As Allied armies pressed toward the Rhine River, Hitler called upon his soldiers to fight even more fiercely. He shouted that whoever gave up a centimetre of German territory while still alive was a traitor to the German people. In a last desperate move Hitler gathered his reserves and 3000 tanks. He hurled them against the American line in the Battle of the Bulge in southern Belgium. The Germans were hoping to reach Antwerp, Belgium, but were slowed down by strong American resistance. Eventually the German advance was halted and the retreat began. Hitler had lost 120 000 men and 600 tanks.

Meanwhile the Russians were swarming across Eastern Europe on their way to Berlin. Although everywhere the Germans resisted with skill and determination, they could not hold back the attack that was coming on all sides. By April 1945 the Russians were in the German capital of Berlin. Berliners fought heroically to defend their city, even using veterans and school boys to try and prevent the inevitable. But by now it was too late. The diary of a captured officer records the plight of Berlin in these last days:

German refugees move back through the Canadian lines.

27 April

Continuous attack throughout the night ... Telephone cables are shot to pieces. Physical conditions are indescribable. No rest, no relief. No regular food, hardly any bread. We get water from the tunnels and filter it ... Masses of damaged vehicles, half-smashed trailers of ambulances with the wounded still in them. Dead people everywhere, many of them frightfully cut up by tanks and trucks.

The end could not long be delayed. By 8 May 1945 fighting in Europe was all over.

Since March 1945 Hitler had more and more shut himself off from the truth. He had retreated into his bomb-proof bunker deep in the earth below the Chancellery building in Berlin. When Russian troops were only a few blocks from the Chancellery, Hitler realized it was all over. He married his blonde companion Eva Braun, and then dictated his last will and testament. In his will he again attacked the Jews and blamed the whole war upon them. He ordered the Germans to fight on and accused his generals of deserting him. Later the same day Hitler learned that the Italian dictator, Mussolini, had been captured and killed by partisans. Mussolini's body had been strung up by the heels in a public square in Milan. This convinced Hitler that he should not suffer the same fate. On 30 April 1945 Hitler shot himself. His bride took poison. According to the instructions he left, their bodies were carried out of the bunker, soaked in gasoline, and set on fire. For the next several hours the bodies burned until they were reduced to unrecognizable remains. One week later Nazi Germany ceased to exist. V.E. day, Victory in Europe day, had arrived. The long struggle in Europe was over.

Though the war in Europe was over, Japan had still not been defeated. Heavy air raids against Japan were carried out by the United States. President Roosevelt of the United States had died in the last days of the war and been replaced by President Truman. In July 1945 President Truman warned the Japanese to surrender or risk being totally destroyed. The Americans now had a powerful new weapon, the atomic bomb. On 6 August 1945 an American bomber appeared in the sky above Hiroshima. It carried a package about a metre long that would change the nature of war forever. The bomber was named the Enola Gay and it carried an atomic bomb. In a few seconds the city of Hiroshima was covered by a giant mushroom cloud of smoke and dust. A lightning-like flash covered the whole sky. Sixty per cent of the city's built-up area was destroyed by fire and the blast. Seventy-one thousand were dead or missing, and 68 000 were injured. Nearly all buildings within a kilometre of the blast had been flattened. An eye witness in Hiroshima described the blast:

> I looked up and saw a lightning-like flash covering the whole sky, blinding my eyes ... Outside all around I found dead and wounded. Some were bloated and scorched. Such an awesome sight. Their legs and bodies stripped of clothes and burned with a huge blister. All green vegetation from grasses to trees, perished in that period.

Still the Japanese did not surrender. Three days later a second atomic bomb was dropped on the city of Nagasaki. Another 35 000 Japanese were killed and 60 000 were injured. Now the Japanese were ready to give up. On 10 August 1945 Japan surrendered to General Douglas MacArthur, the American commander in the Pacific. At last World War II was over.

The Nazi Death Camps

The Allies, mopping up in Europe in 1945, were horrified when they found the Nazi death camps. In these camps millions of the enemies of Nazism had been imprisoned and killed. Some were there because they were Jews and Hitler hated Jews. Others were political prisoners who had dared to speak out against the Nazis.

Dachau and Bergen-Belsen were typical of the camps in Germany. Here large numbers of Jews, communists, and Protestant and Roman Catholic clergy were imprisoned. All able-bodied men and women were put to work on the Nazi war effort. At least 5 000 000 slaves were working in Germany by 1944. In some of the camps medical experiments were carried out on helpless human beings who were used as guinea pigs.

As European countries were occupied by the Nazis, the Jews in those lands were also sent to concentration camps. When Poland was invaded, all the Polish Jews were driven into ghettos. Sections of large cities like Warsaw were walled off and the Jews were forced to live in the ghetto. Rations in the Warsaw ghetto were reduced to starvation levels. For example, the following diet was provided:

per person per month

2 kilograms flour
185 grams sugar
2 litres of milk
100 grams of bread

Nutritionists have calculated that the average intake of calories was 170-230 calories per day in this ghetto. Normal intake of calories would be about 2000. In the Warsaw ghetto as many as twenty people lived in a room measuring four metres by six metres. There was little or no heat, despite the -25°C temperatures in the Warsaw winter of 1940. Epidemic typhus and dysentery spread unchecked. Bodies were left in the streets unburied. There were continuous raids, searches, and beatings by the Nazis. Jews were dying by the thousands, but not fast enough to please Hitler.

In long and secret talks with Himmler, the head of the German Gestapo, Hitler devised one of the most outrageous schemes in human history. He decided that every Jewish man, woman, and child would be transported to concentration camps and exterminated (killed). This, he called the 'final solution' to the 'Jewish problem' in Europe.

At places like Auschwitz and Treblinka in Poland, millions of Jews were worked to death or sent straight to the gas chambers. At Auschwitz the victims were crowded into gas chambers that were disguised as showers. The shower rooms were sealed up and Zyklon B gas was dropped into the chambers through a small opening in the ceiling. It took from three to fifteen minutes to kill all those confined within the chamber. The bodies were then removed by a special detachment of prisoners. Gold fillings from the teeth of the victims were yanked out, melted down, and made into gold bars. Other valuables such as watches, bracelets, and rings were also deposited by Himmler in secret bank vaults for future use. Then the corpses were placed in ovens for cremation. Six thousand could be gassed *in a day* at Auschwitz.

At other camps in Eastern Europe the victims were made to dig their own graves, and then were shot in the back by Gestapo sharpshooters.

Some of the most moving stories of bravery and heroism have come out of the death camps. At Auschwitz there was an eighteen-year-old girl, Rosa Robota. Rosa and many of her friends were forced to work for the Nazis in a gunpowder factory. They planned to steal enough gunpowder to blow up the crematorium and the gas chambers. Every day a dozen girls smuggled out small quantities of explosives hidden in the hems of their dresses. The explosives were buried around the camp until there was a sizeable stockpile.

On the afternoon of 7 October 1944, they successfully blew up Number 3 Crematorium. The Gestapo were enraged by this act of sabotage. An investigation was begun and Rosa and the girls were arrested. Every day Rosa was beaten, and after four days of torture the Nazis hanged her.

Hours before her death Rosa Robota managed to smuggle out a message from the death cell. It read, 'Be strong and brave.' The message helped give strength to others in Auschwitz who would become victims of Hitler's 'final solution'.

By the end of the war Hitler had destroyed over one-third of the Jews in Europe. It is estimated that 6 000 000 human beings, among whom Anne Frank was one, were put to death. Their only crime was that they were not members of the 'master race'.

War in the Mediterranean Area

1940 June	Italy invades France.
November	Italy invades Greece.
	Italian armies suffer heavy defeat at the hands of the British in north Africa.
	Hitler sends German forces – the Afrika Korps under General Rommel – to assist Mussolini.
1942 January	Rommel defeats British at Tobruk. He takes 30 000 prisoners.
October	The British forces under General Montgomery defeat Rommel at the battle of El Alamein.
	The British army sweeps westwards along the north African coast.
November	American and British forces under General Eisenhower land in Algeria.
1943 May	German and Italian forces are trapped.
12 May	General von Arnim is forced to surrender his 267 000 German soldiers in Tunisia.
10 July	Allied forces, including Canadians, invade Sicily. 'Operation Huskey', as this operation is called, takes thirty-eight days to capture the island. German forces from Sicily escape to Italy.

25 July	Mussolini is placed under arrest.
3 September	Italy surrenders. Italy makes peace with the Allies.
September	Allies land on southern tip of Italy and fight their way northwards against stiff German opposition.
1944 June 4	American forces enter Rome (the first European capital city recaptured from the Germans).
1945 April	Mussolini shot.
	Venice and Milan captured by Allies.

Christmas at Ortona 1943
Christmas dinner in the shelled, broken church in Ortona. Candles and white table-cloths ... not four hundred metres from the enemy, carol singers, the soldiers coming in in relays to eat a Christmas dinner – men who hadn't had their clothes off in thirty days coming in and eating their dinner, and carol singers singing "Silent Night".

The Canadians perfected a type of street fighting that would become standard for the rest of the war. The steep streets of Italian towns were blocked with rubble, and therefore tanks were useless. Nearly every house held an ambush as German snipers hid themselves in the top floors. Canadian soldiers fought their way house by house. They used explosives to knock holes through the walls of adjoining houses. Then they would race through the smoking gaps with their machine-guns chattering. This tactic of street fighting is called "mouse-holing".

War in the Pacific Ocean Area

1941	Japanese attack American possessions at Pearl Harbor, Guam, Wake Island, Midway Island, and the Philippines.
	Japanese bomb British bases at Hong Kong and Singapore.
	Japanese destroy two British battleships – *Repulse* and *Prince of Wales*.
	Japan threatens to invade Australia.
1942	U.S. air-sea victories at the battle of the Coral Sea and Midway Island prove to be the turning point against the Japanese forces.
1943	Threat removed from Australia.
	The Allies are ready for a full-scale offensive.
	British and other Allied forces fight jungle warfare against the Japanese in Burma.

1944   Invasion of the Philippines at Leyte Island under the command of General Douglas MacArthur of the United States. More men go ashore at Leyte than land at Europe on D Day.

American forces capture island after island from the Japanese – Guadalcanal, the Carolines, and the Marianas.

American bombing of Japan begins.

1945   After desperate fighting, American forces recapture the Philippine Islands.

Battle at Iwo Jima – 20 000 American casualties.

American and British troops capture the island of Okinawa just 480 kilometres from Japan.

British remove Japanese from Burma.

Atomic bomb dropped on Hiroshima.

Atomic bomb dropped on Nagasaki.

Japan asks for surrender, ending World War II.

In September 1941 Canada was asked by Britain to contribute 2000 troops to help defend Hong Kong in case of a Japanese attack. When the attack came in 1941, 290 Canadians were killed. Others were taken as prisoners of war by the Japanese. A total of 264 Canadians perished in the prison camps where the conditions were horrible. Four soldiers were shot trying to escape. A diphtheria epidemic killed another fifty who were denied proper medical care. After the war several Japanese commanders were given life sentences for barbarism.

By 1943 the United States was spending $9 billion a month on the war effort.

1943 Canadian transports drop tonnes of supplies into jungle clearings in Burma and make countless flights to bring out casualties from the fighting area.

1944 One of the greatest naval battles in history takes place at Leyte Island. The Americans virtually wipe out the Japanese navy. The U.S.A. sinks 3 battleships, 6 aircraft carriers, 10 cruisers, and destroys 400 Japanese aircraft.

The Japanese usually refuse to surrender no matter how heavy the odds against them. If the end is in sight, desperate Japanese often tie bombs around their waists and hurl themselves into American trenches. Japanese pilots fly suicide missions. They purposely crash their one-man planes onto the decks of American battleships. They are known as kamikaze pilots. To die in battle for their homeland seems to be the most glorious thing they could do.

William Stephenson

Canadians only found out about some of our heroes long after the war was over. These were the men and women who risked their lives as intelligence agents. They worked behind enemy lines collecting information about secret enemy movements and activities. One of these agents was William Stephenson, whose code name was 'Intrepid'.

Stephenson was born in 1896 near Winnipeg. He served in World War I, and later became a friend to Winston Churchill. When World War II broke out in 1939, Churchill named him Britain's Chief of Intelligence.

Early in 1939 one of Hitler's top secret coding machines, called Enigma, was smuggled into Britain. Stephenson and his team managed to break the Enigma code. After that, the British were able to decode Germany's signals. Thus they were able to know many of Hitler's decisions almost as soon as he made them. By breaking this 'unbreakable code', Intrepid's department saved thousands of Allied lives and shortened the length of the war.

Another of Intrepid's key operations was Camp X, located just east of Toronto. Here secret agents were trained and intelligence-gathering devices were tested. For example, one-man submarines and underwater demolition equipment were tried out in nearby Lake Ontario.

Ian Fleming, the creator of the fictional undercover agent James Bond, trained at Camp X. It was Fleming who said, 'Stephenson worked himself almost to death carrying out undercover operations and dangerous assignments that can only be hinted at.' The man called Intrepid was knighted for his services, and has since retired to live in Bermuda.

Digging Deeper

What is meant by the term 'turning point of a war'? Where do you think the turning point came in World War II? Explain your reasons.

1

In World War II many reporters travelled with the Allied armies. Class members can research and write brief articles as 'on-the-spot' reporters. The articles could be organized into a class newspaper on the war years. Here are some events that could be investigated:
a) the bombing of German cities;
b) life as a crew member on a large bomber;
c) living in a prisoner-of-war camp;
d) the D Day invasion;
e) sailing with a convoy across the North Atlantic;
f) life as an undercover agent behind enemy lines;
g) what it was like when the German surrender was announced.

2

In the years since the dropping of the atomic bombs on Hiroshima and Nagasaki, many people have questioned the wisdom of President Truman's actions. Do you believe that the United States was justified in dropping the bombs on a largely civilian population? You are an advisor to President Truman. Outline what you consider to be the pros and cons (arguments for and against) using the bombs on Japan.

3

Today there are atomic weapons hundreds of times more powerful than the bombs dropped on Hiroshima and Nagasaki. The world knows that a war fought with atomic weapons could mean the end of all human life. Do you believe any nation would be justified in using atomic weapons today?

4

Do some research to discover the part played by Canadian soldiers in the Italian campaign of World War II.

5

Some students might like to research the role played by American forces in the war in the Pacific. The topic could be presented under the headings
a) how the War began;
b) the American campaign in the Pacific;
c) Japanese kamikaze pilots;
d) the defeat of Japan.

6

26

THE WAR ON THE HOME FRONT

Conscription Again!

The conscription issue raised its ugly head again in World War II. This time Mackenzie King was determined not to let the question tear the country apart as it had during World War I. All the bitter feelings and hostility between the French and English over the conscription issue were in danger of flaring up once more.

At the beginning of the war Mackenzie King promised that conscription for overseas service would not be introduced. Determined to avoid the French-English split of 1917, the Liberals made this pledge to French Canada. However, as the war went on, the military situation began to deteriorate. Prime Minister King found himself in a corner. Many English-speaking Canadians began to call for compulsory military service. Britain had applied conscription from the start, and when the United States entered the war, they too introduced full conscription. Many Canadians whose sons or husbands were voluntarily fighting overseas resented the fact that other Canadians could escape wartime service. To meet public pressure, the government introduced compulsory military training, but for home defence only. The National Resources Mobilization Act called up single men for the defence of Canada or for conscription into war industries. They hoped that once enlisted, many soldiers of the home defence army (nicknamed the 'Zombies') would volunteer to go overseas. Some did but many did not.

By 1942 Mackenzie King realized that there was a strong pro-conscription feeling in most of the country. He decided to go to the nation with a plebiscite, which is a direct vote of all citizens on an issue of major national importance. Canadians were asked in the plebiscite if they were in favour of releasing the government from its repeated pledges that it would not introduce conscription for overseas service. English Canada answered with an overwhelming 80% 'Yes', but 72% of the province of Quebec said 'No'. English Canada was reassured by the vote. To satisfy Quebec, Mackenzie King emphasized that conscription was not yet

Mackenzie King and
Winston Churchill.

necessary, and would only be used as a last resort. His famous
statement about the policy was purposefully vague because it
could be taken favourably by either side. King said, 'Not necessarily conscription, but conscription if necessary.'

In 1944 many citizens now said that conscription was necessary. Colonel Ralston, Minister of National Defence, had been
to Europe to inspect the troops. He discovered that the army
was desperately short of men. Men who had been wounded two
or three times were being sent back to the front lines to fight.
When Ralston returned to Canada he urged the Prime Minister
and Cabinet to bring in conscription immediately to maintain
the Canadian forces overseas. Colonel Ralston had considerable
support in the Cabinet, but Mackenzie King still was determined to avoid conscription if at all possible. The Prime Minister fired Ralston, and replaced him with A.G.L. McNaughton.
General McNaughton was a popular retired army officer who
believed he could raise the required soldiers by voluntary means.
Though McNaughton tried valiantly, within a few weeks it was
clear he would be unsuccessful. McNaughton reported that
morale in the army was now collapsing. There were even threats
that some officers would not serve unless conscription was
brought in.

As a last resort King turned to Louis St. Laurent, the leading
cabinet minister from Quebec. King explained to St. Laurent the
desperate situation in which the Liberal party found itself.
There was real danger that King's government would collapse.
With St. Laurent's co-operation, the Prime Minister announced
a total of 16 000 draftees would be sent overseas, but no more for
the time being. Only 13 000 of the draftees were sent overseas
before the war ended.

The motion to send 16 000 draftees overseas passed in the House of Commons by a majority vote of 143 to 70. Only one minister from Quebec, C.G. Power, resigned from the Cabinet. He protested that the government had broken its pledge to French Canada. There was some rioting in Quebec City and Montreal when the results of the vote were announced. However, the response in French Canada was not nearly as violent as it had been in 1917. Mackenzie King had won a victory for unity. Reasonable citizens in Quebec realized that King had tried hard to prevent conscription in order to keep the country together. He had done all he could to put off conscription as long as possible. He had paid attention to French-Canadian opinion. Although the French Canadians were unhappy about conscription, they gave Mackenzie King credit for doing his best.

Mackenzie King's conscription policy was probably one of his greatest political achievements. He had been ruthless when he fired Colonel Ralston. Some of his critics accused him of being a delayer and bending to every change of public opinion. But King had remembered and learned from the tragic experience of 1917. This time the conscription crisis did not tear apart the Liberal party nor did it succeed in dividing French and English Canada beyond repair.

A Thousand Words: The Propaganda War

In World War II psychological warfare played a major part in military strategy. This type of warfare uses propaganda. Emotional symbols were used in an attempt to influence the behavior of people. These symbols could be the flag, the family, the homeland, or the wickedness of the enemy. It was believed that one picture was worth a thousand words. In Nazi Germany Dr. Goebbels was Hitler's propaganda minister, and the Allies also established a Psychological Warfare Division. Even in Canada there was a Wartime Information Board responsible for wartime propaganda.

During World War II propaganda was aimed at four main targets: enemies, Allies, neutrals, and the home front. When the enemy is the 'target', propaganda emphasizes the theme of eventual defeat. When aimed at the Allies, propaganda stresses unity, loyalty, and victory. For neutral countries propagandists concentrate on the righteousness of their cause. On the home front, propaganda emphasizes the need for effort and sacrifice to achieve victory.

Whether the propaganda was a poster, a radio program, or a film, the message was always the same. In Canada the Wartime

Information Board tried to instill pride and confidence in the
country, to inspire sacrifice, to show the consequence of defeat,
and to convince people that the Allies would win the war.

POSTER PROPAGANDA

Examine the following posters and decide

- who is the intended target?
- who is the sender of the message?
- what is the message of the poster?

- what is the purpose of the poster?
- how is the message relayed?
- what is the effect of the poster?

Women Roll up Their Sleeves for Victory

The Allies were committed to the idea of 'total war'. This meant using population and resources to the fullest extent. Both Canada and Britain brought women into the armed services early in the war. In 1941 the army created the Canadian Women's Army Corps. The air force formed the Canadian Women's Auxiliary Air Force, which was later changed in name to the Royal Canadian Air Force (Women's Division). A short time later the Women's Royal Canadian Naval Service was created. By the end of the war, women in uniform numbered 21 624 (C WAC), 17 018 (RCAFWD), and 6781 (WRCNS). Another 4500 women were in the medical services.

Women in uniform.

Overseas the CWAC's were not sent into front-line combat with the infantry and tanks. They did essential work, however, behind the lines in army headquarters. Although women did not fly planes or serve on ships, as radio operators they helped to guide back to base those who did. In regimental first-aid posts and in general hospitals in Europe and Britain, nurses and Red Cross workers treated the wounded and dying. Besides their nursing duties, they took time to read and write letters for the wounded, cheer up their patients, and look after their mental as well as physical wounds.

A woman who served near the front recalled her wartime experiences:

> I was a Red Cross Corps worker so my job wasn't actually in surgery or a real nurse's job in the field, but we had to do all we could to help.
>
> Some men were cheery, asking for a cigarette, joking. Some were in shock through loss of blood and just torn-up bodies ... and some of these were the ones who were dying. You got to know. They had this look about them, a whiteness, a look in their eyes. Some would die while you sat beside them. One did once, a young boy from Ontario, and he died as I was reading the last letter he got from his mother. He'd asked me to do it. He let out this kind of sigh and his head fell down a bit and then lifted up a bit and then fell down again and I knew he was gone. He had a lot of steel in his chest. I suppose he never had much of a chance.
>
> It was a time when you could work twelve hours a day and another four if you wanted to, and you'd crawl into the tent just dead. The bombing didn't bother us. The shelling. Sometimes it sounded like thunder rolling across the lake, just like at home at the cottage, hour after hour, and it got to be part of you. If it was on, you didn't actually hear it, but when it stopped you did.

Similarly, women played a vital role in war industries at home. As in World War I, the war helped to prove that women could perform tasks as well as men. In 1939 there had only been 638 000 women in the work force in Canada. By 1944 there were 1 077 000. Traditionally only unmarried women worked, but now it became the patriotic thing for all women to help 'fight Hitler at home'. Overalls and the bandana became the symbol of service to Canada. Women by the thousands operated riveting machines in shipyards, welded parts in airplane factories, and worked on assembly lines in munitions plants. In rural areas they ran farms almost single-handedly while the men were away fighting. Jobs that had traditionally been done by men were now done effectively by women. These included work in lumber mills and as streetcar and bus drivers.

The government set up a Women's Division of the National Selective Service under Mrs. Fraudena Eaton. The task of the Women's Division was to recruit as many women as possible into vital wartime work. In ads in newspapers, in store windows, and in movie theatres women were urged to 'back the boys up to bring them back'. At first single and childless married women were sought for employment. However, as more and more workers were needed, married women with children were encouraged to take full or part-time jobs. In Ontario and Quebec the government established child-care facilities for women working in war industries. Married women were temporarily allowed to earn more money without their husbands having to pay higher income tax. Indeed salaries for women did rise significantly dur-

Making hats for the Armed Forces.

ing this time. Women in the aircraft industry received an average weekly wage of $31, which was more than double what women earned before the war.

Women who could not serve in uniform or work in war industries still played a vital role as volunteers. They packed parcels for prisoners of war and knitted sweaters and socks for the fighting men overseas. They worked in service clubs and canteens serving coffee and sandwiches to Canadians in uniform and Allied soldiers training in Canada.

Some people see the women's contribution to the labour force during World War II as a great breakthrough in expanding the traditional roles of women in Canadian society. But for many women the breakthrough was only temporary. Following the war, women often lost their jobs to returning servicemen. Also, the tax concessions to married women were removed and the government-sponsored day nurseries were discontinued. It seemed as if the government wanted married women to return to their homes and children or to the traditional female occupations such as teaching, nursing, and domestic services.

Government Control

As part of the commitment to 'total war', the government assumed a great deal of control over the Canadian economy. The War Time Prices and Trades Board (WTPTB) froze prices, wages, and rents in order to keep down the cost of living. It drastically reduced the number of luxury goods that could be manufactured. Because wool was scarce, the WTPTB forbade the making of men's suits with vests, double-breasted jackets, cuffs, and pleats. Similarly, women's fashions were also influenced by the lack of material. The style became streamlined with tight, knee-length skirts, small hats, and close-fitting jackets.

To finance the war, the Canadian government increased direct taxes on individuals and corporations, and placed high sales taxes on luxury goods. Canadians were urged to buy Victory Bonds. Famous personalities such as the popular Montreal-born movie actress Norma Shearer encouraged Canadians to purchase Victory Bonds. To the credit of Canadians, two-thirds of the Canadian cost of the war was raised through the sale of Victory Bonds. That is, individual Canadians and corporations loaned money to the government which was to be repaid with interest after the war. Of the $18 billion paid by Canada for the war effort, $12 billion was raised through the generosity of Canadians.

THE EFFECT OF WORLD WAR II ON CANADA

When war broke out in 1939, Canada was almost totally unprepared. Nevertheless, the country did its utmost to make a vital contribution to the war effort. By 1945, Canada emerged with an important place in world affairs.

In the first place, Canada made a major contribution of men, munitions, food supplies, and raw materials. In 1939 Canada's three military services totalled just over 10 000 men. By 1945, 1 086 771 Canadians had worn a uniform, of whom 49 252 were women. Among these, fatal casualties numbered 22 964 for the army, 17 047 for the air force, and 1981 for the navy. In a nation of slightly over 11 000 000 at the end of the war, these figures represent a great loss. Similarly, in terms of war production, Canadians worked miracles. Starting from almost nothing, Canadian plants turned out 800 000 motor vehicles, 16 000 aircraft, 900 000 rifles, 200 000 machine-guns, 6500 tanks, over 400 cargo vessels, and nearly 500 escort vessels and mine sweepers.

Secondly, as in World War I, Canada's economy was strengthened by the war. In 1939, Canada still suffered the effects of the Depression. Unemployment was widespread and the economy just beginning to recover from the economic slump. By 1945 the Canadian economy was booming. The gross national production of goods tripled. Such materials as asbestos, aluminum, coal,

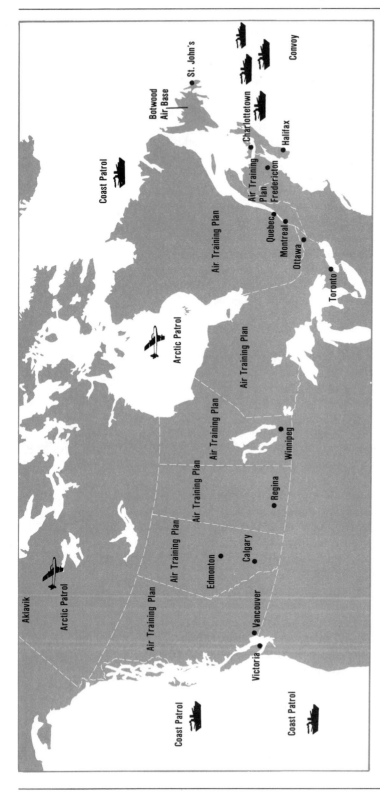

British Columbia

The products of B.C.'s forests and rivers are tuned to the war effort. The entire 1942 catch of salmon was shipped to Britain. The Pacific ports vie with the Atlantic in shipbuilding. The Pacific Coast Militia Rangers was formed when Japan entered the war; it is modelled after the Home Guard of Britain.

Prairie Provinces

In the clear skies of the Canadian Prairies have been trained many world famous pilots of the R.A.F. and the R.C.A.F.
The industrial resources of its towns and cities are working exclusively for the common cause, turning out guns, locomotives, uniforms, etc.

Ontario

The energies and resources of Ontario are geared to the war effort. Its great motor car and farm implement factories are manufacturing armoured vehicles, guns and planes. To its established industries many new plants have been created and are now producing planes, shells, explosives and smallarms for the common cause.

Quebec

Quebec produces 75% of the asbestos used by the Allies. Aircraft, tanks, guns, shells, warships and merchant vessels are produced in its industrial centres. 50% of Canada's newsprint is made in Quebec and it is a new source of strategic war metals and minerals.

Maritimes

From Canada's eastern ports have sailed 13 000 vessels carrying 77 000 000 tons of cargo to the United Kingdom. 99% of this tonnage has reached Britain.

Military Growth

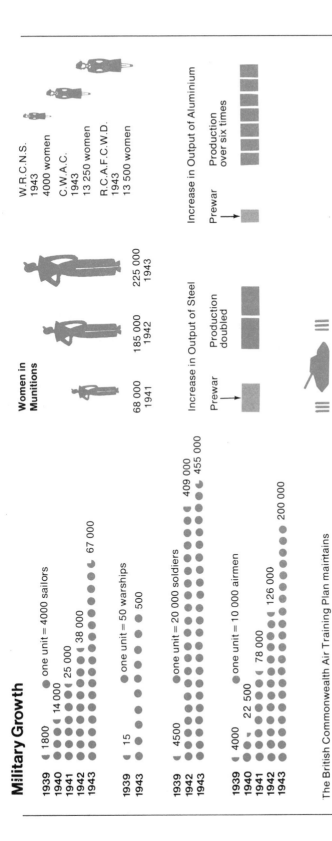

one unit = 4000 sailors

1939 1800
1940 14 000
1941 25 000
1942 38 000
1943 67 000

one unit = 50 warships

1939 15
1943 500

one unit = 20 000 soldiers

1939 4500
1942 409 000
1943 455 000

one unit = 10 000 airmen

1939 4000
1940 22 500
1941 78 000
1942 126 000
1943 200 000

The British Commonwealth Air Training Plan maintains 154 Flying Schools in Canada. 60% of its graduates are Canadian and 50% of its cost is borne by Canada.

The Canadian Red Cross

There are 2 096 608 members and 31 789 branches of the Canadian Red Cross Society. Since the outbreak of war over 21 300 000 articles have been sent overseas. In 1941 was inaugurated the Prisoners of War Service. 10 000 food parcels are sent per week.

Women in Munitions

68 000 — 1941
185 000 — 1942
225 000 — 1943

W.R.C.N.S. 1943 — 4000 women

C.W.A.C. 1943 — 13 250 women

R.C.A.F.C.W.D. 1943 — 13 500 women

Increase in Output of Steel

Prewar → Production doubled

Increase in Output of Aluminium

Prewar → Production over six times

War Productions

1914-18	$1 002 672 413
1941	$1 200 000 000
1942	$2 600 000 000
1943	$3 700 000 000

Canada is manufacturing $1 000 000 000 in War Materials and equipment for the U.S.A. Almost all the motor transport used by the 8th Army (Libya) is made in Canada. Canada is the fourth largest producer of war supplies and equipment among the Allies.

manganese, chemicals, and paper, all contributed to the war and made Canada's industries expand rapidly. The production of key agricultural goods such as wheat, flour, bacon, ham, dried eggs, and canned meat and fish also experienced an economic boom.

Thirdly, the most striking consequence of the whole crisis was a new international status for Canada. Canada emerged from the war respected by the other nations of the world. At the same time, Canada seemed prepared to accept new responsibilities in maintaining world-wide peace. In a very real sense the war had assisted Canada in establishing its place as a 'middle power' among nations.

Digging Deeper

1 Is government propaganda necessary and important in war-time? Why? Is it important during peacetime? Why? What sorts of propaganda would you accept during peacetime?

2 During the Second World War many family farms and factories were run by Canadian women. What were the effects of the war effort on women's roles in society? What changes came about at the end of the war? Did these changes improve or hinder women's struggle for equality?

3 During the war the government established a day-care program for children whose mothers were working in wartime industries. How important do you think this program was in getting women involved in the war effort? Today there are over a half-million children under age six whose mothers work. What community services do you think should be offered to assist working mothers? Can society afford these services that allow women to work? Are these services seen as important priorities in your community?

4 Twice in the 20th century the issue of conscription nearly tore the Canadian nation apart. Compare and contrast the two situations, accounting for the different outcome of the 1944 crisis.

5 Try making propaganda posters. Different groups may be assigned various targets:
a) enemy – Nazi Germany or Japan;
b) Allies – Britain or France;
c) neutrals – the United States before 1941;
d) the home front – perhaps the conscription issue.

27

THE INTERNMENT OF JAPANESE-CANADIANS: A CASE STUDY IN HUMAN RIGHTS

Shock and anger gripped the Canadian people when they heard the Japanese had attacked the American naval base at Pearl Harbor on 7 December 1941. That same night the Royal Canadian Mounted Police swept down on the Japanese community in British Columbia and began to make arrests. In the next few days thirty-eight 'dangerous individuals' and 'troublemakers' were rounded up. In the months that followed all Japanese

Japanese-Canadians on the way to an internment camp.

nationals (people born in Japan but living in Canada) and Canadian citizens of Japanese descent were imprisoned under the Wartime Emergency Powers Act. They were taken from their homes, packed into trains, and usually sent to internment camps in the interior of British Columbia. The stronger men were assigned to work on road construction in northern British Columbia and Ontario. Others were used as farm labourers in the sugar beet fields of Alberta and Manitoba. Men who resisted were separated from their families and sent to a prisoner-of-war camp in Angler, Ontario.

It did not seem to matter to the Canadian government whether these people were born in Japan or Canada. In fact, more than 14 000 were second-generation Japanese born in this country. Another 3000 were naturalized Canadian citizens. There was no appreciation of the fact that 200 Japanese-Canadians had fought in the Canadian army in World War I. Canada and Japan were at war, and all Japanese-Canadians were considered to be potentially dangerous.

Most of the people of Japanese descent lived in British Columbia. Many were fishermen who owned small boats and fished for salmon along the British Columbia coast. Others worked in fish canneries or owned small plots of land where they grew fruit and vegetables for the Vancouver market. A few owned neighbourhood grocery stores or restaurants, or worked as domestic servants in the homes of the wealthy of Vancouver. Now their property was taken away and their businesses were ruined.

Discrimination was nothing new for the Japanese in Canada. The first known settler in Canada from Japan was Manzo Nagano. He is said to have stowed away on a British freighter docked at Nagasaki, not knowing where it was headed. When it stopped at New Westminster in May 1877, he jumped ship. Most of the early Japanese immigrants who followed Nagano to Canada came as labourers for the coal mines, lumber camps, and railways. Their intention was to make a fortune and return home. However, many ended up staying in Canada. Because there were few Japanese women to marry in Canada, marriages were arranged with women in Japan, by using photographs. The women would later join husbands whom they had never seen. These women became known as 'picture brides', and in 1913 some 300 to 400 women arrived through this kind of arrangement. Though many non-Japanese were shocked by this practice, it was consistent with Japanese custom. These marriages worked amazingly well because in Japan the marriages were more the joining of two families rather than two individuals.

When they first arrived, Japanese immigrants in Canada were

often praised for their hard work and eagerness. But their eventual success as farmers or fishermen alarmed and frightened many people in British Columbia. They were soon seen as tough competitors. White farmers and workers who felt their jobs might be threatened stirred up racist feelings and warned of the 'Yellow Peril'. Racist feelings surfaced in Vancouver in 1907 when 5000 whites rioted through the Chinese and Japanese communities. Store windows were smashed and the crowd chanted 'Down with the Japs' and 'Keep Canada White'. Japanese were excluded from higher-paying jobs in mining, denied the right to vote in British Columbia, and barred from public service and professions.

It is probably not surprising that anti-Japanese feeling flared up again in British Columbia during the war. The shock of Pearl Harbor and the treatment of Canadian prisoners of war in Hong Kong turned Canadian public opinion against the Japanese-Canadians. On the day war broke out a Japanese-Canadian girl recalled how a man approached her on the street and spat in her face. Resentment was so bad that a Chinese woman wore a sign around her neck that said 'I'm not a Jap, I'm Chinese'.

Japanese fishermen were the first group to be evacuated. Rumours that spread like wildfire suggested Canada would be attacked at any minute and that the fishermen were navy officers sent to spy on British Columbia waters. About 1200 Japanese fishing boats were seized by the Canadian government

Round-up of Japanese-Canadian fishing boats.

and their owners sent to the interior of British Columbia. One fisherman remembered:

To this day I don't know what they thought about these fishing boats. They were our living. They were small boats made of wood. We had no radar, no radio, no echo sounder. Just tiny little vessels with their chuggy little motors and space for the fish we caught ... And they said we were charting the coast and waterways ... Why, we could go into Vancouver any time and buy British Admiralty charts of every single kilometre of the coast. But try and convince people that we were not spies, that we were not spying ... But oh no, no way. As far back as the late 1890s they had determined that they would kick the Japs off the river.

The R.C.M.P. was satisfied that the few Japanese who were possibly dangerous had already been arrested. The Canadian navy saw no problem now that the fishermen had been removed from the coast. The Chief of the General Staff reported to the government, 'I cannot see that they [Japanese-Canadians] constitute the slightest menace to Canadian security.' Still, politicians and British Columbia citizens were not satisfied. They continued to demand that all Japanese-Canadians should be interned. In February 1942 the Canadian government decided to move all the Japanese-Canadians away from the coast to inland centres. The Government did this for two reasons: to prevent spying which could lead to an enemy invasion, and to protect Japanese-Canadians from being harmed in anti-Japanese riots.

At first they were housed in the cow barns at Hastings Park in the Exhibition Grounds in Vancouver. Then most were sent by special trains to six ghost towns in the interior of British Columbia. They were allowed to take sixty-eight kilograms of clothing, bedding, and cooking utensils for each adult. In towns such as New Denver, Slocan, and Greenwood, they were housed in crude frame huts. Two bedrooms and a kitchen had to be shared by two families. Until 1943 there was no electricity or running water. Living conditions were so bad that food packages from Japan were sent through the Red Cross to interned Canadians in British Columbia. In these remote communities they were kept under constant surveillance by the R.C.M.P. Japanese veterans of the First World War were also paid to watch over the settlement and report anything out of the ordinary. About 3650 Japanese-Canadians were sent to work as farm labourers east of the Rocky Mountains. At Angler, Ontario, the men were actually surrounded by barbed wire and guarded by veterans. Those considered to be the most dangerous were made to wear uniforms with red targets sewn on their backs.

▲ Inside the kitchen of an internment camp.

◄ A men's dining room in an internment camp.

When Japan surrendered, the Canadian government considered sending all Japanese-Canadians back to Japan. This would have included many born in Canada who did not speak or understand any language but English. The deportation fortunately never took place because a large number of Canadian citizens protested that this would be dishonourable and unfair to the Japanese-Canadians. About 4000 made up their own minds to return to Japan in 1946.

Those who did remain in Canada did not have an easy time adjusting in the post-war years. Only a small number went back to British Columbia. Instead they spread out across the country. Citizens of Japanese descent were finally given the right to vote federally in June 1948, and in British Columbia elections in 1949.

Many of the Japanese-Canadians were bitter when they found out after the war that their land had been sold, often at a fraction of its value. They had been told that the government would hold their belongings in trust.

Checking the documents of Japanese- Canadians.

When we left we had to turn over our property to the Custodian of Enemy Property for safekeeping. Now that meant to us that when the war business was over we'd get our property back. Some just put everything in a bedroom and put a lock on the door and thought it would be safe. Some just left the stuff and people could walk in and take what they wanted. That happened. Oh yes. Often.

It was a terrible shock when we learned that this safekeeping business meant nothing, that all of our stuff had been sold at auction. There are people who were never told that they lost all their goods by confiscation because the Custodian just couldn't bother looking after it all. Others would get a cheque or a credit saying so much was due to them, but there were some people who got no money at all. Now that wasn't right. That safekeeping thing caused a lot of bitterness. People would say, 'That's all we had and now we've got nothing.' It made a lot of people pretty mad. First they take us from our homes and stick us in a dump, and now this.

One man's house sold for $50 at a government auction, and its contents for $8.50. Another man's fishing boat sold for $150, a fraction of what it was worth. Most people felt that they received from the government between 5% and 10% of the real value of their property and possessions. In 1946 a Japanese Property Claims Commission was set up by the Canadian government. It was to review the claims of those who felt they had not been treated fairly for their confiscated property. Although in some cases additional money was made available, it never fully compensated for what had been lost.

Digging Deeper

Should the internment of the Japanese-Canadians have occurred? Why or why not? Who was responsible? What does this episode teach us about our Canadian society?
Do you think a minority group could be interned today? Why or why not?
Why were the Japanese-Canadians interned and not the German-Canadians?

1

Role playing:
Role play a meeting in which the following people discuss whether the Japanese-Canadians should be interned during World War II.
a) Prime Minister Mackenzie King;
b) Chief of the General Staff (General Stuart);
c) a British Columbia politician;
d) a Canadian-born leader of the Japanese community;
e) a non-Japanese fisherman on the British Columbia coast;
f) a representative of a British Columbia labour union;
g) a lawyer interested in civil rights disputes;
h) a person with a son in a Japanese prisoner of war camp;
i) a citizen of British Columbia fearful of a Japanese attack on British Columbia.

2

A Values Inquiry

A Child in a Prison Camp by Shizuye Takashima is the true story of a young Japanese-Canadian girl's experience in an internment camp during World War II. 'Shichan', as she was known to her friends, has written of the three years during which she and her family were isolated in a camp. During the spring of 1944 she recorded a discussion her family had. They were trying to decide whether they should stay in Canada or go back to Japan.

Spring 1944

The war with Japan is getting very bad. I can feel my parents growing anxious. There is a lot of tension in the camp; rumors of being moved again, of everyone having to return to Japan. Kazuo and his family leave for Japan. Many are angry they have left us. Some call them cowards, others call them brave! I only feel sad, for I liked Kazuo so much, so very much.

Father shouts at mother, "We return to Japan!" "But what are we going to do? You have your brothers and sisters there. I have no one. Besides, the children ...." "Never mind the children," father answers. "They'll adjust. I'm tired of being treated as a spy, a prisoner. Do what you like; I'm returning!"

I can see Mrs. Kono looks confused. "My husband is talking of returning to Japan, too. I think it's the best thing. All our relatives are still there. We have nothing here." Yuki stares at her. "It's all right for you, Mrs. Kono, you were born there, but we weren't. I'm not going. That's all!" And she walks out of the house.

Mother gets very upset. I know she wants to cry. "I don't want to go to Japan, either," I say. "They're short of food and clothing there. They haven't enough for their own people. They won't want us back."

All of a sudden I hate that country for having started the war. I say aloud, "Damn Japs! Why don't they stop fighting?" Father glares. "What do you mean 'Japs'? You think you're not a Jap? If I hear you say that again I'll throttle you."

I see anger and hatred in his eyes. I leave the room, go out of the house. I hear him say loudly to mother, "It's all your fault. You poison our children's minds by saying we're better off here."

And another argument starts. I am getting tired of it, and confused. I feel so helpless, and wish again I were older, then maybe I could go somewhere .... But I do not hate the people in Japan.

I know Yuki doesn't hate them either, really. It's all so senseless. Really, maybe children should rule the world! Yuki tells me it is wrong for father, because of his anger at the wrong done towards him and us, to expect us to return to his country: "Sure, we're Japanese. But we think like Canadians. We won't be accepted in Japan if we go there."

A Child in Prison Camp
©1971, Shizuye Takashima
published by Tundra Books of Montreal

Questions:
1. What problems do Shichan's family face?
2. Describe what each member of the family would like to do.
3. Describe the behaviour of each member of the family. How does their behaviour relate back to their feelings about what is important to them?
4. Point out the ways in which the beliefs of mother, father, and Shichan are similar and different.
5. Suggest reasons why each person feels the way he/she does.
6. What other alternatives are available for the family?
7. Name some possible consequences for the family if they stay in Canada, or if they go back to Japan.
8. Pretend you are each of the people mentioned above. What would you do about this situation?
9. Why did you decide on this course of action, and what might be some of the consequences you would have to face?
10. What do you think Shichan meant when she said, 'Why can't children rule the world?'

Japanese Bombs Dropped From Balloons in World War II Still Pose Deadly Threat

Hundreds of deadly Japanese balloon bombs aimed at Canada and the United States in World War II are still lying around in isolated areas. They may still be capable of maiming and killing people today. Experts warn that the lethal, unexploded bombs could still be a hazard to hikers and campers in remote areas.

Late in the war the Japanese launched a scheme to send balloons across the Pacific. They were released into the strong winds that blow over the Pacific Ocean from the west in the late winter and early spring. The idea was that the balloons would float across the Pacific, drop in North American forests, and start spectacular forest fires.

The balloons, made of six layers of tough mulberry paper, were about ten metres in diameter. They were filled with hydrogen gas, and the explosive device hung down below.

It is estimated that the Japanese launched 9000 of these balloons, but only 296 were recovered in the United States or Canada. Not one forest fire was started. Fortunately the forests are rain-soaked or snow-covered in the winter and spring. Thus the fire balloon campaign failed. Only one of the bombs is known to have taken casualties. A woman and five children were killed in Oregon on 5 May 1945 when they found and disturbed a balloon bomb. Other bombs landed from Alaska to Mexico and as far inland as the Manitoba-Ontario border. Military officials warn that the bombs may still be explosive. Anyone finding one should not handle it, but report its location as quickly as possible to the authorities.

Questions:

1. How serious was the threat of the Japanese balloon bombs to North America?
2. Did Canada's knowledge of the deadly balloons justify the internment of the Japanese-Canadians?

28
PLANS FOR PEACE

On the decks of the giant U.S. battleship *Missouri*, the Japanese formally surrendered to the American general, Douglas MacArthur. Eyewitnesses recalled the event. On the slate grey battleship, American admirals and generals, and British, Russian, French, and Chinese military officials gathered for the signing ceremony. The Japanese Foreign Minister and the Chief of the Imperial Staff were ushered on board. After a short speech by General MacArthur, they were led to a table and told to sign the Terms of Surrender. With expressionless faces, they put their signatures to a document that acknowledged the total defeat of Japan. General MacArthur then took a fountain pen from his pocket and placed his signature on behalf of the United States. MacArthur hesitated a moment, and then he stepped forward: 'Let us pray that peace be now restored to the world, and that God will preserve it always.'

Even before the war ended, the Allies started making plans for the peace that would follow the surrender of Germany and Japan. They agreed on the need for a new international organization to maintain peace and security after the war. The old League of Nations, formed to keep peace after World War I, had been a failure. Despite this failure, President Roosevelt of the United States, Prime Minister Churchill of Britain, and later Premier Stalin of Russia, were determined to set up an international organization where governments could settle differences that might otherwise lead to war. It was agreed that an international conference would be held at San Francisco in April 1945 to sign a formal charter or constitution.

Fifty nations took part in the San Francisco conference, including Canada. 'We, the peoples of the United Nations, determined to save succeeding generations from the scourge of war, which twice in our lifetime has brought untold sorrow to mankind ... do hereby establish an international organization to be known as the United Nations' (Preamble to the Charter of the United Nations). The member nations agreed to band together to remove any threat to world peace (collective security). They further promised to give economic, military, and political help to improve world conditions and to establish world peace and security. Canada believed in this idea of collective

THE UNITED NATIONS SYSTEM

● Principal organs of the United Nations

● Other United Nations organs

○ Specialized agencies and other
autonomous organizations within
the system

Main Committees ●

Standing and ●
procedural committees

Other subsidiary organs ●
of the General Assembly

**TRUSTEESHIP
COUNCIL**

**GENERAL
ASSEMBLY**

**INTERNATIONAL
COURT OF
JUSTICE**

United Nations Relief and Works Agency for ●
Palestine Refugees in the Near East **UNRWA**

United Nations Conference ●
on Trade and Development **UNCTAD**

United Nations Children's Fund **UNICEF** ●

Office of the United Nations High Commissioner ●
for Refugees **UNHCR**

Joint UN/FAO World Food Programme ●

United Nations Institute ●
for Training and Research **UNITAR**

United Nations Development Programme **UNDP** ●

United Nations Industrial ●
Development Organization **UNIDO**

United Nations Environment Programme **UNEP** ●

United Nations University **UNU** ●

United Nations Special Fund ●

World Food Council ●

**ECONOMIC
AND
SOCIAL
COUNCIL**

● Regional commissions

● Functional commissions

● Sessional, standing and
ad hoc committees

UN Chart

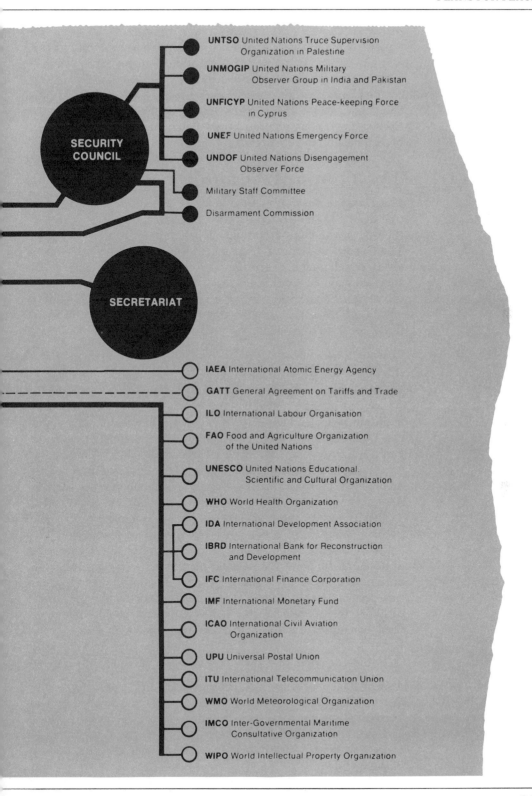

SECURITY COUNCIL

UNTSO United Nations Truce Supervision Organization in Palestine

UNMOGIP United Nations Military Observer Group in India and Pakistan

UNFICYP United Nations Peace-keeping Force in Cyprus

UNEF United Nations Emergency Force

UNDOF United Nations Disengagement Observer Force

Military Staff Committee

Disarmament Commission

SECRETARIAT

IAEA International Atomic Energy Agency

GATT General Agreement on Tariffs and Trade

ILO International Labour Organisation

FAO Food and Agriculture Organization of the United Nations

UNESCO United Nations Educational, Scientific and Cultural Organization

WHO World Health Organization

IDA International Development Association

IBRD International Bank for Reconstruction and Development

IFC International Finance Corporation

IMF International Monetary Fund

ICAO International Civil Aviation Organization

UPU Universal Postal Union

ITU International Telecommunication Union

WMO World Meteorological Organization

IMCO Inter-Governmental Maritime Consultative Organization

WIPO World Intellectual Property Organization

security. The two world wars had emphasized the need for nations to stand together against any kind of aggression (hostile, war-like acts). By signing the charter, Canada offered money and resources on the side of peace.

The United Nations has six major parts. The chart illustrates the organization: The General Assembly, Security Council, the Secretariat, Economic and Social Council, International Court of Justice, and the Trusteeship Council.

The General Assembly

The *General Assembly* is made up of all the member nations that belong to the United Nations. Each member pays a share of the cost of the United Nations, depending on its ability to pay. The General Assembly discusses and debates such problems as aid to developing countries and international use of the sea. It suggests ways of settling disputes that arise in various parts of the world. Each nation has one vote. If the General Assembly votes for U.N. action on a matter, it is turned over to the Security Council to be decided.

The Security Council

The real centre of power in the United Nations is the *Security Council.* It has the authority to take military or other action to maintain peace and security. Five nations are permanent members of the Security Council – the United States, the U.S.S.R., Britain, France, and the People's Republic of China. These powerful nations are known as the 'Big Five'. Ten non-permanent members are elected to the Security Council by the General Assembly for a term of two years.

The 'Big Five' must approve all the major decisions of the Security Council. In other words, each of these five powers can 'veto' or block Council decisions. When the U.N. Charter was drafted, these powerful nations demanded the right to veto, arguing that since they would have to provide most of the military security forces, they had the right to block any action they disliked. It was hoped that the veto power would seldom be used, but unfortunately this has not been the case.

The Secretariat

About 4000 workers from all parts of the world form the *Secretariat* or the working staff of the U.N. It is headed by the Secretary-General who is nominated by the Security Council and elected by the General Assembly. He is the chief administrator and must co-ordinate the activities of the U.N. in all parts of the world.

Lester Pearson at the U.N.

The Economic and Social Council

The *Economic and Social Council* works for world peace by try-ing to eliminate the economic and social conditions that could cause war. In the days that immediately followed World War II this council concentrated on providing relief for war refugees. Later, it introduced programs to raise living standards and pro-mote human rights. Many agencies set up by the Economic and Social Council carry out its goals. One of the most important agencies is the United Nations Educational, Scientific, and Cul-tural Organization (UNESCO). It has built schools, research facili-ties, and cultural centres in many of the underdeveloped areas of the world. Another is UNICEF, the United Nations International Children's Emergency Fund. Money collected on Hallowe'en is used to help children in war-ravaged countries and in places that have been struck by floods and other natural disasters. The World Health Organization (WHO) is concerned with problems of world health and medical research.

The International Court of Justice

This court was set up to try to settle disputes between nations in a peaceful manner. Unfortunately no member can be compelled to attend. However, the court does rule on cases in which the member nations have agreed to abide by its decision.

The Trusteeship Council

The *Trusteeship Council* was set up to take care of those colonies taken from the defeated countries of both world wars. Many of these colonies were in Africa. The goal of the council is to administer the trusteeships until they can become independent. At present only one trust territory remains: the Pacific Islands once owned by Japan.

It was hoped in 1945 that the United Nations Organization would be able to avoid the problems experienced by the League of Nations. President Roosevelt was determined that this time the United States would join the world organization. The U.S.A. was now the greatest power in the world and led the way in supporting the U.N. The permanent headquarters of the United Nations was built in New York City. American participation, as well as that of the U.S.S.R., made the U.N. much stronger than the old League had been. The U.N. was further strengthened by the fact that it had the power to use military force if necessary. The League of Nations never had such a provision.

In the League, unanimous approval was required of all members before action could be taken. The U.N. is stronger because its Security Council may act if a majority (including each of the 'Big Five') approves an action.

The other great strength of the United Nations was that it recognized that world peace depended on more than taking united action against aggression. For this reason the Economic and Social Council, with its many agencies, set out to attack the problems that could lead to war: poverty, disease, energy needs, food and water shortage, pollution, and unemployment.

Digging Deeper

1

Select one of the agencies of the United Nations (such as UNESCO, UNICEF, and WHO). Do some research to find out what work the agency does. You may wish to write to the Information Division of the United Nations, New York City, for particular details. Present a short report to your class where you describe the agency's functions and evaluate its achievements.

In the left-hand column are five weaknesses of the League of Nations. In the right-hand column describe the features of the United Nations that try to correct the weaknesses of the League.

2

LEAGUE OF NATIONS	UNITED NATIONS
i) The United States was not a member.	
ii) Russia and Germany were major countries that did not join.	
iii) There was no military force to back up the League's decisions.	
iv) All members had to agree on any action to be taken.	
v) No emphasis was placed on improving economic and social conditions of people in the world.	

Some people have said that the Economic and Social Council of the United Nations has done more for world peace than the Security Council. Do some research on the work of the Economic and Social Council in order to explain what they mean. Do you agree with this opinion? Why or why not? Why is the Security Council often unable to take action when conflicts break out between nations?

3

Set up a Security Council meeting in class. With students role-playing representatives of the fifteen member nations, debate an issue of world concern.

4

Refer back to the summary chart of themes at the end of Unit One (page 54). Using the chart as a model, make a chart for Unit Five. On the chart trace the development of those themes through this unit.

5

29

KING AND ST. LAURENT

THE LAST DAYS OF MACKENZIE KING

In 1945, refugee camps in Europe were filled with hundreds of thousands of people. Many had seen their homes destroyed and their families separated. Many had survived the Nazi concentration camps. Thousands saw their homelands now being taken over by the Russians, and refused to live under communist rule.

Even after the war ended, shortages and hardships remained a way of life in Europe. Families lived among the ruins of bombed-out buildings. A few lumps of coal, a bar of soap, or a small package of coffee were considered luxuries. It was almost impossible to obtain any kind of meat, and desperately needed medicines were in very short supply.

At the United Nations the refugees were known as 'displaced persons'. In Canada they were often referred to intolerantly as D.P.s. Gradually, though, Canada began to open its doors to welcome an increasing number of displaced persons. All through the 1930s and early 1940s Canada's immigration policy had been very restrictive. That is, Canada had only been accepting people from white Commonwealth countries. When only 7576 immigrants came to Canada in 1942, it marked the lowest number to arrive since 1860. Now that the war was over, Canada began to return to an open door policy. For one thing, Canada needed trained people for post-war development. But the policy was also changed for humanitarian reasons. The suffering of so many thousands in Europe could not be allowed to continue. In the year 1948, 50 000 refugees immigrated to Canada. Immigration played an important role in the expansion of Canada's population after the war. Starting slowly with war brides and displaced persons, the flow built up in the decade of the 1950s. In 1957 it reached 282 164 people, the highest total since 1913.

The first to arrive in Canada were the war brides with their children. This is not too surprising, considering that one in five Canadian soldiers who went overseas as bachelors came home married. In late 1944, the first of 40 000 war brides began arriv-

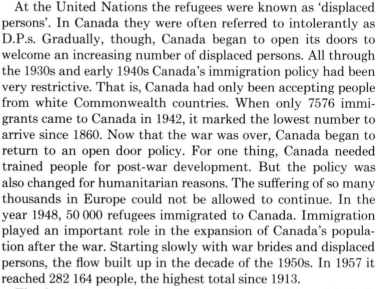

British war brides arriving in Canada.

ing in this country. Twenty thousand children were brought along with them.

The Canadian Wives' Bureau was set up in London, England to prepare the war brides for their new life in Canada. Charlotte Whitton, at that time a social worker, wrote a brochure which was given to all war brides overseas. It was full of practical information for women about living in Canada. It included such items as tips on how to order from the mail order catalogue and the sleeping arrangements on Canadian trains. The Red Cross and the Y.W.C.A. also did their part to help the war brides settle in. But all the help in the world could not prepare some of them for what they found upon arriving in Canada. Many Canadian boys had exaggerated how well-off they were at home. Many a war bride arrived expecting to find the modern home she had been promised. Instead she found herself alone on an isolated farm with no conveniences. Other women had to live with in-laws who were complete strangers until their husbands returned home from Europe. A few of the war brides were so homesick and discouraged that they went back to their own country. However, most stayed, adjusted, and took up their new lives in Canada.

Two war brides remember their first impressions of Canada.

I really hadn't the slightest idea what to expect when I arrived in Quebec. We stayed three months in St. Jean and then moved to Drummondville where we settled. Of course, I'd known that my husband was a French-speaking Canadian, but it was quite

≫→

a shock to find that his relatives spoke no English at all. Although his family was a bit put out that he'd married une Anglaise (and a Protestant one at that), they were very good to me.

My husband and I had two great days in Saskatoon when I arrived. We'd never had a real honeymoon in England, and those two days were all we could afford. Then we took the train to his home town, Birsay, Saskatchewan. At that time it was an all-day trip to cover the 160 kilometres. What a welcome awaited us at Birsay station. I felt like the Queen of England! All the people of the village and surrounding farm area were there to welcome me. I met my in-laws, two lovely people who still had their Yorkshire accents.

In the two decades after World War II, more than two and a half million came to Canada as immigrants. Although about one-fifth went on to settle in other countries, the majority stayed and lived in Canada. The largest group came from Great Britain, followed by Italy, the United States, Germany, Greece, Portugal, Poland, and the Netherlands.

Both of these last two groups had strong wartime connections with Canada. The Polish army had fought alongside the Canadians in northwest Europe and Italy. Polish fliers had trained in Canada, and after the war, many Polish refugees decided to make Canada their home. Doctors, lawyers, engineers, and highly-trained technical people were among the Polish immigrants. Many took jobs as dishwashers and janitors, and worked very hard in order to get established in Canada.

The Dutch also had a soft spot in their hearts for Canada. Canadians had helped to liberate Holland from the Nazis. Crown Princess Juliana of the Netherlands had lived in Ottawa during the war. A room in the Ottawa Civic Hospital had been declared Dutch territory so that her third daughter could be born on 'Dutch soil'. After the war 30 000 Dutch people – mostly farmers – began to arrive in Canada. For years Holland expressed its gratitude to Canada with an annual gift of tulip bulbs which bloom in the springtime in the parks of Ottawa.

There was one very important difference between the immigrants of Laurier's time and those who came after World War II. Most of the latter settled in urban centres in central Canada or British Columbia. At the opening of the century, immigrants had settled largely in rural areas. Ontario received about 50 per cent of the mid-century immigrants, Quebec 25 per cent, British Columbia 10 per cent, and the combined prairie provinces about 12 per cent. Only 3 per cent settled in the Atlantic region. The typical immigrant of the early 1900s had been a farmer or a labourer. The immigrant of the late 1940s and early 1950s was usually a skilled worker or a professional person.

Mackenzie King had led Canada through the Second World War. In fact he had been prime minister longer than any man in the Commonwealth. He had been leader of the Liberal party since 1919, when he had been chosen to succeed Sir Wilfrid Laurier. But by now he was tired and sick, and in 1948 King gave up the leadership of the party. When he retired, a long era in Canadian politics ended.

The following are some assessments of Mackenzie King. Which would you agree with and why? Which do you disagree with and why?

'Very few people it would seem had loved King; not many even liked him; but vast numbers had voted for him.'

'He has been hated and adored. My own guess is that historians will not be able to deny him the elements of great statesmanship.'

'He left Canada a more independent community than he had found it.'

'His zeal for national unity ... helped to prevent an explosion that would have made things much worse.'

'He had some unpleasant characteristics.'

'King was at his best when the political storms were at their worst.'

'He genuinely believed he was doing good things for the people and for the nation.'

THE ST. LAURENT YEARS 1948-1957

Louis St. Laurent was the second French-Canadian prime minister in Canadian history. He had been a prominent corporation lawyer in Quebec City who had come to Ottawa and entered politics out of a wartime sense of duty. He was fluently bilingual. His popularity in Quebec had greatly helped Prime Minister King and the Liberals to carry that province during the conscription crisis in 1944. During the federal election campaign of 1949, St. Laurent spent so much time patting the heads of small children and kissing babies that a reporter had nicknamed him 'Uncle Louis'. The nickname stuck with St. Laurent and conveyed the image of a kindly, elderly gentleman.

Newfoundland Joins Confederation

On 1 April 1949, Newfoundland, including Labrador, became Canada's tenth province. It is said that some people on that island hung black flags out the window and wore black arm-

Joey Smallwood.

bands in protest. Others gathered in community halls to celebrate becoming Canadians.

Newfoundlanders had flatly rejected Confederation in 1867, preferring to keep up their historic ties with Britain. Sir John A. Macdonald was disappointed when Newfoundland rejected Confederation. He had once remarked, 'The Dominion cannot be considered complete without Newfoundland. It has the key to our front door.'

Since 1855 Newfoundland had been self-governing. The world-wide depression of the 1930s, however, had hit the island very hard. The government went broke and had to accept British administration and assistance. After World War II, Joseph R. Smallwood began to urge fellow Newfoundlanders that it was time to join Canada. Smallwood, a former organizer of a fishermen's union, publisher, and radio personality, became the driving force for Confederation. It was a tough fight. The anti-Confederationists warned that it would mean the end of Newfoundland. Confederation would bring economic ruin. The Roman Catholic Church feared that Confederation would mean the end of Roman Catholic education. But Joey Smallwood held out the promise of the baby bonus. Newfoundland families were large families. A family of 9 or 10 was not considered overly large. The promise of a monthly allowance from the Canadian government for each child seemed like a fortune to most Newfoundlanders. Indeed in 1949 conditions for most people were poor by any standard. There was a shortage of schools, hospitals, roads, and jobs. If Newfoundlanders believed Joey Smallwood, all they would have to do would be to join Canada and then sit back and wait for the cheques to arrive!

ARE YOU IN THIS LIST?

To All Mothers: Confederation would mean that never again would there be a hungry child in Newfoundland. If you have children under the age of 16, you will receive every month a cash allowance for every child you have or may have.

To All War Veterans: Canada treats her Veterans better than any other country in the world. She has just increased their War Pensions 25%. Under Confederation you will be better treated than under any other form of government.

To All Wage-Workers: All wage-workers will be protected by Unemployment Insurance. Newfoundland, under Confederation, will be opened up and developed. Your country will be prosperous. Your condition will be better.

To All Over 65: You would have something to look forward to at the age of 70. The Old Age Pension of $30 a month for yourself, and $30 a month for your wife ($60 a month between you) will protect you against need in your old age.

To All Railroaders: You will become employees of the biggest railway in the world, the C.N.R. You will have security and stability as C.N.R. employees. Your wages and working conditions will be the same as on the C.N.R. Under any other government you face sure and certain wage-cuts and lay-offs. You, your wives and sons and daughters and other relatives should flock out on June 3 and vote for Confederation.

To All Building Workers: Under Confederation Newfoundland will share fully in the Canadian Government Housing Plan, under which cities and towns are financed to build houses. 1000 new homes will be built in St. John's under this Plan.

To All Light Keepers: You will become employees of the Government of Canada. Your wages and working conditions will be greatly improved. You will be treated just the same as the light-keepers in the 5 Canadian light-houses already in Newfoundland.

To All Postal-Telegraph Workers: You will all become employees of the Government of Canada, at higher salaries and much better working conditions.

To All Customs Officials: You will become employees of the Government of Canada, at better salaries and much better working conditions.

To All Gander Workers: You who are now employed by the Newfoundland Government will become employees of the Government of Canada. The Department of Transport of the Government of Canada will operate Gander. They will not try to make Gander pay by cutting you down and trying to make you pay the costs of operating the Airport. Everybody on Gander will be better off under Confederation.

To All Fishermen: The cost of living will come down. The cost of producing fish will come down. The Government of Canada will stand back of our fisheries. The Fish Prices Support Board of Canada, backed by Canada's millions, will protect the price of your fish.

To All Newfoundlanders: The cost of living will come down. The 120 000 children in our country will live better. The 10 000 Senior Citizens of our country will be protected in their old age. Newfoundland will be linked up with a strong, rich British nation. Newfoundland will go ahead with Canada.

The Confederate, May 31, 1948

In a direct public vote on the issue (referendum), Newfoundlanders voted by a narrow majority – 52 per cent to 48 per cent – to join Canada. Smallwood was appointed the province's premier. By the terms of union, Newfoundland received the same financial benefits as other provinces as well as special assistance because of its unstable economy and low standard of public services. The federal government took over the island's public debt and the operation of the Newfoundland Railway.

THE ECONOMIC BOOM

A tall pillar of flame and smoke shot up into the Alberta winter sky. The crowd of oil workers, geologists, and officials let out a whoop and a cheer. It was 13 February 1947, and the fabulous Leduc Number 1 oil well near Edmonton had just come in. That day a new stage in Alberta's oil and gas boom began.

Oil company crews had been exploring for oil intensively in the West since 1913. But until the Leduc strike about ninety per cent of Canada's total output was coming from the Turner Valley near Calgary and Norman Wells in the Northwest Territories. By 1947 Turner Valley production was falling off by about ten per cent a year. Thus, when Leduc Number 1 started pumping, oil hysteria swept the country again. Almost overnight sleepy little towns near Edmonton became boom towns. Soon more than 1200 wells were steadily producing in the Leduc area.

Drilling for oil on the prairies.

In a sense Leduc marked the beginning of the post-war economic boom in Canada. However oil was just one of the natural resources that led to the dynamic growth of Canada's economy after 1945.

In every area of economic activity new production records were set. At no time before had Canada experienced such tremendous expansion. When the Ungava Peninsula in northern Quebec became the centre of high-grade iron ore mining operations, tent cities sprang up overnight in the bush. A great aluminum smelter was built at Kitimat far up the British Columbia coast. Construction began on a railway to Great Slave Lake to assist the development of mining resources in the Northwest Territories. Uranium from northern Saskatchewan, and from Elliot Lake and near Bancroft in Ontario went into the production of new American nuclear weapons. Britain and the United States contracted to buy as much uranium as Canada could produce. Potash development in Saskatchewan did much to improve the economy of that province in the 1950s and 1960s.

The construction of refineries, processing plants, and the world's longest oil and gas pipeline added to the prosperity of Canada.

During the post-war economic expansion in Canada new resources began to take the place of the old ones. For a long time wheat had been Canada's leading export. Now wheat stood in third place in Canada's trading list. Newsprint and lumber moved into first place. Next came resources that were unknown or reasonably unimportant exports before World War II – uranium, natural gas, oil, iron ore, and chemical products. With the development of these new resources Canada's economy became much more diversified.

EXPORTS AND IMPORTS (1958)

MAJOR EXPORTS FROM CANADA	MAJOR IMPORTS TO CANADA
newsprint	machinery and parts (non-farm)
lumber, timber	automobile parts
wheat	petroleum
wood pulp	electrical equipment
aluminum	automobiles
uranium	engines and boilers
nickel	tractors and parts
copper	iron and steel products
iron ore	aircraft and parts
asbestos	other farm machinery, tools, and parts
farm machinery and tools	cotton fabrics
barley	paper products
beef cattle	coal

Canada's oldest and strongest trade links have always been with its partners in the North Atlantic community – the United States and Britain. Before World War II Canada's exports went mostly to Britain and other parts of the world, and Canada's imports came mostly from the United States. During the war Canada's trade with Europe declined because of the U-boat menace. At the same time close trading relationships grew up between Canada and the United States. In the post-war years the American economic boom made the United States the fastest-growing market for goods in the world. Canada's geographic

Hydro-electric station near Cornwall, Ont.

relation to the United States made it possible to take advantage of this large market. Besides, Canada had most of the resources the United States needed and wanted. The trade friendship between these two countries was further strengthened by the tremendous flow of American capital into Canada. The money came in to help with the large-scale development of Canada's natural resources. Technical know-how was also borrowed from the Americans. The fact that Canadians share many of the same tastes as Americans also improved trade on both sides of the border. In the post-war years the United States became Canada's chief customer.

CANADA'S TRADE PARTNERS (1958)

EXPORTS TO (in millions of dollars)		IMPORTS FROM (in millions of dollars)
$1326.5	Britain and Western Europe	$823.5
22.6	Eastern Europe	10.2
14.9	Middle East	73.3
63.9	Africa	27.9
245.2	Asia	144.4
52.6	Australia	32.7
239.8	South and Central America	291.2
2808.1	United States	3460.1

Opening of the St. Lawrence Seaway.

Canada and the United States were now each other's best customers. Most Canadians thought this was a good thing. Huge American markets for Canadian goods meant more jobs for Canadians and a high standard of living. Heavy American investment in Canada was helping to develop our resources and finance major industrial projects. However, some informed Canadians warned that American domination of the Canadian economy was a serious threat. There was a real danger that some major industries such as oil, minerals, and paper could some day be completely owned by the Americans. These Canadians were also alarmed by the growing trade imbalance: Canada was importing more goods from the United States than it was exporting across the border. As early as 1957 a Royal Commission on Canada's economic prospects, headed by Walter Gordon, warned of the danger of too much foreign ownership in the Canadian economy. It strongly advised the Canadian government to make policy decisions about this important issue.

More than any other project of the 1950s, the construction of the St. Lawrence Seaway illustrates Canada's spectacular industrial growth. For years Canadian and American officials had talked of improving the inland waterway route of the St. Lawrence River and the Great Lakes. This would allow ocean-going ships to travel as far as the western end of Lake Superior. It would also be possible to harness the rapids of the St. Lawrence River for hydro-electric power. Both Ontario and New York State desperately needed the extra power that this project could produce.

Although the joint plan had been discussed thoroughly, the

Americans continued to hesitate. American railroads were afraid they would lose business if ocean vessels could steam directly to cities such as Detroit and Chicago. In 1951 Canada decided to go ahead with the construction of the St. Lawrence Seaway on its own. Only at the last minute did the Americans decide to join in. The United States probably realized that once built, the Seaway would be entirely within Canadian territory and control, unless the project was a joint agreement. So the Americans decided to join in.

The planning and design of the Seaway, and most of the construction, was carried out by Canadians. The control dam required by the power project flooded a large area between Cornwall and Iroquois in Ontario. Entire communities had to be removed and new homes were built for 6500 people. Sixty-five kilometres of the C.N.R. were rerouted and Highway 2 was relocated. The St. Lawrence Seaway was officially opened 26 June 1959 by Queen Elizabeth II for Canada and President Eisenhower for the United States. This project is an outstanding example of the strong commercial ties that bind the Canadian and American economies.

Political Developments

Under the Liberals, Canada took several further steps towards becoming a completely independent nation. The Supreme Court of Canada was set up in 1949. Nine justices of the Supreme Court became the final court of appeal for Canadians. No longer would Canadians be allowed to appeal the decisions of their court cases to the Privy Council in Britain.

In 1952 Vincent Massey became the first Canadian-born governor-general of Canada. This prominent Canadian had played an important part in producing the 1951 Massey Report. The report had pointed out the danger of the growing American influence on Canada's culture. Radio, films, books, television, art, music, and even sports in Canada were all in danger of being swamped by the American influence. Massey pointed out that one solution would be to set up an organization called the Canada Council to promote the Canadian arts. This was done in 1957, and Canada Council money still helps to encourage and support artists, scholars, musicians, and writers. In his years as governor-general, 1952 to 1959, Vincent Massey visited all areas of Canada. He wanted to give Canadians a sense of pride in their country and a sense of national identity.

As the election of 1957 approached, the Liberal government seemed old and tired. The Prime Minister himself, Louis St. Laurent, was seventy-five years old. The Liberals had been in power since 1935 and seemed to have lost touch with the people.

To many it seemed that the government no longer listened to the people of Canada. A wild and bitter debate which broke out in Parliament in 1956 showed just how bad things had gotten. The Liberals had decided to finance the building of a trans-Canada pipeline, which in itself was a good idea. The pipeline would carry natural gas from its source in Alberta to markets in Ontario, Quebec, and the United States. In Parliament the Opposition wanted to ask questions. Why was the government loaning $118 million to a pipeline company that was eighty-three per cent owned by Americans? How much of the natural gas would end up in the United States? Was the Trans-Canada Pipeline Company getting too generous a deal from the Canadian taxpayer?

C.D. Howe, the cabinet minister in charge of the pipeline, was impatient to get construction started. He did not want to sit around the House of Commons debating the issue. The government forced the bill through Parliament using closure. This is a special rule limiting the amount of time that a bill may be discussed in Parliament. The Opposition raised a storm of protest, but the bill was passed by the Liberal majority. Forcing the pipeline bill through Parliament hurt the St. Laurent government. Now John G. Diefenbaker, leader of the Conservatives, had a major issue on which to fight the next election. Diefenbaker claimed that by using closure, the Liberals had trampled on the rights of Parliament. He thundered that this was one more example of the American takeover of the Canadian economy. Above all, Diefenbaker argued that the Liberals had been in power too long and had lost touch with people's feelings. In the election of June 1957, 112 Conservatives were elected to 105 Liberals. John Diefenbaker became prime minister. In another election the following year, there was a Conservative landslide in Canada. The Conservative Party won by the largest majority of any party since Confederation (Conservatives 208; Liberals 49; C.C.F. 8). For the first time since the days of John A. Macdonald, the Conservatives won a large number of seats in Quebec (50 of 75).

Digging Deeper

a) Research the reasons why Newfoundland rejected Confederation in 1867.

b) List the factors you think were important in persuading Newfoundlanders to vote for joining Confederation in 1949.

1

In 1949 the people of Newfoundland voted in a referendum to join Canada. How many other provinces joined Confederation in this way? Why do you think the referendum was important in Newfoundland's case?

2

30

DIEFENBAKER AND PEARSON

Prime Minister John Diefenbaker and U.S. President Dwight Eisenhower.

Early one morning in 1909 a fourteen-year-old newsboy talked to Sir Wilfrid Laurier. The boy resolved then and there that one day he too would be prime minister. By 1958 John George Diefenbaker had reached his goal. He was the prime minister of Canada and leader of the party with the greatest majority in Parliament in history.

The road to political power had not been easy for John Diefenbaker. He was born in rural Ontario near Owen Sound, but his family settled on a homestead in northern Saskatchewan in 1903. One summer he was a travelling book salesman and slept 'in almost every haystack in Saskatchewan'. In 1919 he graduated with a law degree from the University of Saskatchewan and became a prairie lawyer. Over and over in his early career Diefenbaker suffered defeat. Among these defeats was the time he did not get elected mayor of Prince Albert. Four times he was defeated in provincial and federal elections before he won a seat in the House of Commons in 1940. And twice he was rejected by his Conservative party for the leadership before they turned to him in 1956.

Diefenbaker was the first prime minister of Canada of neither British nor French background. He was intensely proud of his German background and was conscious that he represented a large number of Canadians who were neither British nor French. He brought into politics the sort of people who had not been there before: a Chinese Member of Parliament, a Ukrainian Minister of Labour, and an Indian Senator. For the first time a woman, Ellen Fairclough, was named to the federal Cabinet. Mrs. Fairclough's appointment as Secretary of State represented a breakthrough in public service for all women. Diefenbaker was also proud of his family's days as homesteaders in the West. He saw himself as the champion of the common man. Indeed he had the tremendous ability to appeal to ordinary Canadians and win their devotion. Long experience as a criminal lawyer had made him a dynamic and persuasive speaker. On stage or before television cameras he revealed a kind of political charisma. This meant that by the strength of his personality and his spell-binding oratory, he was able to stir up many Canadians and win their support.

The following excerpts are from a speech by John Diefenbaker in which he presented his 'vision' of what Canada could become. This speech was made on 12 February 1958.

Ladies and gentlemen, we started in the last few months, since 10 June, to carry out our promises, and I can tell you this, that as long as I am Prime Minister of this country, the welfare of the average Canadian will not be forgotten.

This national development policy will create a new sense of national purpose and national destiny. One Canada. One Canada, wherein Canadians will have preserved to them the control of their own economic and political destiny. Sir John A. Macdonald gave his life to this party. He opened the West. He saw Canada from East to West. I see a New Canada – a Canada of the North.

We will open that northland for development by improving transportation and communication and by the development of power, by the building of access roads. We will make an inventory of our hydro-electric potential.

Canadians, realize your opportunities! This is only the beginning. The future program for the next five to seven years under a Progressive Conservative Government is one that is calculated to give young Canadians, motivated by a desire to serve, a lift in the heart, faith in Canada's future, faith in its destiny.

This is the message I give to you my fellow Canadians, not one of defeatism. Jobs! Jobs for hundreds of thousands of Canadian people. A new vision! A new hope! A new soul for Canada ...

≫⟶

> To the young men and women of this nation I say, Canada is within your hands. Adventure. Adventure to the nation's utmost bounds, to strive, to seek, to find, and not to yield. The policies that will be placed before the people of Canada in this campaign will be ones that will ensure that today and this century will belong to Canada. The destination is one Canada. To that end I dedicate this party.

Questions:

1. Why would Diefenbaker feel he was following in the footsteps of John A. Macdonald?
2. Pick out the elements in the speech that would appeal to the 'average Canadian'. Explain your answer.

Over the next four years the Diefenbaker government produced some impressive legislation. Much of it was concerned with working towards the vision of Canada outlined by Diefenbaker. Money was poured into badly-needed housing. A great irrigation and power project was begun on the South Saskatchewan River. Federal money helped construct the Trans-Canada Highway linking all the provinces. Many kilometres of 'roads to resources' were built in the North. In the field of radio and television, the government set up the Board of Broadcast Governors to supervise the quality of broadcasting. Canadian Indians were given voting rights equal to those of all other Canadians.

Perhaps of all the programs, the one that gave Diefenbaker the greatest sense of accomplishment was the Canadian Bill of Rights. Citizens of many countries had their rights guaranteed by their constitution. In Canada these rights had been upheld by custom and tradition rather than by law. Now in 1960 an act of Parliament was passed granting Canadians the traditional freedoms:

- Freedom of speech (right to state an opinion without being afraid of government or law).
- Freedom of assembly and association (right to hold meetings, parades, and join clubs).
- Freedom of religion (right to worship as you please).
- Freedom of the press (right to publish opinions without fear of the government or law).
- Right of the individual to equality before the law (right to a fair trial, legal council, and protection against being unfairly imprisoned).

Unfortunately, the Bill of Rights in Canada is not 'entrenched'. That means it is only an act of the federal Parliament and is not written into the constitution. Therefore it could be changed, as could any other act of Parliament.

One of the greatest successes of the Diefenbaker government was a series of massive wheat deals. Tremendous wheat surpluses had piled up on the prairies in the 1950s. Granaries, port terminals, and prairie grain elevators were jammed with wheat which farmers were unable to sell. Diefenbaker understood the desperate economic situation of the farmers. He succeeded in arranging huge wheat sales to the People's Republic of China and other communist nations. A backlog of 19.9 million tonnes of wheat were exported and Diefenbaker won the unending political support of prairie farmers.

In spite of these successes, Diefenbaker's appeal to Canadians began to fade. In 1959 both Canada and the United States went through an economic slowdown. By 1962 unemployment figures in Canada had climbed higher than in any year since the Depression. That same year the Conservative government devalued the Canadian dollar to 92.5¢ of American currency. The

purpose of this move was to discourage foreign imports, to stimulate Canadian exports by making them cheaper to buy, to encourage foreigners travelling in Canada, and to discourage Canadians from travelling in other countries. However, the government's action was unpopular. The people tended to blame the government for the country's economic problems.

Although he had had tremendous backing in Quebec in 1958, Diefenbaker did not seem to understand the needs and hopes of that province. Few members of Parliament from Quebec were given important Cabinet positions. In 1959, however, Diefenbaker did appoint General Georges Vanier, a French Canadian, as governor-general. This could not stop Quebec enthusiasm for the Conservative government from fading.

Difficulties with the United States over the defence of North America also were problems for the Diefenbaker government. In 1958 Canada signed an agreement with the United States setting up the North American Air Defence Command. Canada and the United States were to share air forces and air defence systems. Despite the agreement, the Diefenbaker government refused to accept nuclear warheads for the Bomarc B, a surface-to-air missile. Diefenbaker felt that arming the Bomarcs with nuclear warheads would set back the hopes for nuclear disarmament in the world. His opponents argued that the Bomarc without nuclear warheads was useless. The government's indecision over the question of nuclear weapons added to growing criticism of Diefenbaker. The Cabinet itself split over the issue, and

A Bomarc missile.

three ministers (including the minister of defence) resigned while several others decided to retire from federal positions. The Conservative party, which a few years before had won the largest victory in history, was a shambles.

The early 1960s saw the revival of two smaller political parties. The first of these was the C.C.F. In the election of 1945 the C.C.F. party won twenty-eight seats. By 1958 their number in the House of Commons had dropped to eight. In 1961 a convention was held by the C.C.F. and the Canadian Labour Congress to found a new party. It would be called the New Democratic Party. It was hoped that the party would gain support from farmers, the educated middle class, and labour. The colourful and energetic Premier of Saskatchewan, T.C. 'Tommy' Douglas, agreed to be leader.

The New Democratic Party stood for such things as full employment, free education, Canadian control of the economy, public ownership of important natural resources, and a national medical insurance plan.

Tommy Douglas.

Almost from the beginning the N.D.P. showed greater signs of success than the C.C.F. In 1962, nineteen N.D.P. members were elected to the House of Commons. Support was drawn mainly from industrial and mining regions of Ontario and British Columbia.

The Social Credit Party also went through a reorganization period in 1961. A new national leader, Robert Thompson, was chosen. Social Credit had been in power in the provincial governments of Alberta since 1935 and British Columbia since 1952. However, in the federal election of 1958, it had won no seats. To everyone's surprise, Social Credit did very well in the election of 1962. The party had one main campaign argument. It was that the country's economic difficulties were the result of the heavy national debt that had developed with the Conservative government. Twenty-six members were elected from Quebec, and four from western Canada. The Quebec wing of the party was led by a fiery car dealer from Rouyn, Quebec, Réal Caouette. Social Credit success in Quebec was probably the result of dissatisfaction many Quebeckers felt with both Liberals *and* Conservatives. In 1963 Caouette and most of the Quebec wing broke away from the party to form the *Ralliement des Créditistes* (Social Credit Rally). When they did this, Social Credit lost any hope of being a truly national party. The *Ralliement des Créditistes* is based solely in Quebec.

In the election of 1963, the Liberal Party was able to attack Conservative mismanagement of the economy. They also criticized the government's indecision on defence policy and Canada's worsening relationship with the United States. On 8 April 1963 the Canadian public decided. The Conservatives were defeated and the Liberal party formed the government in Canada.

Lester 'Mike' Pearson, the new prime minister, was a sharp contrast to Diefenbaker. Pearson had become leader of the Liberal party when Louis St. Laurent retired in 1958. When Pearson was only seventeen he had enlisted in the army to fight in the First World War. At the time he was transferred to the Royal Flying Corps, an officer said to him, 'Lester is not a very belligerent name for a man who wants to be a fighter pilot. We'll call you Mike.' The name stuck. After the war 'Mike' Pearson taught at the University of Toronto, and then joined the Department of External Affairs. Pearson enjoyed a successful diplomatic career, which included being Canada's ambassador to the United States. He had also been active in the United Nations from its beginning, and had been President of its General Assembly 1952-53. He had gained international respect for helping create the U.N. Emergency Force in the Suez crisis of 1956. For his contribution to world peace, he received the Nobel Prize for peace in 1957. Unlike Diefenbaker, Pearson was soft-spoken and never really seemed at home in the give-and-take of the House of Commons debates.

During the time Pearson was prime minister, his government pushed forward reforms in many fields. A medical insurance plan and a Canada pension plan were set up. The Company of Young Canadians was set up to help such groups as the Indians, and the urban and rural poor. The Company sent Canadian volunteers to help people help themselves and gain self-respect.

Two important steps were taken in the field of defence. The nuclear warheads that the Diefenbaker government could not decide on were installed on Canadian missiles in 1963. Also, the Liberal government made the three branches of the Canadian armed forces into one joint command. By joining the army, navy, and air force, the government hoped to improve Canada's peace-keeping capacity and create a more effective fighting force.

In 1963 the Pearson government set up a Royal Commission on Bilingualism and Biculturalism (Bi and Bi Commission). It was to examine the relations between French and English Canadians and to consider Quebec's role in Confederation. For some time French Canadians had been complaining that they did not feel like equal partners in Confederation. The Commission studied the issue for several years. It concluded that Canada was passing through its greatest crisis. Among the major recommendations of the Bi and Bi Commission were the following:

i) Canada should be officially declared bilingual by making French and English the official languages of the federal Parliament and courts;
ii) New Brunswick and Ontario should officially declare themselves bilingual provinces;
iii) provinces where the minority group is more than ten per cent should provide government services in both English and French;
iv) the region of Ottawa-Hull should be made a national capital area and should be officially bilingual;
v) students in all provinces should be given a chance to study both official languages;
vi) more French Canadians should be employed in the federal government;
vii) in Quebec, French should be the main language of work, government, and business.

By 1970 many of the major recommendations of the Committee had been carried out.

Partly to please Quebec, the Liberals decided to adopt a new Canadian flag. It would replace the Canadian Red Ensign with its Union Jack in the upper corner and the Canadian Coat of Arms diagonally opposite it. The Ensign was disliked by many French Canadians because of its close association with Britain. Many non-French Canadian citizens also thought it was time for Canada to have its own distinctive flag. The design of the new flag submitted to Parliament by the Liberals purposely avoided British and French symbols – the Union Jack and the fleur-de-lis. Instead, there were three red maple leaves sprouting from a single stem on a white background. At each end of the flag were vertical blue bars. The colours red, white, and blue were the only historical connection. The flags of both Britain and France contain these three colours.

In Parliament John Diefenbaker led the opposition to 'Pearson's Pennant'. Diefenbaker, proud of Canada's British connections, wished to keep the Red Ensign. He was not alone. Many veterans who had fought bravely under the Red Ensign in two world wars did not want to see it replaced.

Months of controversy followed. Finally a Parliamentary committee made up of members from all parties recommended a new design. It was a single red maple leaf on a white background with red borders at each end. Diefenbaker and some of the Opposition hoped to delay the passing of the flag bill. Their plan was to filibuster. Filibustering means talking on endlessly until the plan has to be dropped so the government can go on with other business. For thirty-three days Opposition members stated and restated their reasons for rejecting the new flag. Neither side would give in. Finally the Liberal government ended the debate by using closure. At 2:30 in the morning of 15 December 1964 Canada's new red maple leaf flag was officially passed. It was a scene full of emotion. As the vote was announced (163 for, 78 against) the M.P.s rose to their feet to sing 'O Canada' and 'God Save the Queen'.

Raising the new Canadian flag.

Certainly the happiest feature of Pearson's term as prime minister was the celebration of Canada's centennial year 1967. Canada marked the one-hundredth birthday of Confederation with many ceremonies and celebrations throughout the year. The biggest celebration was the International Exposition, 'Expo 67', held at Montreal. During the summer of 1967 Pearson was host to a steady stream of state visitors, including Queen Elizabeth II and Prince Philip.

As centennial year drew to a close, Pearson announced his decision to retire as leader of the Liberal party. In the final speech to his party, he mentioned those achievements of which he was most proud. They included the introduction of the new flag and centennial year. But Pearson went on to stress the need for national unity: 'We who believe in our country must work with a passionate intensity to see that Quebec separatism doesn't happen; that the Canadian dream does not end but is realized in a Canadian destiny worthy of those who have brought us so far in our first century.'

Document Study:

The Bi and Bi Commission challenged both English and French to make serious changes in their attitudes in order to make Confederation work.

From evidence so far accumulated, it appears to us that English-speaking Canadians as a whole must come to recognize the existence of a vigorous French-speaking society within Canada, and to find out more about the aspirations, frustrations, and achievements of French-speaking Canadians, in Quebec and outside it. They must come to understand what it means to be a member of a minority, or of a smaller partner people, and to be ready to give that minority assurances which are unnecessary for a majority. More than a century ago, Sir John A. Macdonald wrote to an English-speaking friend: 'Treat them as a nation and they will act as a free people generally do – generously. Call them a faction and they become factious.' They have to face the fact that, if Canada is to continue to exist, there must be a true partnership, and that the partnership must be worked out as between equals. They must be prepared to discuss in a forthright, open-minded way the practical implications of such a partnership.

On the same evidence, it seems to us that French-speaking Canadians for their part must be ready to respond positively if there are to be truly significant developments towards a better partnership. It would be necessary for French-speaking Quebeckers to restrain their present tendency to concentrate so intensely on their own affairs, and to look so largely inward. Problems affecting all Canada are their problems too. They would need to beware of the kind of thinking that puts 'la nation' above all other considerations and values. They too, like the English-speaking, should forget the conquest and any psychological effects they think it left. They would have to avoid blam-

⟫→

ing English-speaking Canadians for shortcomings which are their own and at times, to remember that English-speaking Canadians have their feelings too. They, as well as the English-speaking, must remember that, if a partnership works, each party must give as well as get.

Bi and Bi Royal Commission

Question:
Read the quote from the Royal Commission carefully. Make a chart in your notebooks in two columns labelled 'What the English should do' and 'What the French should do'. Summarize in your own words the recommendations to both cultural groups.

Digging Deeper

1   Why do governments in Canada change hands? List as many reasons as you can. Why did Canadian electors reject the Diefenbaker government in 1963? What brought the Liberals to power in 1963?

2   Lester Pearson held at least six major jobs in his lifetime: wartime pilot, university professor, ambassador, politician, secretary of state for external affairs, and prime minister. What skills do you think Pearson must have had to have held each of these jobs?

3   Why are symbols, such as a flag, important to a country?
Why would some groups of people be strongly opposed to a new flag?
Try to think of some other symbols that represent Canada.
What are the symbols of the province in which you live? Does your school or community have special symbols? How do you feel when you see these symbols used?

4   Do some research to find out which native peoples had the right to vote in federal elections before 1960. Find out which provinces allow native peoples to vote in provincial elections.

31

CANADA IN THE POST-WAR WORLD

On the night of 5 September 1945 an international drama began to unfold in Ottawa. Igor Gouzenko was a young clerk in the Soviet embassy in Ottawa. He decided to defect and live permanently in Canada. He smuggled 109 top-secret documents out of the embassy under his shirt. His idea was to turn the secrets over to authorities in return for a new start in life in Canada.

For thirty-six hours no one would take Gouzenko seriously. A member of Prime Minister King's staff even suggested that he return to the Soviet embassy and replace the documents! By this time Gouzenko was desperate. The theft had been discovered and Soviet embassy officials had broken into Gouzenko's apartment. Fortunately, a neighbour called the Ottawa police. They arrived just as Gouzenko was being hustled away by the Russians. Finally the R.C.M.P. were convinced that Gouzenko was telling the truth.

The documents Igor Gouzenko turned over contained shocking information. They revealed that a massive spy ring was operating in North America out of the Soviet embassy in Ottawa. From the files provided by Gouzenko, the police were able to discover several top agents working in Canada, the United States, and Britain. In Canada the agents included two colonels, a navy officer, a squadron leader, a member of parliament, and clerks in government offices. In the United States and Britain the trail led to the arrest of scientists who had worked on the first atomic bomb. Since the United States was the only nation that had the atomic bomb, the U.S.S.R. was desperate to have atomic information.

Canadians were shocked by the news. The thing that astounded them most was that the U.S.S.R., a former wartime ally, was spying on its friends. But nations that are allies during a war often quarrel when the war is over. The main reason for this is that they become rivals for the control of the nations they have defeated. This was certainly true after the end of World War II. Both the United States and the U.S.S.R. came out of the war as superpowers, stronger than any of the other nations. They could be expected to compete to establish influence over

Germany and Japan. The U.S.S.R. was the leading communist nation and seemed determined to spread communism into the countries of eastern Europe it had taken over from Germany. The United States worried that the spread of communism would mean strict government control over the lives of people in eastern Europe. In Britain, Winston Churchill said that the Russians were stretching an 'iron curtain' of secrecy around eastern Europe. This was the beginning of the 'Cold War'.

The term 'Cold War' originally meant that the two superpowers would try to defeat each other by any means short of actual fighting. It would be a 'cold', not a 'hot' war. The Cold War has, however, included several armed conflicts. But there has never been an actual declaration of war between the United States and the U.S.S.R.

The first open clash in the Cold War between the two superpowers was in 1947. It was caused by events in Greece and Turkey. In Greece political confusion followed World War II. Greek communists were struggling with supporters of the Greek king for control of the government. The U.S.S.R. was helping the Greek communists. At the same time Stalin was trying to seize oil-rich lands on the Black Sea in Turkey.

President Harry Truman announced that the United States would help Greece and Turkey and any other nation threatened by communism. The United States would follow a policy of 'containment'. They would try to 'contain' or stop the spread of communism anywhere in the world. This policy became known as the Truman Doctrine. With American military and economic help, Greece and Turkey were both able to resist communist pressures at this time.

There were, however, serious problems in other parts of Europe as well. Much of Europe lay in ruins after World War II. The United States was determined to help rebuild Europe and stop the influence of the U.S.S.R.

The American secretary of state, George C. Marshall, announced the European Recovery Plan, or the Marshall Plan, as it has become known. This was a huge self-help program of American economic aid for Europe. Vast amounts of machinery, raw materials, food, and building supplies were sent to help Europe recover from the war. Canada was already giving aid to Europe, but welcomed the opportunity to assist in the Marshall Plan. In the first year (1948), Canada shipped $706 million in goods to war-torn countries. During the five years of the plan, $13.5 billion of supplies were given to sixteen European nations by the United States and Canada. As western Europe recovered and became more prosperous, the possibility of a communist takeover faded.

The war had given a tremendous boost to the Canadian economy. Our great natural wealth meant that we were one of the few nations who could help the war-shattered world. There was a marked change in Canada's foreign policy following World War II. A country's foreign policy is the planned relationship that it sets up with other nations of the world. It is designed to achieve certain national goals such as trade, friendship, defence, commerce, and immigration. Following the war there seemed to be a new willingness for Canada to play an active part in great events on the world scene. Prime Minister King was determined that Canada would play an important part in the post-war world. Obviously Canada could not influence international politics as much as the great powers – the United States, the U.S.S.R., Britain, France, and China. But neither was Canada a small, weak, or unimportant country. Because of Canada's natural resources, military might, size, and political stability, Canadians looked at their country as a 'middle power'. King established a foreign policy to help make Canada a middle power.

Canada's foreign policy from 1945-1970 was based on four major areas of concern:

1. support of the North Atlantic Treaty Organization for defence;
2. support of the United Nations to promote world peace;
3. co-operation with the United States in continental defence;
4. co-operation within a strong Commonwealth.

Canada and NATO

The year 1948 was a crucial one in the Cold War. The U.S.S.R. was continuing to expand, first by trying to take control of the city of Berlin, and then by moving their troops into position to seize Czechoslovakia. The United States, Canada, and other Western powers viewed this expansion with alarm. They decided to take joint action to defend themselves.

On 4 April 1949 the North Atlantic Treaty Organization (NATO) was formed. Twelve nations signed the treaty. They were Belgium, Britain, Canada, Denmark, France, Iceland, Italy, Luxembourg, Netherlands, Norway, Portugal, and the United States. (By 1955 these countries had been joined by Greece, Turkey, and West Germany.)

Canada's Prime Minister St. Laurent was an early supporter of a defence alliance. St. Laurent realized that the weakness of the United Nations was that it had no permanent armed force of its own. The U.N. was not able to defend Canada against a possible Soviet threat. St. Laurent said in the House of Commons, 'We are fully aware ... of the inadequacy of the United Nations at the present moment to provide the nations of the world with the security which they require. The realities of this situation must be faced.'

Prime Minister Louis St. Laurent and military personnel.

The NATO alliance committed its members to collective security. This meant a kind of safety in numbers, because all members banded together and promised to defend each other in the event of an attack. Thus it was hoped that the combined strength of the NATO alliance would discourage the U.S.S.R. from taking any hostile action against NATO members.

Canada's contribution to NATO has cost hundreds of millions of dollars in armed forces, aircraft carriers, and military equipment. Canada's attempt to have NATO move into economic cooperation as well has not met with much success. NATO has remained a military pact.

The U.S.S.R. responded in 1955 to the creation of NATO by forming its own military alliance, the Warsaw Pact. Its members were the U.S.S.R., Albania, Bulgaria, Czechoslovakia, East Germany, Hungary, Poland, and Rumania. Thus in 1955 Europe was again divided into two hostile camps – NATO and the Warsaw Pact.

Support of the United Nations

Canada was one of the original signers of the Charter of the United Nations. It was dedicated to supporting U.N. activities. When war broke out in Korea in 1950, Canada showed it was willing to help the United Nations keep peace in the world.

The Korean War was the first real test of the U.N.'s peacekeeping ability. The Koreans had been an independent people for centuries. They had been taken over by Japan in the early 1900s. When Korea was liberated at the end of World War II, the Soviet army occupied the northern half of the country. A communist government was established there. American troops occupied the southern half. The 38°N parallel was the border. The United Nations had been trying to re-unite the Koreas with no success.

In June 1950 a powerful North Korean army invaded South Korea. It seemed likely that the heavily-armed North Koreans would take over the entire country.

The matter was brought to an emergency meeting of the Security Council of the United Nations. At that moment the Soviet delegate was refusing to attend (boycotting) the Security Council. The Security Council was therefore able to agree to take action. It ordered North Korea to withdraw its forces. It called on members to send military forces to Korea. General Douglas MacArthur was appointed to command these U.N. troops. Most troops were from the United States, but other nations, including Canada, did contribute to the peacekeeping effort. Canada sent one infantry brigade, three naval destroyers, and an air transport squadron, about 8000 men in all. (Four hundred and six Canadians were killed in the Korean War, and over one thousand were wounded.) Canada had shown the world that it was prepared to play a responsible role as a middle power.

The Korean War ended in 1953 with a truce. Both sides agreed to stop fighting. The United Nations' action had saved South Korea. However, the war did not succeed in uniting the two Koreas. Both sides were back to a line approximately where they had started in 1950.

In 1956 a situation arose which could easily have developed into a major war between the superpowers. Egypt's head of state, Colonel Nasser, decided to take over the Suez Canal. The canal was a vital trade route in the Middle East. Ships could travel from the Mediterranean Sea to the Red Sea and Indian Ocean through the Suez Canal. The Egyptian action greatly alarmed Israel, Britain, and France. These nations retaliated by attacking Egypt. The U.S.S.R. threatened to send missiles for use by Egypt. The United States warned that it would step in if the U.S.S.R. intervened. A very dangerous chain reaction was building up.

Frantic activity took place at the United Nations. Members desperately looked for a way to reduce the tension. Lester B. Pearson was at that time Canadian Secretary of State for External Affairs. Pearson persuaded the General Assembly to order all foreign troops out of Egypt. Then he convinced the U.N. to set up a United Nations Emergency Force (U.N.E.F.) which would be positioned between the rival armies.

The U.N.E.F. was Pearson's brainchild. Its members were to be drawn from middle powers who had no personal interest in the dispute. The Force would not fight unless attacked. Instead, it would observe, investigate, mediate, and report back to the U.N. General Assembly. The Force would be composed of 6000 soldiers. One thousand were Canadians. Major-General E.L.M.

Burns of Canada would command the U.N. force.

In the days that followed, Egypt, Israel, Britain, and France obeyed the ceasefire. The U.N.E.F. succeeded in bringing peace to the Middle East. Much credit for this success must be given to Lester Pearson. For this achievement, Person was awarded the Nobel Peace Prize in 1957. It was a great honour for him and for Canada.

The U.N.E.F. managed to keep the Egyptians and Israelis apart for eleven years. However, within a few days of its removal in 1967, fighting once more broke out in the Middle East. In 1973 another Arab-Israeli war developed. United Nations forces were once more stationed in the disputed area. The Middle East remains today an area of high tension.

Canada continued to help keep peace in several troublespots in the world. Canadians were sent to the Congo (now Zaire) in 1960-1964. In 1964 Canada contributed to the U.N. peace force in Cyprus in the Mediterranean. In 1965 Major-General Bruce Macdonald of Edmonton led a U.N. observer group to supervise the truce between India and Pakistan.

Co-operation with the United States in Defence

By the mid-1950s, both the United States and the U.S.S.R. had developed guided missiles that could carry nuclear warheads capable of wiping out a large city. One ten-megaton hydrogen bomb was at least forty times more powerful than the atomic bomb dropped on Hiroshima. Lying directly between the U.S.S.R. and the United States, Canada was in an important position. Missiles fired from the U.S.S.R. at the United States could reach their target in a matter of hours. Since the U.S.S.R.'s missiles would probably be fired across the North Pole, a means of early detection would have to be found. Suddenly the Canadian Arctic became of immense strategic importance.

The permanent Joint Board of Defence was reorganized. Three chains of radar stations were built to detect an air invasion of North America. The Pinetree Radar System was built along the Canadian-American border. Along the 55°N parallel was the Mid-Canada Line, and the Distant Early Warning Line (D.E.W.) was situated along the Arctic coastline. Ships and aircraft provided radar surveillance on both the Atlantic and Pacific coasts.

This co-operation between Canada and the United States was further increased in 1958. The North American Air Defence Command (NORAD) was set up. NORAD brought the air defence of the two countries into a fully-integrated joint command. The commander is an American, the deputy-commander is a Canadian. Deep within the Cheyenne Mountain in Colorado the operation centre for NORAD was constructed. If there was a nuclear attack by the U.S.S.R., the defence of North America would be directed from NORAD headquarters. From here nuclear missiles could be fired in retaliation against the U.S.S.R. It was hoped that the NORAD defences would keep the U.S.S.R. from ever striking North America.

Co-operation Within a Strong Commonwealth

The Commonwealth of Nations grew out of the old British Empire. Many of Britain's former colonies were gaining their independence. However, they chose to stay together in a voluntary organization of independent states known as the Commonwealth. All the member nations acknowledged the British monarch as head of the Commonwealth, though not necessarily the head of state of all member countries. Countries of many different languages, religions, races, and cultures share membership in the Commonwealth.

Canada played a major role in keeping the Commonwealth truly multi-racial. In 1961 South Africa wished to continue as a member of the Commonwealth after becoming a republic. Canada was unhappy with South Africa's policy of racial segregation and the privileged position of the white population. Prime Minister Diefenbaker argued that South Africa's racial policy was not consistent with the Commonwealth ideal of co-operation and equality among the races. Diefenbaker knew that many African and Asian members would not stay in the Commonwealth if one nation, South Africa, openly practised racial discrimination. South Africa decided to withdraw its application for continued membership.

Canadians have one of the highest standards of living of all the Commonwealth countries. Therefore Canada has done a great deal to give economic aid to all parts of the Commonwealth. In 1950 the Colombo Plan was set up by India, Pakistan, Ceylon, Australia, New Zealand, and Britain. The organization was later joined by Canada, the United States, Japan, and a number of countries in Southeast Asia. Its purpose was to give technical and financial help to developing countries in Asia.

It was hoped that through the Colombo Plan living standards throughout Asia would be improved. Canada has been a major supporter of the plan. In the first year $25 million was pledged for factories and equipment. A nuclear power generating plant was given to India, a cement factory to Pakistan, and aid in irrigation and transportation systems was given to several countries. Under the plan Canadian universities, governments, and industries have educated students from developing countries. Thousands of young people have studied medicine, forestry, education, agriculture, and administration. By 1973 Canada had contributed $2 billion to the Colombo Plan.

Digging Deeper

1

Following is a list of terms used in this chapter:

middle power   superpower
Truman Doctrine   foreign policy
cold war   Colombo Plan
Marshall Plan   Warsaw Pact

Use each term correctly in a sentence to show you understand its meaning.

2

What were the goals of the Truman Doctrine and the Marshall Plan? How successful were these policies?

3

Germany was defeated and heavily damaged at the end of World War II. Was the United States wise to help rebuild Germany and make it an ally? Explain your point of view.

4

Why was the Korean War called an international police action? Did its outcome strengthen or weaken the security of the world? Explain your answer.

5

To broaden your understanding of Canada's role as a peacekeeper, individual students or groups can investigate one or more of the operations in which Canada played a part:

- Kashmir 1949;
- Korea 1950-1954;
- Palestine 1954;
- Viet Nam, Cambodia, Laos 1954;
- Egypt 1956-1967;
- Lebanon 1958-1959;
- Congo 1960-1964;
- West New Guinea 1962-1963;
- Yemen 1963-1964;
- Cyprus 1964;
- India-Pakistan 1965-1966.

Research could be summarized in a chart form under the headings:
- causes;
- Canada's role;
- Canada's impact during the crisis;
- significance for Canada.

Canada is a member of both the United Nations and NATO. What are the arguments for and against our membership in these organizations?

6

Discuss how Canada's foreign policy between 1945 and 1967 might have affected the attitudes of people in other countries to Canadians.

7

Are there any advantages in having the United States responsible for Canada's defence? What are the disadvantages?

8

Do some research on the Commonwealth:
- On a world map, mark the location of the Commonwealth countries.
- Why was it founded?
- Which nations have joined since it was founded and why?
- Which nations have left since it was founded and why?
- What does the Commonwealth do today?
- What advantages and disadvantages are there for Canada in being a member of the Commonwealth?

9

Debate: Canada should help the poor people in our own country instead of sending foreign aid to far-away countries.

10

32

THE ASBESTOS STRIKE: A CASE STUDY

Asbestos workers.

The province of Quebec had the largest asbestos plant in the world. Asbestos is a fibrous material that neither burns nor conducts heat. This makes it very valuable to many industries. Forty per cent of the world's supply of asbestos came from Quebec. Almost all of it was exported to the United States.

In February 1949 over 2000 workers of the American-owned Johns-Manville plant in Asbestos, Quebec, went on strike for higher wages. Their major demand was a 15¢ an hour wage increase. This would bring them up to $1.00 per hour. They were also asking for an increase in paid holidays to nine per year, and double-time for work on Sunday. In addition, they were worried about getting the asbestos dust cleaned up in the mills and the town. The dust was dangerous to their health. At the beginning of the strike the townspeople joked that when the miners stopped working, they had accidentally hit on the best way to get rid of the dust.

The Union Nationale government of Quebec under Premier Maurice Duplessis had always been strongly opposed to labour unions. Unions in Quebec were tolerated only if they remained weak and if the workers were opposed to strikes. It was Duplessis' view that the employer offered jobs to the people of the community and workers should be grateful for the employment provided by the companies. In Quebec a union could be outlawed if it had any communists among its leaders. Since Duplessis himself had the final say on who was a communist, this law could be used against any union of which he disapproved.

The Quebec Premier declared the Asbestos strike illegal and sent in the Quebec provincial police. Duplessis accused the strike leaders of being saboteurs, that is, people seeking to cause trouble. The workers complained of police brutality and unfairness to the strikers. The strike continued.

As the strike dragged on into May, it grew more ugly. Johns-Manville had begun to use strikebreakers. Some were old employees and some were new ones brought in from outlying towns and villages. So the company was still producing asbestos, but at a much reduced level. Through all of this, Duplessis continued to support the anti-union American company. A letter from the Chairman of the Johns-Manville Company to Premier Duplessis thanked him for

> ... the firm support which you and your government have given us in seconding our efforts to maintain ourselves in an adequate position. It was a great comfort for me this morning to be able to assure our board of directors of your constant support, as well as the protection which continues to be accorded to our properties and our strikebreakers and others working in the plant.

In the meantime, the strikers' families suffered hunger and real need. They were especially annoyed when they found out that the strikebreakers had been given a 10¢ an hour wage increase. To the men who had gone on strike demanding only 5¢ an hour more than that, it seemed like a real slap on the face. Tensions erupted. The strikers set up barriers and roadblocks on routes leading into the town, smashed windows of strikebreaker's homes, and threatened non-striking workers. And at one of the demonstrations some visiting journalists were even arrested. Among them was Pierre Elliott Trudeau.

On a day known as 'bloody Thursday' the strikers tried to interrupt factory production by stopping strikebreakers on their way into the plant and by picketing company property. When the strikers stopped a car with four police officers in plain clothes, one of the policemen fired two revolver shots. With that the crowd went wild. The police were hauled from the car, kicked, and beaten into unconsciousness. The strikers were now in complete control of the town.

Early the next morning 400 provincial police went into the town to restore order. This time the role of strikers and police was reversed. Heavily armed with shotguns, sten guns, revolvers, tear gas, and billies, the blue-and-brown clad officers finally restored order. Two hundred miners were arrested. Several miners were savagely beaten – a reporter for *Time* magazine described this as 'sickening'. Gradually peace returned to the town of Asbestos, but great bitterness remained. Most of all it was directed against the provincial police. Jean Marchand, strike leader, released a signed statement to the press. In it he compared the behaviour of the provincial police to 'Hitler's elite troops'.

The strike dragged on for another two months until a settlement was reached. The workers went back with a 10¢ an hour increase in wages and two more paid holidays. But at least a hundred miners remained out of work because the strikebreakers had been kept on by the company. The workers had gained very little.

Maurice Duplessis. ▲

One of the most significant aspects of the Asbestos strike was that the Roman Catholic Church had publicly opposed the government of Quebec. The Church had supported the workers, raised money to feed their families, and acted as a mediator between the company and the strikers.

The Asbestos strike marked the beginning of rapid social changes that were coming in the province of Quebec. During the late 1940s and early 1950s, Quebec was shaken by a series of long, bitter, and often violent strikes. Quebec was starting to emerge into a modern industrial province. The labour unions were beginning to challenge the rigid rule of the Duplessis government. Rapid changes in Quebec's society and economy were soon to follow.

The Asbestos strike attracted the attention and changed the thinking of several young Quebec thinkers. Among those who took part in the strike were several men who would soon make names for themselves. Jean Marchand, the union leader, would go on to a federal cabinet post. The reporter who covered the story for the newspaper *Le Devoir*, Gérard Pelletier, would become a cabinet minister and the Canadian ambassador to France. Pierre Elliott Trudeau, who had been present during part of the 142 day strike, later edited a book of essays and articles about it. Eventually, of course, he would become prime minister of Canada. They were among many other Quebec thinkers sympathetic to the strike who became leaders of Quebec and Canada in the 1960s. The strike was a turning point in their lives.

Digging Deeper

ROLE-PLAY   1

Set up an imaginary commission to investigate the Asbestos strike. More than half the class should play the role of strikers. Others may play the role of owners and managers of Johns-Manville. A few students may take the role of judges. The role cards and questions for each group to work on are below.

Strikers

You are the workers and you have gone on strike to force the company to meet your demands. The cost of living has risen but your wages have remained the same. You are fighting to get the asbestos dust cleaned up in the plant and the town.

With these things in mind, consider the following questions and try to develop the attitudes and opinions of the strikers.

1. As a worker why do you think you went on strike?
2. Are your reasons justified? Why?
3. Find out all you can about asbestosis.
4. Who are your leaders and supporters?
5. What are the demands of the workers?
6. Why does management oppose you?
7. Do you think management has the right to bring in strike-breakers? Why?
8. Do you think violence is justified in trying to win your case?

Owners

You are the bosses, the owners, and the managers of the factories. The workers at your plant in Quebec have gone on strike, causing you to lose money and profits. With these things in mind, answer the following questions and try to develop the opinions that you think management would have.

1. As an owner, why do you think the workers went on strike?
2. Were the workers justified?
3. Why do you oppose the strike?
4. Should people have the right to strike? Why or why not?
5. Should management have the right to bring in strikebreakers? Explain your answer.
6. What role do you think the police should play in the strike?
7. If the strikers give up, will you allow them back to work without punishing them?

Judges

You are the judges in this case. Try to find out exactly what happened and try to make a decision about who was right. In this strike there has been violence and property loss. Two groups in society with different attitudes and opinions are in conflict. Listen to both sides and ask questions. Keep order so that all sides of the controversy may be heard in court. Do not hesitate to tell people to let someone else speak, if necessary. If workers or bosses are merely sitting there, try to get their opinions. You may direct questions to individuals if you wish. Make up some questions in advance to ask both sides.

2

View the film *Mon Oncle Antoine* (1971, NFB). It is an interesting portrayal of life in a Quebec asbestos town. Watch the film and try to visualize the conditions of the miners in the 1940s. Find out what changes have taken place since then (hours of work, wages, conditions of work, benefits).

33

THE QUIET REVOLUTION IN QUEBEC

In order to understand what happened in Quebec after World War II, you must have some understanding of the relations between the French and English in Canada. Use the following quiz to check your own knowledge of early Canadian history. As you take up and discuss the answers with your class, you will be learning some facts about French Canada. Any events in the early history you are not sure about should be checked out in library books or other texts (*Exploration Canada* and *Flashback Canada*) and reviewed.

1. The capital city of Quebec is a) Montreal b) Sherbrooke c) Quebec City.
2. Outside of Quebec the largest portion of French Canadians live in a) Prince Edward Island b) Alberta c) New Brunswick.
3. The first French-Canadian prime minister was a) Sir Wilfrid Laurier b) Louis St. Laurent c) Arthur Meighen.
4. The percentage of the population of Ontario that is French Canadian is about a) 2% b) 10% c) 30%.
5. The early French settlers in North America treated the native peoples a) as friends b) with neglect c) with persecution.
6. Canada is a bilingual country. What percentage of Canadians can carry on a conversation in both French and English? a) 6% b) 13% c) 47%.
7. In the history of Canada since its discovery by Cartier in 1535, the French have controlled Canada a) for much less time than the British b) for a little less time than the British c) for about the same amount of time as the British.
8. Ever since the battle of the Plains of Abraham, French Canadians have felt a) like conquered people b) second class citizens c) both of the above d) none of the above.
9. After an uprising in 1837 in Quebec, Lord Durham recommended that a) the French should be assimilated (taken over completely) by the British b) the French should all be sent back to France c) the French in Quebec should be allowed to set up their own country.

$\gg\!\!\rightarrow$

10. Which French-Canadian Father of Confederation most helped to persuade his people to believe in a united country? a) Antoine A. Dorion b) George Etienne Cartier c) Etienne P. Taché.

11. Confederation was a compromise worked out to a) put down the French Canadians once and for all b) prevent French Canada from joining the United States c) make Quebec a full and equal partner with the other provinces.

12. In the eyes of Quebec Louis Riel was a hero. In English Canada he was seen as a traitor. This was because a) Riel led the Métis in a struggle against English settlement on the prairies b) Riel was a French-speaking Roman Catholic c) Riel was a symbol of the division between French and English Canada d) all of the above reasons.

Maurice Duplessis, premier of Quebec from 1936 to 1939 and 1944 to 1959, ruled Quebec with an iron hand. Duplessis was called Le Chef, the Chief. His government was a one-man rule. It was generous and dedicated, but it could also be harsh and dictatorial. Opponents called the age of Duplessis 'la grande noirceur', which means the great darkness. Certainly Quebec's resources were developed under Duplessis, mostly with American money. But development in Quebec was often done in a corrupt manner. For almost every bridge, road, or hospital built, Duplessis expected something in return. He demanded political favours, campaign funds, or votes. And he got them.

Some characteristics of Maurice Duplessis are described by Pierre Laporte:

At Shawinigan Duplessis once declared that if the voters re-elected a member of the Opposition, a bridge needed for the heavy local traffic would not be built. They were warned. And when they elected a Liberal Opposition member anyway, the bridge was not built while Duplessis was alive.

In Verchères County, Duplessis said during a political meeting in 1952: 'I warned you not to elect a Liberal candidate. You did not listen to me. Unfortunately your riding did not receive any of the grants that could have made it a happier place in which to live. I hope you have now learned your lesson and that you will vote against the Liberals this time.'

Until 1956 the secondary roads of the Verchères County remained in a lamentable condition. A priest had to ride a tractor for over eight kilometres to reach the parish church of St. Anatole. A physician was unable to get to a patient because the roads were impassable. So it was no surprise when the farmers of this riding declared, on the eve of the 1956 election: 'We have elected a Liberal in 1944, 1948, and 1952. This time we are going to vote for new roads.'

Although Duplessis was creating a new industrialized Quebec, he emphasized the old ways of thinking. Quebec society was largely closed to outside influences. The Roman Catholic Church and the old French-Canadian ties to the land were emphasized in order to keep Quebec separate from the rest of Canada.

In September 1959, while visiting northern Quebec, Maurice Duplessis had a stroke and died. The age of Duplessis was over. One-man government began to crumble away. Pressures for change were suddenly let loose in Quebec. Reforms began almost immediately. But the real change came when the new Liberal government under Jean Lesage was elected in 1960. It was the beginning of the 'Quiet Revolution'.

Lesage gathered around him an impressive team of cabinet ministers which included René Lévesque as minister of natural resources. The 'Quiet Revolution' of the Liberals promised to do two things. One was to improve the economic and social standards of the people of Quebec. The other was to win greater recognition for all the French in Canada.

One of the first programs of the Liberals was for the government to take over control of hydro-electric power companies. This also included the building of the Manicouagan Power Dam, one of the largest in the world. French-Canadian engineers from all parts of Canada and the world returned to Quebec to work on the project. The phrase used was '*on est capable*' or 'we can do it!'

Another slogan of the Quiet Revolution was '*maîtres chez nous*', meaning 'masters in our own house'. The government began to replace programs that the church had previously run. These included hospital insurance, pension schemes, and the beginnings of medicare. To do this the Quebec Liberals had to struggle with Ottawa for a larger share of the tax dollar.

One of the most sweeping reforms was the modernization of the entire school system. In the past the schools of Quebec had been run by the church. Most of the teachers were priests, nuns, or brothers. They provided a good education, but it was not the sort of training in business and technology Quebec now needed. Lesage wanted a government-run school system that would equip modern Quebec with brains in engineering, science, business and commerce.

The new freedom of expression in Quebec gave rise to a flood of books, plays, and music about the French culture in Quebec. In the theatre Gratien Gélinas became one of the most popular contemporary playwrights. The 1960s saw a tremendous output of Quebec movies. French-Canadian film makers have always been far more successful than English-Canadian film makers. One reason for this is that Quebec films do not have to compete with American films for audiences. New directors like Claude

Robert Charlebois, a popular folksinger from Quebec.

Jutra began to emphasize in their films themes drawn from Quebec life. Of all the artists, the singers of Quebec in the 1960s used political themes and messages the most. The song '*Mon Pays*' by Gilles Vigneault won an international award at the Brussels Music Festival in 1965. This song describes Vigneault's tender feelings towards his 'country' – Quebec – and his French-Canadian heritage.

But all was not well in the province of Quebec. Things were going badly between the French and the English. There was almost no real personal contact between the two founding cultures of Canada. Hugh MacLennan used the phrase, 'two solitudes', meaning that the English and French in Quebec and Canada seemed to live parallel but completely separate lives.

The Royal Commission on Bilingualism and Biculturalism showed that the 'two solitudes' were not always equal. The study showed a breakdown of average male wages in Quebec by ethnic group. At the top of the economic ladder were the Quebeckers of British origin. Their average annual wage in 1960 was $4940. Average wages then declined through a number of other ethnic groups: Scandinavian, Jewish, German, Polish, and Asian. All of these other groups were largely English-speaking. Then, almost at the bottom of the economic scale, were the French-Canadian Quebeckers. Their average annual wage was $3185. Another complaint was that most of the top jobs in the province of Quebec were held by English-speaking persons.

Although the French greatly outnumbered the workers of British origin in Quebec, twice as many British as French held high paying, high-status professional and managerial jobs. Thus the French, eighty per cent of Quebec's total population, were among the least favoured in their own province. The Commission report warned that Canada was going through the worst crisis of its history. Unless there was a new and equal partnership between the founding cultures of Canada, a breakup was likely to result.

Some Quebeckers suggested that the only solution to Quebec's problems was separatism. Separatism is the desire of a province to break away from the Canadian union. The separatists, as they were called, demanded immediate independence for Quebec. They said that as long as Quebec was associated with the rest of Canada, French Canadians would never be treated as equals.

The idea of separatism was not new in Quebec. Often in troubled times between the English and French, someone raised the possibility of Quebec leaving Confederation. This occurred when Louis Riel was hanged, and again when the Canadian government introduced conscription in 1917. During the Quiet Revolution of the 1960s, a small but influential group in Quebec began to talk seriously again about separation.

One of the early separatist groups of the 1960s was the *Rassemblement pour l'Indépendance Nationale* (RIN). One of its founders, Dr. Marcel Chaput, wrote a book that shocked English Canada called *Why I am a Separatist*. In it he described the way a French Canadian is made to feel inferior every day of his life.

- The French Canadian's country is the whole of Canada, but he is accepted only in Quebec.
- The French Canadian is told that he belongs to the great French civilization, but at the same time he hears someone speak of 'those damned Frenchmen'.
- The French Canadian is forced to be bilingual; the others are unilingual.
- The French Canadian hears nothing but praise at school and elsewhere for the beauty of the French language; he is obliged to learn English.
- The French Canadian is told that Canada is a country which united two cultures; he has difficulty getting service in west Montreal [English-speaking areas] if he uses French.
- The French Canadian enters the French university only to study from American text-books.

- The French Canadian is told all about national unity, but he is ordered: 'Stay in your province.'
- The French Canadian hears people insist that Canada is an independent country; every day he sees another country's queen on his coins and on his stamps.

The *Front de Libération du Québec* (FLQ), founded in 1963, was a smaller but more radical group of separatists. The FLQ had no leader, but was a collection of separate cells or groups of young people. Their idea was to use terrorism as a weapon to achieve independence for Quebec. A number of bombs were exploded, mostly in Montreal, and at least one person was killed.

A mail-box bomb explodes in Montreal.

Another separatist group, the ALQ (*l'Armée de Libération du Québec*), became even more violent. They robbed banks to get money and raided arms depots of the Canadian Armed Forces for ammunition. They set bombs in letter boxes in the English-speaking districts of Montreal and attacked army barracks. A favourite slogan of many of the separatist groups was '*Québec Libre*' – 'Free Quebec'.

Between 1963 and 1970, it is estimated that there was a terrorist bombing somewhere in the province once every ten days. Terrorism did not result in the independence of Quebec, as hoped for by the FLQ and other separatists. However, it did help alert many English Canadians to the grave problems in the heart of Canadian Confederation.

Many French-Canadian nationalists in Quebec were not separatists. They believed that separatism had no future. The answer lay in a strong federalism in which French Canadians could play a full role in a genuinely bicultural Canada. You will recall that Canadian federalism is the type of government in which several provinces are brought together under one central government, though the provinces have their own provincial and local governments. Three prominent Quebeckers who believed in federalism, and thought it could be made to work in Quebec, went to Ottawa in 1965 as Liberal members of the Canadian Parliament. They were Pierre Trudeau, Jean Marchand, and Gérard Pelletier, sometimes referred to as the 'Three Wise Men' from Quebec.

Bombing in Montreal.

In the Quebec provincial election of 1966, the people again turned to the Union Nationale under Daniel Johnson. Johnson was elected premier on the slogan 'Equality or Independence'. He warned Ottawa that Confederation had only a few years left to change or break up. Unless Quebec was given 'special status' in Confederation, it would have to separate and go its own way as a separate nation. This demand for 'special status' included control over economics, social welfare, and housing, and sufficient tax powers to carry out these responsibilities. Quebec also wanted to be able to deal directly with foreign governments in matters of culture and education. This last demand especially was rejected by Ottawa, which claimed complete control in international affairs.

The conflict between Ottawa and Quebec was dramatized in August 1967 by a visit of the president of France, General De Gaulle. De Gaulle came to Canada at the invitation of the Que-

THE NEW KING CHARLES: DE GAULLE CONTEMPLATES A DISTANT CORNER OF THE GRAND DESIGN

bec government to inspect the magnificent site of Expo '67. He sailed up the St. Lawrence River on board a French missile cruiser, *Colbert*, and was given an excited welcome when he landed at Quebec City. From there he travelled to Montreal in an open car. All along the route, which was lined with the Quebec and French flags, De Gaulle was cheered by enthusiastic crowds. Canada's flag was nowhere to be seen. At a reception held by the city of Montreal, President De Gaulle appeared on a balcony to address a wildly-cheering throng, many of whom were separatists. He told the people that he felt that day as he had on the day France was liberated from the Nazis in 1944. He ended his speech with the resounding cry, '*Vive le Québec libre!*' ('Long live free Quebec'). '*Québec libre*' had been the well-known slogan of separatists and terrorists since 1963. De Gaulle seemed to be giving his enthusiastic support to the separatists in their struggle for the liberation of Quebec.

Canadians watching De Gaulle on television were stunned by his comparison of their government to that of the Nazis. Prime Minister Pearson was outraged by De Gaulle's interference in Canadian affairs. Pearson issued a sharp statement to the press, labelling as 'unacceptable' De Gaulle's encouragement to 'the small minority of our population whose aim it is to destroy Canada'. The Prime Minister went on to say that 'The people of Canada are free. Every province in Canada is free. Canadians do not need to be liberated. Indeed, many thousands of Canadians gave their lives in two world wars in the liberation of France.' General De Gaulle cancelled the rest of his trip to Ottawa and returned immediately to France. Until De Gaulle's retirement in 1969, relations between France and Canada continued to be tense because of this affair.

Meanwhile protests, demonstrations, and violence continued in Quebec. René Lévesque had already left the Liberal party and started the Movement for Sovereignty-Association. In 1968, with part of the RIN, he formed the Parti Québécois (PQ). Lévesque always opposed terrorism and insisted on democratic and moderate means for achieving independence. While the independence movement was growing in Quebec, Pierre Trudeau had taken over as leader of the Liberals and prime minister when Pearson resigned in 1968. On the eve of the election, 24 June 1968, the St. Jean Baptiste parade was held in Montreal. Prime Minister Trudeau stood on the platform with the special guests. In the crowd were some radical separatists determined to demonstrate against Trudeau. The parade turned into a riot. People began throwing bottles and rocks. Most of the guests on the platform dashed inside for safety, but Trudeau remained on the platform. The people of Canada, watching on television, saw their Prime Minister standing firm against the radical separatists. The next day Trudeau won a resounding majority in the election. It was a vote of confidence from English Canada and much of moderate Quebec.

In April 1970 the Liberals also won a victory in the provincial election in Quebec. They had a new leader, Robert Bourassa. After a decade of turbulence and change, Bourassa appeared to represent stability for the province. However, as we shall see, the Bourassa years were far from quiet in Quebec.

Digging Deeper

1

Place the following events in French-English relations in chronological order, from the earliest to the most recent:
- Manitoba Schools Question
- Confederation
- the execution of Louis Riel
- conscription crisis of World War I
- election of Sir Wilfrid Laurier
- the conquest
- rebellion in Lower Canada
- exploration of the interior of North America by Radisson and Groseilliers
- Lord Durham's report

2

Review the contributions to Canada of early French-speaking individuals:
- Mother Marie de l'Incarnation
- General Montcalm
- Samuel de Champlain
- Louis-Joseph Papineau
- George Etienne Cartier

3

Duplessis was fond of saying, 'There wouldn't be employees without employers.' What does his statement mean? How did his actions during the Asbestos strike illustrate this belief?

34

SPOTLIGHT: THE '50s AND '60s

Sputnik

The space age began in 1957. In October 1957 the U.S.S.R. launched the first satellite into space. The world was astonished! People were no longer confined to the earth's surface – and space captured everyone's imagination. The success of Sputnik I was followed a month later with Sputnik II, which carried a dog into orbit. The United States launched their Vanguard I in 1958. The space race was on!

In 1961, the Russian Yuri Gagarin was the first man to travel in space. He was closely followed by two Americans, Alan B. Shepard Jr. in a sub-orbital flight, and John Glenn, who circled the earth three times in the Friendship 7 capsule.

In 1969 the world watched in awe as Neil Armstrong, followed by Edwin Aldrin, walked on the moon's surface. This was certainly one of the most impressive space accomplishments since the first Sputnik was launched in 1957. Since then many men and a woman have made long flights in orbiting satellites to explore the secrets of our solar system. Unmanned craft have also explored the planets of Mars, Venus, and Jupiter to try to increase our knowledge of the universe.

Suburbs and Urbanization

New growth of Canadian cities was a result of the post-war expansion. More industrial jobs in cities, and the conveniences of city living made Canada's rural population fall from thirty-eight per cent in 1951 to twenty-six per cent in 1966. By the mid-1960s Montreal was still the largest urban centre, although Toronto was growing fast. Vancouver remained in third position, but Ottawa was challenging Winnipeg for fourth place.

Almost overnight suburbs mushroomed all around the cities. Developers began to build planned communities using the neighbourhood plazas or schools as their focus. The spread of suburbs led to fads in home design and decorating. Every house had a picture window and, if possible, an attached garage or carport. Inside, white woodwork was popular and the living room now featured three walls painted one colour, and the fourth covered with wallpaper.

In the garage was the car that made suburban living possible in the first place. During the 1950s Canadians bought 3 541 381 passenger cars. Each year's model seemed to grow longer, lower, and wider. North Americans believed that 'bigger was better', so enormous V-8 engines, two-tone colours, and power steering were added. Outlandish tail-fins became the fad of the 1957 and 1958 models.

Hula hoop

In the 1950s there was no fad quite like hula-hooping. The idea was supposed to have come from Australia where bamboo hoops were used. North American hoops were made of plastic. Hula hoop manufacturers made $45 000 000 from the fad in one year. An impressive record was set by ten-year-old Pamela Brown of Brantford, Ontario when she twirled a hoop for 3 hours and 5 minutes, an estimated 15 938 twirls.

Rock 'n' Roll and Elvis

It all began in 1954 when Elvis Presley wrote and recorded a couple of nice lively tunes for his mother's birthday. The recording engineer liked what he heard, and called Elvis back in a couple of months to cut a single called 'That's All Right, Mama'. A Memphis disc jockey started to give it a spin on the radio, and orders poured in. It seemed that Elvis had something special. Elvis was not sure what it was, but later remarked, 'I don't want it ever to end.'

Many teenagers considered Elvis Presley the 'King of Rock 'n' Roll'. They screamed and shouted when he sang 'Love Me Tender', 'Hound Dog', or 'Heartbreak Hotel' in concert, or saw him in such movies as 'Blue Hawaii' and 'Kid Galahad'.

When he died at his Graceland Mansion in August 1977, thousands of fans paid their respects to the 'King' who had given rock 'n' roll its style two decades before.

Elvis Presley at Maple Leaf Gardens.

Beatles

In 1964 teenagers discovered the Beatles. To the shock of adults, young people copied shaggy Beatle haircuts, bought Beatle buttons, watches, wigs, dolls, and wallets, and repeated Beatle lyrics, such as 'She loves you, yeah, yeah, yeah', over and over again. Sociologists called 'Beatlemania' a form of protest against the adult world. They said it could not last. The experts were wrong. The boys from Liverpool, England were recognized as making the most important advances in popular music in our era. The 1960s belonged to the Beatles. The 1950s was the era of the solo singer, but with the popularity of the Beatles the 1960s saw the growth of musical groups.

Stratford

During the 1950s Canadians began to get serious about setting up a distinctive Canadian theatre. In the sleepy little town of Stratford, Ontario, Tom Patterson had an idea. He persuaded Tyrone Guthrie, a famous director, to produce a Shakespearian festival at Stratford. In a circus tent beside the Avon River, the Stratford Shakespearian Festival held its first season in 1953. Year after year the crowds continued to come until the Festival Theatre was eventually constructed.

Stratford's success became an inspiration for theatres across the country. Drama lovers built the Neptune Theatre in Halifax, the Manitoba Theatre Centre in Winnipeg, Theatre New Brunswick in Fredericton, and similar theatres in many other centres across Canada.

Thanks to Stratford and these others, Canadian actors and actresses have become internationally known. These include Kate Reid, Jessica Tandy, Lorne Greene, William Shatner, Christopher Plummer, Don Harron, and Gordon Pinsent. Though some of these actors and actresses went to the United States or Europe to establish their reputation, many did get their start in Canadian theatres such as Stratford.

Ballet

In 1951 a twenty-nine-year old ballerina named Celia Franca founded the National Ballet of Canada. Celia and Betty Oliphant travelled more than 8000 kilometres across Canada in search of talent. Three hundred auditions were held in schools and public halls. From these, twenty-eight dancers were chosen. The Company could only afford to pay the dancers $25 per week, and $5 more for performances. But they opened their company that year to rave reviews in Toronto and Montreal. Then they went on tour throughout southern Ontario. Because

The Beatles.

The Toronto Dance Theatre performing.

of the drive of Celia Franca and others like her, ballet has won an important place in the hearts of Canadians.

Similar companies sprang up around the same time. These include the Royal Winnipeg Ballet and Les Grands Ballets Canadiens in Montreal.

Television

Can you imagine what it was like not to have television? Did you realize TV did not become widespread in Canada until the 1950s? People living along the American border were able to pick up American programs before that. However, it was not until 1952 that the C.B.C. introduced its television service. Even then stations were few and far between, and television was not available in the less populated regions of Canada until years later. The screens were small, everything was in black and white, and the pictures were often lost in a snowstorm of dots. But television caught on quickly. By 1954 Canadians owned more than a million television sets.

By the end of the 1950s, television had completely revolutionized Canadian life. Eating habits changed when families bought TV tables so they could eat their meals in front of the set. Children were watching so much television that homework suffered. Children's viewing habits became an urgent topic at hundreds of parent-teacher association meetings. Conversation ceased when guests who didn't own a set dropped in. They were motioned to sit down and be quiet. Family life itself underwent great changes because of television. Families that used to go to church on Sunday evening, or play games or visit relatives, suddenly found themselves watching the 'Ed Sullivan Show'.

Among the favourite Canadian shows and entertainers were comedians Wayne and Shuster, Tommy Hunter on 'Country Hoedown', 'Front Page Challenge', and 'Hockey Night in Canada'.

Literature

The fifties and sixties saw the emergence of several important Canadian novelists and poets. Among them were Mordecai Richler, Hugh MacLennan, Irving Layton, Robertson Davies, Leonard Cohen and Margaret Laurence.

Gabrielle Roy

Gabrielle Roy was born into a French-Canadian family in St. Boniface, Manitoba, the youngest of eleven children. She loved to write short stories in French and her mother encouraged her to do so, even though the situation of a French-Canadian writer in Manitoba seemed hopeless at that time.

In two of her novels, *The Street of Riches* and *The Road Past Altamont*, she recounted her childhood experiences in rural Manitoba. One of her best known works, *The Tin Flute*, describes the poverty and pride of the people of the St. Henri district of Montreal. This novel was chosen by the Literary Guild of America in 1947 as the book of the month.

Gabrielle Roy now lives in Quebec City where she feels at home among fellow French-speaking Canadians. She has commented on the issue of Quebec separatism, saying, 'My great hope would be that Quebec would realize itself as a fully distinct part of Canada, and stay Canadian, bringing to Canada a part of its riches.'

Hugh Garner

Hugh Garner's family moved to Canada from England when he was six years old. They settled in Toronto's Cabbagetown district, a poor and run-down part of the city.

Garner dropped out of school in grade 10 and held a variety of low-paying jobs after that. When the Depression hit, Garner, like thousands of young men, set off across Canada and the United States on the freights. Later he wrote about those days, telling 'the stories of ordinary people, living ordinary lives, happy or sad about everyday things of life.'

Many of his short stories have been adapted for television. They are hard-hitting and often show the seamy side of life. But Garner was one of the first Canadian writers to show that the urban poor were good subjects for fiction.

Digging Deeper

Refer back to the summary chart of themes at the end of Unit One (page 54). Using the chart as a model, make a chart for Unit Six. On the chart trace the development of those themes through this unit.

35
LIFE BEGINS AT ONE HUNDRED

CANADA BEGINS ITS SECOND CENTURY

At ten minutes to midnight the lights of Parliament Hill flickered off. In a few minutes it would be 1 July 1967. A crowd of 50 000 people on the lawns of the Parliament Buildings held sparklers aloft to light up the night sky. Suddenly the sky blazed with red, white, blue, and green fireworks. Then at midnight the carillon chimed 'O Canada' and the huge throng joined in singing. As the anthem ended, there followed an outburst of cheering, clapping, and horn honking such as Ottawa had not heard in a hundred years. Many of the party-goers broke open champagne and stayed to dance in the streets until the sun dawned on the first day of Canada's second century.

1867 | 1967

The capital's welcome of Canada's one-hundredth birthday was repeated all across the country. Canada broke into a frenzy of Dominion Day parades, picnics, and pageants. Church bells pealed joyously and were answered by hundred-gun salutes. In Edmonton, Alberta's Premier Manning cut the first slice of a giant, eight-tier birthday cake for thousands of party-goers. At schooner races in Halifax, 20 000 people ate bowls of fish chowder in the Halifax Public Gardens. The crews of eight voyageur canoes, who were racing from Alberta to Montreal, stopped to celebrate with 30 000 Winnipegers at a regatta on the Assiniboine River. Students at Kimberley, British Columbia sewed together 60 bedsheets to make a 610 metre maple leaf flag. And St. Paul's, Alberta, a Centennial-mad town, built a U.F.O. landing pad to welcome any little green visitors to the Centennial celebrations.

There was scarcely a city, town, or village in the country without a new Centennial park, library, or concert hall to dedicate. In Prince Edward Island Premier Campbell led a ceremony of rededication to Confederation. It was here in Charlottetown in 1864 that the Fathers had first met to discuss union. In nineteen cities and towns, great-grandchildren of the Fathers of Confederation solemnly laid wreaths at the gravesides of their famous relatives.

Queen Elizabeth helps celebrate the Centennial.

Expo '67.

Most people would agree that the crowning achievement of the Centennial celebrations was the world's fair known as Expo '67 at Montreal. The purpose of the Centennial was to show Canadians and the world an unforgettable picture of our land and its people.

Robert Stanfield.

David Lewis.

As Canada headed into its second century, all three of the major political parties chose new leaders. The first to be chosen was the Conservative, Robert Lorne Stanfield. At a Conservative party convention in 1967 a bitter debate raged. The Conservatives decided to replace John Diefenbaker as leader with Stanfield. The new party leader had been the respected Premier of Nova Scotia. A few months later the Liberal Party met to find a replacement for Lester Pearson, who had chosen to retire. Eight candidates were in the running for the leadership, but the party chose Pierre Elliott Trudeau, a bachelor and a former university professor from Montreal. Three years later David Lewis was chosen to replace T.C. Douglas when he stepped down from the leadership of the New Democratic Party. Thus the three major parties had new national leaders to deal with the changing issues facing Canada as it headed into its second century.

Indeed the whole world was undergoing many social changes in the late 1960s. In both North America and Europe, young people in particular were questioning society's values and points of view. Many decided that the way to challenge society was to protest. There were anti-war demonstrations demanding that the United States remove its forces from the war in Viet Nam. Minority groups such as blacks and native peoples marched to protest the unfair conditions under which their people lived. There were sit-ins in the universities as the students demanded more say in the running of the schools. In Canada there were outbreaks of violence as separatists attempted to draw attention to the problems of the French minority. Another group rebelled by dropping out of society. They became 'hippies'. Outwardly they rejected many of society's values. They wore their hair long and dressed exotically. Experiments with drugs and communal living were common.

Protesters.

It was in this atmosphere of change and rebellion that Pierre Trudeau became prime minister. To many Canadians Trudeau seemed to be the man of the hour. For one thing he was a French-speaking Quebecker. He understood Quebec and would be able to please that province. He was youthful, casual, and informal. He appealed to young people partly because he drove fast sports cars and had been photographed doing jack-knife dives into swimming pools and riding a camel. As minister of justice, Trudeau had convinced people he was cool under pressure, logical, and scholarly. Above all, on television he showed wit and confidence. His charisma on television and at huge political rallies proved to be a real vote-getter.

Trudeau adopted a whole new campaign style. He arrived in many cities by jet, and then descended into a suburban shopping centre parking lot by helicopter. From there he mingled

Trudeaumania.

with the crowd, shaking hands and accepting kisses from admirers. Trudeau made some general remarks to the crowd about building the 'just society'. Hecklers were put down easily with quick-witted replies. He ended by challenging Canadians to take a chance on the future and vote for the Liberals. Smiling for the cameras, he then tossed the flower from his buttonhole to the crowd. In a few minutes he re-entered the helicopter and was whisked away to his next rally. He seemed to be willing to meet the people and discuss the issues with them in plain talk. The crowds loved him. The press called it 'Trudeaumania.'

Next to Trudeau, Robert Stanfield appeared steady but dull. He was particularly uneasy in front of news cameras. Once he complained that every time he left the House of Commons, 'You walk out and they shove a bunch of microphones in your face. In thirty seconds you are expected to produce a profound and intelligent answer to an extremely complicated national issue.' Stanfield's answers were thoughtful and honest, but his slow manner of speaking made him seem indecisive and weak. It is not surprising that Trudeau was elected in 1968, and again in 1972 and 1974, but with reduced majorities.

36

CANADA IN A CHANGING WORLD

As Canada entered its second century, Prime Minister Trudeau called for a complete review of Canada's foreign policy. It was a good time, said the energetic Prime Minister, to examine Canada's relations with other countries of the world. Expo had focused the world's attention on Canada. Now Canada was going to focus its attention on the role it should play in the world.

Beginning in 1968, interested Canadians from all walks of life were invited to take part in what was called the 'Trudeau Review'. Politicians, journalists, professors, business leaders, financial experts, and church and labour leaders offered opinions and advice. The eventual result was the publication in 1970 of six booklets titled 'Foreign Policy for Canadians'. They were to be the blueprint for Canada's foreign policy in the 1970s and beyond.

Canadians were informed that Canada now had six basic national goals:

1. to help the Canadian economy grow stronger;
2. to keep Canada independent;
3. to work for peace and security;
4. to promote fairness and equality for everyone;
5. to improve living conditions for all people;
6. to protect our natural environment (conservation).

What were the reasons for the Trudeau Review? For one thing, the major nations of Western Europe had now recovered from the effects of World War II. Canada's importance in defending Europe was now far less crucial than it had been in the two decades following the war. Britain was moving closer to its European neighbours for trading purposes. Canada recognized that this could mean becoming totally dependent upon the United States for trade and defence. Japan and China were re-emerging as great powers and many new nations in Africa were becoming independent. At the same time, many thoughtful Canadians were beginning to worry about increasing American control over all aspects of Canadian life. Many were also critical of the Amer-

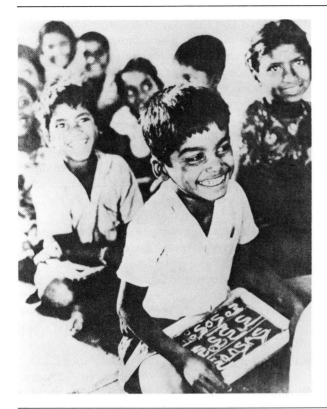

A UNICEF school in India.

ican involvement in the war in Viet Nam. They thought the Americans should withdraw their troops from Viet Nam in the interest of world peace. For all these reasons, it seemed like a good time for Canada to take a hard look at its foreign policy.

The Trudeau Review decided there were three possible paths the government could follow:

1. it could leave foreign policy as it was in the past, or,
2. it could seek to be tied even more closely with the United States, or,
3. it could seek to develop trade and friendly relations with other countries in order to reduce Canada's dependence on the United States.

This last path, later called 'The Third Option', was the policy the Trudeau government decided to pursue.

Canada and Europe

Canada's friendship with Europe seems very natural considering the vast number of Canadians who are of British, French, or other European descent. Many recent immigrants have also come from Europe, and they maintain strong ties with their country of origin.

In 1975 Britain joined the European Economic Community (the European Common Market). The Common Market is a group of Western European nations who trade freely with each other without tariffs. Canadians worried because Britain, as a Common Market member, would no longer be able to offer low tariffs to Commonwealth nations. Yet it was vital that Canada should trade more with Europe in order to reduce our dependence on the United States. Prime Minister Trudeau's frequent trips abroad were part of an effort to develop closer ties with the Common Market. He wanted to promote the sale of Canadian technology, especially nuclear power plants. He also wanted to attract more European investment to Canada. In July 1976, an important step was taken. Canada and the E.E.C. signed an Agreement for Commercial and Economic Co-operation. The agreement promised to increase trade, investment opportunities, and a sharing of scientific and technological information between Canada and the Common Market countries. Swedish and French car manufacturers have already established branch plants in Nova Scotia and Quebec. Money from several European nations is being invested in Canadian real estate and industry.

Prime Minister Trudeau also visited the U.S.S.R. Since Canada geographically lies between the two superpowers, Trudeau wanted to build up ties of friendship with the U.S.S.R. He also realized that the U.S.S.R. had great experience in northern development. This could be useful to Canada in developing the Arctic. Furthermore, Canada wished to trade with the U.S.S.R. and its Eastern European allies. In April 1973 a $200 million sale of wheat and barley was made to the U.S.S.R. Another sign of increasing good will between Canada and the U.S.S.R. had been an agreement signed two years earlier to exchange scientific, technical, and cultural information. The hockey games that followed between Team Canada and the U.S.S.R. were examples of the increasing openness between the two countries.

Canada and the Pacific

In its search for new trading partners, Canada began to look more seriously at the nations of the Pacific. Canada's geography provided opportunities not just in the Atlantic but also in the Pacific region. Trudeau pointed out that Canada should take advantage of its ringside seat on the Pacific.

The first contact established by the government was with the People's Republic of China. Though the communists had taken over the mainland of China in 1949, the communist government had not been recognized by Canada and the United States. By 1970 Canada and China had exchanged ambassadors and Canada had supported China's admission to the United Nations. It took another two years before the United States recognized Red China. Trudeau paid an official state visit to China in 1973 and at that time China placed a huge order for five million tonnes of Canadian wheat over a three year period.

An important trading relationship has also been built up with Japan, now Canada's third most important trading partner. In 1976 the two countries had signed an agreement to increase their trade – particularly in coal. The Japanese have since invested money in Canadian industries and the development of our natural resources.

As part of the new directions of foreign policy in the Pacific, Canada has continued to build strong trading links with Australia, New Zealand, and other Commonwealth countries in that region. The government has encouraged universities to set up Asian study programs and our immigration policy has been changed to allow more Asians into Canada.

A ceasefire agreement was signed by the United States, North Viet Nam, and South Viet Nam in 1973. Canada agreed to serve on the International Commission of Control and Supervision set up to observe the Viet Nam peace settlement. It soon became obvious that the ceasefire would not work. One Canadian was killed and several others were held prisoner. Therefore, the Trudeau government decided to withdraw Canada from I.C.C.S. duty in July 1973.

Canada and the Rest of the World

The foreign policy review also suggested that Canada strengthen its ties with Latin America. Trudeau visited Mexico, Cuba, and Venezuela in 1976. Our trade with Latin America has increased from $1099 million in 1970 to $3418 million in 1976. Canada has also given an increasing amount of development funds to a number of Latin American countries. When a revolution took place in Chile in 1973, Canada admitted hundreds of refugees.

Canada's major concern in the Middle East has been to bring about a lasting peace to the Arab-Israeli conflict. In 1973 we agreed to return to the Middle East in a peacekeeping role. One thousand and fifty Canadian military specialists became part of the United Nations Emergency Force maintaining the ceasefire by providing supplies, transportation, and communication. After our withdrawal from the I.C.C.S. in Viet Nam, this action reassured other countries that Canada was not abandoning its peacekeeping efforts.

Since the 1950s, many colonies in Africa have emerged as independent nations. Canada has provided large amounts of money, food, and technical aid to these developing nations. This help has been given to both commonwealth and French-speaking African states.

Canada and the United Nations

The Trudeau foreign policy review recommended that Canada work hard to support the United Nations and make it an effective organization for international co-operation. However, the review expressed a growing feeling of disappointment over the U.N.'s lack of power to keep peace in the world. It suggested that Canada try to shift the U.N. emphasis from peacekeeping to social and economic development. Canada has contributed heavily to all those U.N. organizations that are striving to help poor nations and are working for disarmament and human rights. Canada contributes the ninth largest share of the regular annual budget to the United Nations. Since 1946 it has given over $900 million to U.N. organizations. In the 1970s Canada has served on major U.N. peacekeeping missions in Cyprus, the Middle East, and Kashmir.

On 1 January 1977, Canada began a two-year term on the U.N. Security Council. This was the fourth time we had filled one of the non-permanent seats on the Council since the U.N. was set up.

Canada, the Commonwealth, and the French-Speaking Community

Canada has continued to value belonging to the 'family' of nations that makes up the Commonwealth, with the Queen as head of the family. The Commonwealth family is spread throughout the world and is presently made up of thirty-nine countries. As one of the strongest members of the Commonwealth family, Canada has continued to help the smaller and weaker members with generous financial aid. Canada has found that the Commonwealth provides a good framework for peaceful working out of disagreements among family members. The heads of government in the member nations meet every two years, and more than fifty conferences are organized annually under Commonwealth sponsorship. In 1978 Canada was host to the 11th Commonwealth Games in Edmonton, Alberta, and the 12th Congress of Commonwealth Universities.

Since almost one-third of all Canadians are French-speaking, the federal government has sought to strengthen ties with the French-speaking community of the world. These are the countries that are entirely or partially French-speaking, and are known as La Francophonie. Membership involves participating in educational, cultural, and sports activities organized by the various countries. A portion of Canada's foreign aid is directed toward the French-speaking developing nations.

Canada's Foreign Aid to Developing Countries

In Canada a typical Sunday dinner may be a roast of beef, but in much of the world Sunday dinner is no more than a bowl of rice. There are an estimated 4.2 billion people on the earth, and more than 2.5 billion of them live in hungry nations. By the year 2000 those 2.5 billion starving people could double in number. The average Canadian may say, 'I know what hunger is. It's the gnawing feeling you get between meals.' But that is not the kind of hunger that these 2.5 billion people experience. Hunger – real starvation – bloats the stomach, caves in the cheeks, and strips the flesh from the rib cage. And when it is prolonged, it ends in lingering death.

Consider these facts:

- The average income of people living in underdeveloped countries is less than what the average Canadian family receives from the government in family allowance payments.

- Mali has one doctor for every 38 821 people; Canada has one doctor for every 593.

- Canada gave one million tonnes of wheat annually to the world's hungry in 1974-1977. That amount would provide the starving with one slice of bread every five days.

- The U.N. estimates that in Africa and the Far East twenty-five to thirty per cent of the population suffers from malnutrition.

- Bangladesh has one hospital bed for every 9896 people; Canada has one for every 110.

- North Americans spend over $3 billion annually on their pets. This is enough to feed the hungry for a year.

- In Asia, Africa, and Latin America, people go to bed every night wondering if they will have enough food for the next day to keep alive. In the United States and Canada thousands of people go to bed every night wondering if they will have enough will power to stay on their low-calorie diet.

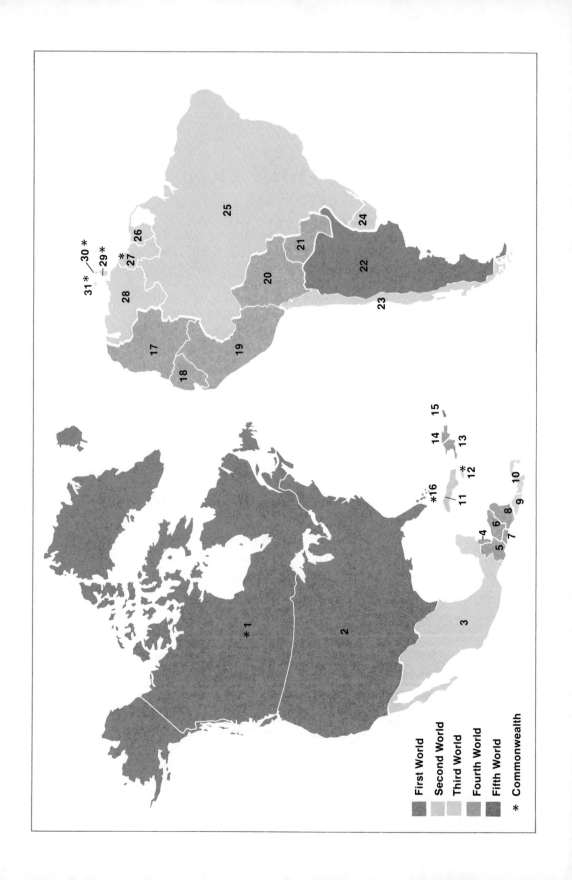

*1 Canada
2 United States
3 Mexico
4 Belize
5 Guatemala
6 Honduras
7 El Salvador
8 Nicaragua
9 Costa Rica
10 Panama
11 Cuba
*12 Jamaica
13 Haiti
14 Dominican Republic
15 Puerto Rico
*16 Bahamas

17 Colombia
18 Ecuador
19 Peru
20 Bolivia
21 Paraguay
22 Argentina
23 Chile
24 Uruguay
25 Brazil
26 Surinam
*27 Guyana
28 Venezuela
*29 Trinidad and Tobago
*30 Barbados
*31 Grenada

Commonwealth Countries

The Bahamas
Barbados
Canada
Grenada
Guyana
Jamaica
Trinidad and Tobago

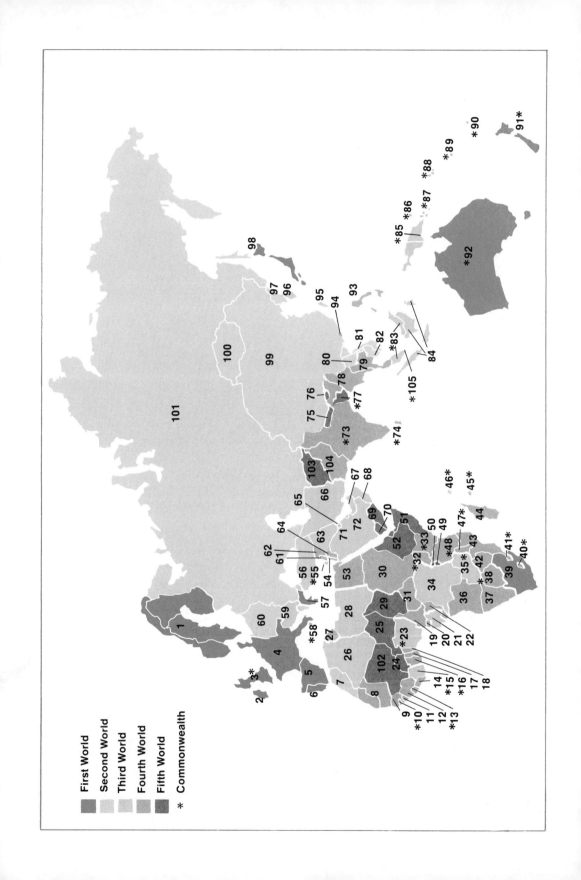

1 Scandinavia
2 Ireland
*3 Britain
4 Western Europe
5 Spain
6 Portugal
7 Morocco
8 Mauritania
9 Senegal
*10 Gambia
11 Guinea-Bissau
12 Guinea
*13 Sierra Leone
14 Liberia
*15 Ivory Coast
*16 Ghana
17 Togo
18 Benin
19 Cameroon
20 Equitorial Guinea
21 Gabon
22 Congo
*23 Nigeria
24 Upper Volta
25 Niger
26 Algeria
27 Tunisia
28 Libyan Arab Jamahiriya
29 Chad
30 Sudan
31 Central African Republic
*32 Uganda
*33 Kenya
34 Zaire
*35 Zambia

36 Angola
37 Namibia
*38 Botswana
39 South Africa
*40 Lesotho
*41 Swaziland
42 Zimbabwe-Rhodesia
43 Mozambique
44 Malagasy Republic
*45 Mauritius
*46 Seychelles
*47 Malawi
*48 Tanzania
49 Burundi
50 Rwanda
51 Somalia
52 Ethiopia
53 Egypt
54 Israel
*55 Cyprus
56 Turkey
57 Greece
*58 Malta
59 Yugoslavia
60 Eastern Europe
61 Lebanon
62 Jordan
63 Iraq
64 Syria
65 Kuwait
66 Iran
67 United Arab Emirates
68 Oman
69 Yemen
70 South Yemen
71 Saudi Arabia

72 Qatar
*73 India
*74 Sri Lanka
75 Nepal
76 Bhutan
*77 Bangladesh
78 Burma
79 Thailand
80 Laos
81 Viet Nam
82 Democratic Kampuchea
*83 Malaysia
84 Indonesia
*85 Papua-New Guinea
*86 Naura
*87 Soloman Islands
*88 Tuvalu
*89 Fiji
*90 Tonga
*91 New Zealand
*92 Australia
93 Philippines
94 Hong Kong
95 Taiwan
96 South Korea
97 North Korea
98 Japan
99 China
100 Mongolia
101 U.S.S.R.
102 Mali
103 Afghanistan
104 Pakistan
*105 Singapore

Commonwealth Countries

Australia
Bangladesh
Botswana
Britain
Cyprus
Fiji
Gambia
Ghana
India
Kenya
Lesotha
Malawi
Malaysia
Malta
Mauritius
Naura
New Zealand
Nigeria
Papua New Guinea
Seychelles
Sierra Leone
Singapore
Soloman Islands
Sri Lanka
Swaziland
Tanzania
Tonga
Tuvalu
Uganda
Zambia

Most of the starving billions are found in the undeveloped countries, or what have come to be called *Third World* countries. Nations are often grouped into three or more categories depending on their wealth and social conditions.

The *First World* includes the advanced industrial nations. They have strong economies, are usually wealthy, and have democratic governments. The United States leads this group. Japan, West Germany, Britain, Canada, Australia, New Zealand, France, and most other western European nations also qualify.

The *Second World* is a term used for the communist countries. These would include the U.S.S.R., the People's Republic of China, Hungary, East Germany, Czechoslovakia, Poland, and other east European communist countries. Generally the Second World is wealthy, but not as rich as the First World.

The *Third World* is made up of all the rest of the countries. Nations that are only beginning to develop their trade and industries belong in this group. So do those nations that claim to be politically non-aligned, that is, independent of both the First and Second Worlds. Many of these countries depend on just one crop or one mineral. Many are also faced with exploding population growth. It is estimated that there are over 200 000 new mouths to feed every day.

In the Third World there are so many sharp contrasts between countries that some experts now insist that there are really five worlds. Arab countries such as Saudi Arabia and Kuwait, which are enormously wealthy from oil resources, might properly be called Third World. The new category *Fourth World* would more properly include countries that have some raw materials and some industrial potential. Such countries need outside help to get their economies going. Peru, the Arab Republic of Egypt, and Liberia could be called Fourth World countries. Those countries that exist in desperate poverty may be referred to as the *Fifth World*. Most have per capita incomes of less than $100 per year and few resources of any kind. They are barely able to feed themselves. Bangladesh, Chad, Nepal, and Afghanistan are said to be in this category. The new categories of Fourth and Fifth World may help us to see the wide diversity of conditions in countries traditionally referred to as Third World.

How does Canada help Third, Fourth, and Fifth World countries? Canada is rich and Bangladesh is desperately poor. The goal of Canada's foreign aid program is to do something to reduce the gap between Canada's wealth and the poverty of Bangladesh and countries like it.

In the past it was often thought that development aid to these countries would automatically help all of the poor people in them. This simply did not happen. Foreign aid supplied by rich nations usually found its way to the small wealthy class (large landowners, government officials, businessmen) in the Third World countries. Little of it got into the hands of the poor for whom it was really intended. In some African nations foreign aid was used by the white minority for military purposes to keep down the black majority. In other Third World countries the money was spent on glamour projects such as stadiums, swimming pools, and convention centres. Recognizing these problems, Canada's foreign aid policies have been reviewed and a new strategy for international development has been adopted.

The Canadian International Development Agency (CIDA) was created in 1968 to co-ordinate all Canadian aid from government and non-government (churches and charities) programs. Among the most important points in our assistance program from 1975 to 1980 were the following:

- Canada will continue and even increase its programs of development assistance.
- Canada will concentrate the bulk of its aid on countries where the per capita income is less than $375 a year.
- Canada will place its major emphasis on helping countries to improve food production and distribution, rural development, education and training, public health, shelter, and energy. As an example, in Senegal, West Africa, fishing is a vital source of food and employment. Three-quarters of the fishermen used dugout canoes. Canada provided outboard motors, helped build and equip workshops for their maintenance, and set up a system for selling the fish caught. From 1970 to 1975, the number of motorized boats rose from 2000 to 4800, and the fish catch nearly doubled. The help from Canada went directly to the fishermen, and the whole country benefited as a result.
- Canada will continue to provide emergency food, aid, and disaster relief to stricken areas of the world.
- About two-thirds of Canada's aid will be direct (bilateral) aid, going from the Canadian government to the government of the Third World country. The rest will be distributed through multilateral programs – given to international agencies such as the World Bank, OXFAM, and UNESCO.
- Canada will strive to raise its foreign aid to reach the United Nations target of 0.7 per cent of Canada's Gross National Product (G.N.P.). G.N.P. is the value of all goods and services produced by the economy of a country in a year.
- Canada will make interest-free loans to developing countries. In the past these loans have been made with the condition that the developing countries buy goods made in

Canada. This was known as tied-aid. In the future Canada will gradually remove the tied-aid restrictions on loans to developing countries.

CANADA'S BILATERAL FOREIGN AID 1977-1978 $636.8 MILLION	
Asia	$230 million
Commonwealth Africa	$100 million
Francophone Africa	$110 million
Latin America	$30 million
Caribbean	$30 million
Emergency Relief	$136.8 million

CANADA'S MULTILATERAL FOREIGN AID 1977 – 1978 $289.3 MILLION This includes:	
World Food Program	$97.5 million
United Nations Development Program	$34 million
Other, including administration	$157.8 million

PERCENTAGE OF GNP SPENT ON FOREIGN AID 1975	
Sweden	0.82%
Netherlands	0.75%
Norway	0.66%
France	0.62%
Australia	0.61%
Belgium	0.59%
Canada	0.58%
Denmark	0.58%
New Zealand	0.52%
West Germany	0.40%
Britain	0.37%
United States	0.26%

Organization for Economic Co-operation and Development

Canada and Defence – NATO and NORAD

In the late 1960s Canada began to have second thoughts about its role in the defence of Europe. Even before the results of the Trudeau Review were published, the government took steps to change Canada's role in NATO. Canada withdrew fifty per cent of its ground troops from European bases. Canadian forces left in NATO would no longer use nuclear weapons. Canada's defence budget for NATO would be frozen at $1.8 billion per year until 1972, one of the lowest budgets of any NATO member. Funds would not be available to replace military equipment that was old-fashioned and out-of-date. The government obviously felt that the role of Canada's armed forces should be concentrated on North American defence and the Arctic.

Canada's changing NATO role obviously upset several of our NATO allies. The West Germans in particular made it very clear that if Canada wished to have trading links with Europe, it must help maintain the NATO defences in Europe. As a consequence, between 1975 and 1977, there was almost a total about-face in Canadian defence policy. Canada bought 128 Leopard 1 tanks from West Germany and 18 Aurora long-range patrol aircraft to guard north Atlantic shipping lanes. Canada is also buying anti-armour and anti-aircraft missiles. It has begun a selection process to find new attack aircraft. In addition the government decided to raise the defence budget by twelve per cent per year for five years. Canada was showing its allies and trading partners that it was returning to a serious commitment to NATO.

Changes in defence policy have also taken place in Canada's role in NORAD. In 1972 the Trudeau government began to dismantle the two nuclear-armed Bomarc missile bases in Ontario and Quebec. The Canadian government felt that the threat of war between the United States and the U.S.S.R. had definitely decreased. Some critics of NORAD even urged that we abandon NORAD completely. They argued that the United States would never allow a foreign power to attack Canada. Other critics of NORAD have complained that the United States often acts without consulting Canada anyway. An example of this occurred in 1973 when American President Richard Nixon placed American forces on world-wide alert. This took place during the Arab-Israeli war. Canadian forces with NORAD were automatically involved. However, the Canadian Minister of National Defence was not officially informed until eight hours after the President had declared the alert.

In 1975 the Canadian government strongly re-affirmed its commitment to the NORAD role. The top two defence priorities were pinpointed as:

1. the surveillance and protection of Canadian territory and coastlines;
2. the defence of North America in co-operation with U.S. forces.

Digging Deeper

1 Examine the six basic national goals of Trudeau's foreign policy. Rank them in order of importance from most to least important. Be prepared to defend your ranking with valid reasons.

2 The following reasons are commonly offered for Canada's foreign aid to developing countries:
a) aid-receiving countries will be grateful and friendly toward Canada;
b) the fortunate countries have an obligation to give part of their wealth to the unfortunate;
c) developing countries will buy manufactured goods from Canada and sell us their natural resources;
d) developing countries will support the First World against the Second World at the U.N.

Explain the meaning of each of these reasons in your own words. Rank these reasons in order of importance to you. Can you suggest any other reasons why Canada should help developing countries?

3 Discuss:
Canada should give aid only to those countries who agree with us politically, and we should ignore those who don't.

4 Debate:
Canada also has poor people. Charity should begin at home. We should spend our money helping people in Canada who live below the poverty line rather than spending our money helping people outside the country.

5 Summarize in chart form Canada's role since 1970 in
Peacekeeping   Defence   Trade   Foreign Aid

6 Sharing the world's resources more evenly would mean sacrifices for Canadians. Would you be willing to reduce *your* living standard to help Third World countries? Why or why not? Would you be prepared to hold a bread and water (starvation) lunch to raise funds and illustrate the problems of the poor? Would your Student's Council be prepared to support a child in a developing country under the Foster Parents Plan?

7 Compare Canadian foreign policy goals from 1945 to 1970 with those of after 1970. How could you explain any change in these goals?

37
QUEBEC
IN CRISIS

5 October 1970

8:15 a.m.

The doorbell rang in the luxurious home of the Senior British Trade Commissioner in Montreal, James R. Cross. Two men carrying a gift-wrapped package told the servant who opened the door that they wanted to deliver it to Mr. Cross. Admitted to the house, they pulled a rifle from the package, seized Cross, and took him away.

11:30 a.m.

Ransom demands from the kidnappers were received at a radio station. They identified themselves as members of the F.L.Q. (*Front de Libération du Québec*) and asked for the release of twenty-three 'political prisoners' being held in jail for bombings and terrorist activities. They also demanded transportation for the kidnappers to Cuba or Algeria, $500 000 in gold bars, and the publication of the F.L.Q. Manifesto (statement of beliefs). The government had forty-eight hours to comply or Cross would be killed.

8 October

The F.L.Q. Manifesto was read over the radio and television network of Radio Canada. The Manifesto called the people of Quebec to revolution, and ended with the words,

> Long live free Quebec! Long live our comrades who are political prisoners! Long live the Quebec revolution! Long live the F.L.Q.

The other demands of the kidnappers were refused by the government.

10 October

Quebec Labour Minister Pierre Laporte was in his front yard tossing a football with his nephew and some other young people. A blue Chevrolet stopped in front of his house and four men with machine-guns shoved Laporte into the back seat. The car sped away. The No. 2 man in the Quebec government had been kidnapped. The Quebec government now began to take the crisis seriously. Premier Bourassa took refuge in Montreal's Queen Elizabeth Hotel surrounded by armed guards. The kidnappers of Laporte identified themselves as a second cell of the F.L.Q.

12 October

In Ottawa federal troops took up positions around government buildings and provided escorts for important government politicians.

14 October

A group of sixteen prominent Quebeckers, including René Lévesque and Claude Ryan, issued a statement. They blamed the federal government for creating an atmosphere of 'military rigidity'. They urged that Quebec be allowed to work out the crisis

Claude Ryan.

on its own, and that the two hostages be exchanged for the political prisoners in jail.

Meanwhile in Toronto, Premier John Robarts of Ontario said there should be no compromise with the terrorists.

15 October

Mass meetings of university students in Montreal expressed sympathy with the F.L.Q. and shouted slogans of revolution. The Quebec Premier asked Ottawa for troops to back up the Montreal and provincial police forces working around the clock to track down the terrorists. Troops of the Royal 22nd Regiment moved into the streets of Montreal to guard public buildings. One thousand paratroopers from Canadian Forces Base Edmonton were flown to the base at St. Hubert just outside Montreal. Armored personnel carriers and soldiers with rifles and submachine guns took up posts in the streets of Montreal.

16 October, 4:00 a.m.

Prime Minister Trudeau, on the advice of the Quebec government, proclaimed the War Measures Act. It was the first time the Act had been used in peacetime. Regulations under the Act outlawed the F.L.Q. and allowed police anywhere in Canada to detain people without charge for up to twenty-one days and without trial for up to ninety days. Now the police and military could arrest people just on suspicion of belonging to the F.L.Q. Asked by a reporter how far the government would go, Trudeau replied, 'Just watch me.'

In pre-dawn raids the police rounded up, among others, fifty members of the Parti Québécois. A total of 465 were eventually arrested. Gerald Godin, now a P.Q. member of the Quebec

National Assembly, recalled how the police smashed down his front door in the middle of the night. 'I got up to investigate, I thought it might be firemen next door, and there were these policemen standing around,' he said. 'I asked them what they were doing there and they said they had come to arrest us.' Godin asked them to produce a search warrant, but 'one gave a little half-smile and told me to turn on the television. I turned it on and there was the announcement that during the night the government had passed these extreme measures.' Godin was held for seven days.

The reaction of the Canadian press to the introduction of the War Measures Act was cautious approval.

Canadian Armed Forces entering Montreal.

18 October

In the early hours of the morning the body of Pierre Laporte was found in the trunk of the same car used to kidnap him. Amazingly the car was parked near the armed forces base at St. Hubert. Laporte had been choked to death with the religious chain he wore around his neck.

The car in which Laporte's body was found.

Canadians waited tensely, wondering what would happen next.

27 October

Barbara Cross went on television to plead with the kidnappers for her husband's life.

15 November

A C.T.V. program, W5, announced the results of a poll in which eighty-seven per cent indicated they were in favour of the introduction of the War Measures Act. Less than six per cent opposed the introduction of this legislation.

4 December

Police surrounded a house in suburban Montreal where James Cross had been held for fifty-nine days. After hours of bargaining, a black Chrysler carrying Cross, the armed kidnappers, and their lawyer drove to the Expo '67 site. The kidnappers surrendered Cross and their arms to a Cuban diplomat. In exchange, the kidnappers were then whisked away to Dorval Airport and flown to Cuba.

28 December

Three F.L.Q. members accused of kidnapping and assassinating Laporte crawled out of a tunnel hidden under a farmhouse south of Montreal. They surrendered to the police and were charged with the murder of Pierre Laporte. The F.L.Q. crisis was over.

The F.L.Q. crisis in October 1970 ended seven years of violence in Quebec. But it did not end the turmoil or the differences between French and English. Most Quebeckers supported the steps taken by the Ottawa government at the time. However, the idea of Canadian soldiers having to keep peace in Quebec was disturbing to most Canadians. In time the feeling grew that Ottawa had over-reacted. Too many questions remained unanswered. Was there really the danger of an 'apprehended insurrection' in Quebec as Trudeau claimed? Were the rumours true that there was a widespread conspiracy about to take over the government of Quebec? If the trouble was in Quebec, why did the government take away the basic civil rights of every Canadian? These questions have never been properly answered by the Canadian government. Thus, much bitterness lingers for the hundreds of people arrested for nothing more than their nationalistic beliefs.

Let us listen in to the conversation of two women discussing the F.L.Q. crisis and the War Measures Act. One is Solange Chaput Rolland from Quebec and the other is Gertrude Laing from Alberta. Their conversation was recorded in 1972 in their book *Face to Face*.

SOLANGE: It is so difficult to explain how we felt when the army was here. The army in Quebec, for whatever reason, is a peculiar symbol. I felt reassured, and at the same time, I hated the army in Quebec. It was the Redcoats again! I know that what I am saying will make our readers jump, but to me, *'l'armée au Quebec, c'est l'occupation!* (the army in Quebec means occupation). I know we *asked* the soldiers to come, because at that time we really thought that a lot of people needed to be protected. But while I was physically reassured, at the same time I was psychologically hurt. *L'armée est au Quebec! Le Quebec est occupé!* (The army is in Quebec! Quebec is occupied!).

GERTRUDE: I think I would have felt the same way if they had come to Alberta to protect me from my fellow-Albertans.

SOLANGE: ... To me, the army was a symbol of English Canada.

GERTRUDE: To me, it represents simply a force that I don't want. I realize that there are times when it is necessary, like taking

GERTRUDE: medicine when you're ill, but I'm sure that psychologically I would have had the same reactions as you.

SOLANGE: You know ... the Patriotes and the revolt of 1837 are very much alive today in Quebec. We seem to be re-living history. Some of the F.L.Q. militants in jail are beginning to sound like heroes for some of our youth. I have even heard that there are classrooms in Quebec where huge posters of Paul Rose, who is accused of the murder of Pierre Laporte, hang on the walls. This is the part which I despise. But to come back to the army, I must say something. The army came once because the government of Quebec asked for protection for some of its citizens. Now there are a number of people in Quebec, and I think I am one of them, who believe that if tomorrow we were to vote massively for the independence of Quebec, the Canadian Government, backed by nine other provinces, would send the army back, not to keep us in Confederation because they want us, but so as not to disrupt the Canadian Confederation.

GERTRUDE: Some Canadians have said quite openly that they would 'send in the troops', but I wonder if they would if the time ever came.

SOLANGE: At the time that Prime Minister Trudeau proclaimed the War Measures Act, did he appear in the eyes of the whole country as the leader that the people had voted into power to put Quebec in its place?

GERTRUDE: If you are thinking that this was the logical result of the election to office of the man who many people expected would 'put Quebec in its place', I would say No.

SOLANGE: I say Yes, Yes, Yes!

GERTRUDE: I don't think this was the feeling of most Canadians. On the other hand, if you mean that at that moment he became the true leader of the country, at any rate of English-speaking Canada (and I think to a large extent French-speaking Canada too), the leader who took the action that most of the people approved of, that most of the world approved of, then I would say Yes. I think he gained enormous prestige even in the eyes of Canadians who up to that point had not been convinced of his leadership. I have to say, however, that personally I found it hard to accept his action; I felt that we didn't need this extreme measure, although certainly I was in no better position than anyone else to know that. I was also very much afraid of the long-term political consequences.

SOLANGE: When the War Measures Act was proclaimed, I was in Winnipeg, and I was awakened that morning with words that still haunt me: 'Ottawa has declared war on Quebec!' You can imagine how I felt! For about ten minutes I really believed this, until by listening to the news, I began to understand that Premier Bourassa had asked the troops to come to Quebec.

There is no doubt that the War Measures Act was a very drastic act. We still don't possess all the facts surrounding the F.L.Q. crisis, but we certainly know now that there was not an armed guerilla uprising planned, that there was not an 'apprehended rebellion', that only thirty-two guns were found, and so on. I believe that our government over-react- ed, but I think I would have done the same thing if I had been in their shoes. What I cannot accept is that the gov- ernment has neither given us the facts, nor admitted that it over-reacted. As a result, we live in a very uncertain atmo- sphere. If the government was sure that there was a possi- bility of open rebellion, they were right to take the steps they did. But since there is nothing to confirm this opinion, are we to suppose that we will once again be occupied if another crisis arises in Quebec?

Questions:

1. To what event in the past was Solange referring when she said 'It was the Redcoats again!'?
2. What do you think Solange meant when she said she was 'psychologically hurt' by seeing the army in Quebec? Can you explain why she may have felt this way?
3. Solange compared the F.L.Q. uprising to the rebellion of 1837. Point out similarities and differences in the two uprisings.
4. Do you think the Canadian government would be justified in sending the army into Quebec to keep it in Confederation? Explain your answer.
5. Explain how the F.L.Q. crisis caused Trudeau to gain 'enor- mous prestige' in the country.
6. Gertrude feared the long-term political consequences of the crisis. Suggest what they might be.
7. How would a Quebecker feel on hearing the words 'Ottawa has declared war on Quebec!'? Why?
8. In what respects did Solange feel the War Measures Act was too drastic? What were her fears for the future? Do you believe her fears were justified? Why?

One of the top priorities of the Trudeau government was to improve the position of French Canadians within Confedera- tion. Even before the F.L.Q. crisis the government had taken steps to give greater recognition to the French language. In 1969 the Official Languages Act was passed. It declared: 'The English and French languages are the official languages of Canada for all purposes of the Parliament and Government of Canada and possess and enjoy equality of status and equal rights and privileges as to their use in all the institutions of the Parliament and Government of Canada.' In other words the act guaranteed that both French and English Canadians could deal with the federal government in their own language. The government also pledged to provide more jobs in the federal government for French-speaking citizens. Until that time only fourteen per cent of the top government jobs were held by the French, even though they made up twenty-five per cent of the population.

The government also tried to encourage regional economic development by providing huge sums of money for this purpose. Of course the money was available for all poor regions of Canada. However, it was hoped that the federal funds for Quebec would help raise the economic level of French Canadians.

In addition, the Trudeau government showed a willingness to try to find ways of revising the constitution. Not only Quebec, but several provinces as well had criticisms of the constitution. Trudeau wanted to revise the constitution in such a way that it would guarantee increasing equality for French and English Canadians. In that way Quebec would not need any special status within Confederation.

Although the F.L.Q. crisis had seemed to end the radical separatist movement in Quebec, moderate separatists continued to grow in number. By 1968 they had formed their own political party, the Parti Québécois, dedicated to Quebec independence. The leader of the P.Q. was René Lévesque, who had been one of the stars of the Lesage administration. He had left the Liberal party in 1967, and within a year the P.Q. had been formed and had 20 000 supporters.

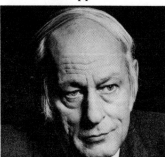

Réne Lévesque.

René Lévesque was born in an isolated village in the Gaspé Peninsula. Because he grew up in the countryside and in a family that was not wealthy, he has always felt very close to the common people of Quebec. It is said that young René learned to read by sitting on his father's lap and listening to great French literature being read. During World War II he left his studies at Laval University to become a war correspondent in Europe. When he returned to Quebec he became a television journalist, explaining the events of the world to the people of Quebec. The popularity of his show earned him a wide audience in his province. In 1960 Lévesque entered provincial politics and was elected to the Assembly as a Liberal. He was one of the moving forces of the Quiet Revolution. Almost single-handedly he brought about the nationalization of Quebec hydro-electricity. He was re-elected in 1962 and 1966.

By 1968 Lévesque and the Parti Québécois were convinced that Quebec should become an independent state. Only by independence could Quebeckers become their own masters with absolute control over their own affairs. Otherwise Quebec would be completely assimilated by the English or completely torn apart by the radical separatists. But separatism for Lévesque did not mean revolution. He hated 'all forms of violence whose only result can be to divide and weaken even further the small nation of Quebec.'

Most political observers in 1968 did not think the P.Q. had much chance of challenging the two leading parties – the Liberals and the Union Nationale. But they did not take into consideration the undercurrents running through the province of Quebec. The P.Q. zoomed off from a standing start, and by November 1976, eight years after it was founded, it would become the provincial government of Quebec.

In the meantime, the Liberals under Robert Bourassa came to power in Quebec. Since the Bourassa government strongly opposed the separatist movement, most Canadians breathed a sigh of relief. The Bourassa government began to build the huge James Bay Hydro-electric Project. The Premier called it the 'project of the century'. Because it would flood and destroy large areas of Quebec traditionally held by Indians, it was strongly opposed by many native peoples' organizations. It was also fought by environmental groups because it would block several of the greatest rivers of the province. Unlike the hydro project of the 1960s, which had been built by French Canadians, the construction and finance of the James Bay Project was by Americans. Most of the power produced will go to the United States.

Similarly, in order to provide jobs for Quebec, the government turned over an enormous block of the province's forests to a giant American corporation. Many people in Quebec criticized these moves. It seemed to be the same kind of concessions that Duplessis gave to the Americans in the 1940s and 1950s in order to attract American investment dollars into Quebec.

The Quebec government, like that of some other provinces,

urged that federal powers be weakened and provincial powers strengthened in some areas. Quebec was especially interested in getting increased provincial control over communications and immigration. Prime Minister Trudeau was prepared to discuss the constitutional changes necessary to satisfy some of Quebec's demands. In June 1971 Trudeau and the provincial premiers met at Victoria, British Columbia to discuss increasing the provincial powers in the constitution. A compromise was reached that seemed to satisfy the provinces and the federal government. However, at the last moment Quebec decided to reject the new constitution. Bourassa said that it did not provide sufficient authority to the province in the field of social security. As a result of Quebec's rejection of the Victoria agreement, the attempt to revise the British North America Act was set aside.

The government of Quebec was intensely concerned about the use of the French language in Quebec and the increasing number of non-French immigrants coming to Quebec. The French language, they believed, was the most important way they could keep alive the French culture. Yet an increasing number of immigrants from Europe coming to Quebec preferred to educate their children in English. Immigrants no doubt believed that if their children spoke English, they could move anywhere in North America and feel at home. In order to guarantee the French language top place in Quebec, the government introduced Bill 22. This Bill proclaimed French as the official language of Quebec. It also ruled that children of immigrant families must attend French schools rather than English. The legislation was widely criticized by non-French Quebeckers and especially by immigrants who had recently come to the province of Quebec.

The Bourassa government was re-elected in 1973 with a strong majority. But the Parti Québécois increased its support and managed to win thirty-one per cent of the votes in the province. During the next three years, Bourassa's government was marred by several scandals and charges of corruption. It seemed unable to do anything about rising prices and increasing unemployment. The province was rocked by one strike after another in the public service: police, hydro workers, teachers, hospital employees, and firemen. As the Bourassa government appeared to be failing, more and more Quebeckers turned to what seemed to be the only attractive alternative – René Lévesque and the Parti Québécois. Many Quebeckers voted for the P.Q. not because they were in favour of separatism but because Lévesque promised them clean, competent government.

Digging Deeper

Did the Canadian government over-react when it brought in the War Measures Act? Can you suggest any other ways in which the government might have handled the threat in Quebec without taking away the civil liberties of all Canadians?

1

What effects would the F.L.Q. crisis have on each of the following? Explain your answers.
a) separatists in Quebec;
b) the English minority in Quebec;
c) Prime Minister Trudeau;
d) people living in other parts of Canada;
e) the Liberal party in Quebec;
f) foreign diplomats and businessmen living in Quebec.

2

Taking a stand: Social protest sometimes involves violence. The F.L.Q. crisis was an example of this. Do you think violence is ever justified in drawing attention to a group's goals? Explain your reasons.

3

38

QUEBEC UNDER THE SEPARATISTS

15 November 1976

For days the public opinion polls had been saying that René Lévesque and the Parti Québécois could win the provincial election. In English Canada nobody wanted to believe that the separatists could ever come to power in Quebec. Even the most dedicated P.Q. members had their doubts. They knew their party would gain in strength, but they held out very little hope of actually winning the election. Then the first election results began to pour in. It looked like the Parti Québécois was going to sweep the province.

The huge crowd that had gathered in the Paul Sauvé Arena in Montreal could scarcely contain its excitement. Over and over they chanted the slogan 'Quebec to the Quebeckers'. Eventually their leader, René Lévesque, arrived and made his way to the platform. By this time the arena was packed to the rafters. When he stepped up to the microphone to speak, the crowd broke into a frenzy of cheering. It was a full five minutes before they allowed him to speak. The Parti Québécois had driven the Liberals from office, winning 68 of the 106 seats in Quebec. For the first time in their history, Quebeckers had elected a government dedicated to the establishment of an independent Quebec. In an emotional speech, Lévesque urged his supporters to keep a reasonable, friendly attitude towards Canada. Then he put forward the challenge, 'Now we have to build this country of Quebec.'

The Parti Québécois victory in Quebec sent shock waves across Canada. As the Task Force on Canadian Unity described it:

That election victory was the culmination of a long historical process; it was also the beginning of a new era in the life of our country. There had been other occasions in Canadian history when provincial governments were elected in opposition to Confederation, but never before had the goal of provincial independence been sought with the firmness of purpose displayed by the leaders of the Parti Québécois. For the first time since it was created in 1867, the Canadian political union faced the genuine possibility that one of its largest provinces might leave.

For many Quebeckers, however, '15 November 1976 announced the hour of freedom.' Others said, 'Quebec is awake now ... We have stood up and we shall not sit down again for quite a while.' A well-known historian from Quebec warned English-speaking Canadians 'to realize the former Canada they were used to exists no more because the old Quebec itself is dead and buried.' The triumphant slogan 'Frogs have teeth' was chalked on walls all over Montreal.

A French-speaking person in Montreal expressed it this way: 'My dear English-speaking countrymen. You are actually kept ignorant of what goes on in Quebec by the news media. A good example of this is that on 15 November you were so ignorant of what was going on in Quebec that you were astonished and almost in a state of collapse after the victory of the Parti Québécois. You never thought that this was possible because you don't know what goes on in Quebec.'

Shortly after the Quebec election, Prime Minister Trudeau described the situation to the Canadian people: 'Quebeckers, like citizens of other provinces, are proud. They seek personal fulfilment in a free and independent way. The central question is whether this growth of freedom and independence is best assured by Canada, or by Quebec alone. Canadians must think about this brutal question now. Not only think about solving it in words, but by deeds, and through their attitudes ... The country will only remain united – it should only remain united – if its citizens want to live together in one civil society.'

The Quebec that the Parti Québécois took over in November 1976 contained about 4.5 million French Canadians and just over one million English-speaking Canadians. That 4.5 million was equal to the population of six provinces put together – Newfoundland, Prince Edward Island, Nova Scotia, New Brunswick, Manitoba, and Saskatchewan. Another 1.5 million French-speaking people lived in other parts of Canada. But 6 million French-speaking people were less than three per cent of the English-speaking population of North America. The fact that so small a French minority survived and flourished in North America has been called in Quebec 'the miracle of survival'.

Small cities and towns of Quebec like Granby, St. Jean, or Chicoutimi looked typically North American, but there was a difference. About ninety-nine per cent of the people in those places lived in French. French was taken for granted as being

Montreal, old and new.

perfectly normal. There were no great conflicts between the English and French here. The few English students in the area were bused to English schools.

However, Montreal presented a much different case. It was here that the two cultures, English and French Canadian, often faced each other and clashed. In the city itself there were 1 200 000 Francophones (French-speaking) and 800 000 of English origin. It was a 60-40 split that made Montreal a lively and enriching place. Until the mid-1970s visitors could come to Montreal, and, apart from some French signs or voices, not realize they were in the second largest French-speaking city in the world. In the eyes of many French Montrealers, that was an insult long endured. The Parti Québécois was determined to make the atmosphere of Montreal more French.

Most of Quebec's English-speaking citizens lived in Montreal. It was said that it was possible and common for English Montrealers to have no real contact with French Montrealers. The English lived in separate neighbourhoods, went to different schools, and attended the English university, McGill. To complicate the problem, most of the immigrants who settled in Montreal chose to join the English-speaking community. They wanted to send their children to English schools because English was the language of North America. And so in the largest city of the province a traditional gulf existed between the two language groups.

Another cause of grievance was that many Québécois believed all the English in the province were rich. They imagined that all the English lived in luxurious mansions in well-off neighbourhoods like Westmount. A popular French-Canadian song spoke of '*les anglais dans les chateaux sur la montagne*' (the English in the castles on the mountain). The French, by comparison, lived at the bottom of the hill in poorer districts of Montreal, such as St. Henri. This picture of Quebec society was not completely true. There were French who lived in splendid homes in places like Laval-sur-le-lac, and there were English who were far from being rich living in places like Point-St. Charles. However, there was an element of truth in this economic grievance. Figures produced in 1970 showed that the average salary for English Canadians in Quebec was $7900. French Quebeckers were at the bottom of the scale, with an average of $6000. To be sure, the gap between French and English salaries had narrowed by twenty-three per cent since 1960. That trend continued during the 1970s, but the gap still existed and the Parti Québécois was determined to do something about the reality of the richer English and the poorer French.

Closely connected to this was the old economic grievance that the bosses were English and the workers were French. If you were French and you wanted to get ahead economically in Quebec, you had to be able to speak English. If you were English, you could be successful in business without knowing a word of French. Again the 1970 average income figures proved that there was a certain amount of truth to this charge. English-speaking Montrealers who did not speak French were at the top of the income scale at $7250. French Montrealers who were not fluent in English were at the bottom of the scale with an average of $5100. In second place were the bilingual Anglophones (English-speaking), and in third place were bilingual Francophones.

In 1972 the Gendron Commission carried out a massive inquiry into all aspects of language use in Quebec. It showed that English was the language of top jobs and promotion in Quebec business. For example, in the Royal Bank of Canada, based in Montreal, only five of its top eighty-five management jobs were held by French Canadians. The government has made a serious effort since then to increase the use of French in private industry to make sure that more French Canadians are given management positions.

An incident occurred in 1976 that illustrated the deep divisions in Quebec over the two official languages. The federal government decided to introduce bilingualism in air and ground communications in all Quebec airports. Up to that time air traffic controllers used French only at five small provincial airports. English-speaking pilots across Canada went on strike protesting the new policy. They argued that English is the universal language of the International Civil Aviation Organization (I.C.A.O.). For safety's sake, they argued, English should be used. Many Canadians supported the English-speaking pilots' point of view. On the other hand, French-speaking pilots maintained that the I.C.A.O. approves the use of English as well as the language usually used at the airport. For nine days English-speaking pilots refused to fly and Canada's air service was paralyzed. The federal government backed down and appointed a commission to report on whether the two languages could be used safely in flight communications. But the damage had been done. French Canadians took the strike as a personal and public insult. Once again their language seemed to be under attack by English Canadians. The commission later reported, after months of study, that flying into bilingual airports in Quebec was no more dangerous than flying into other airports. But the report came out too late. Because of that incident, many French Canadian Quebeckers gave up on Confederation. As René Lévesque himself admitted, this incident helped win tens of thousands of votes for the Parti Québécois.

The P.Q. took steps to do something about the language issue by passing the controversial Bill 101. This bill went even further than Bourassa's language legislation, Bill 22. French was confirmed as the only official language of the province. No business could display a sign in a language other than French. The Quebec agriculture ministry seized and destroyed more than 15 000 unilingual English containers from six Montreal-area Dunkin' Donut Stores. French was made the language of business and commerce. Doctors and nurses lost jobs in hospitals because they could not speak French fluently. Probably the most controversial section of the bill concerned the language of education. Immigrants and all future immigrants to Quebec would not be allowed to send their children to English-speaking state schools. This was particularly resented. It meant that immigrants from the United States, Britain, and all parts of Europe coming into Quebec would be forced to educate their children in French. English-language schools would be allowed to continue in Quebec. They would be limited to children already enrolled in the English system or to children having at least one parent who received his or her elementary education in an English school in Quebec.

Anglophones in Quebec were dismayed with the new language charter. Some businesses announced that they were having difficulty in getting employees with school-age children to accept transfers to their Montreal offices. Under Bill 101, families of English-Canadian businessmen transferred temporarily to Quebec would be compelled to send their children to French schools.

The Task Force on Unity commented on this issue as follows:

We firmly believe that children of all Canadian citizens who move to another province should continue to have access to educational services in the language, be it French or English, in which they would have obtained them in their former province of residence. It seems to us to be only just and fair that every French and English person have access to essential health and social services in his or her principal language wherever numbers warrant; the same applies to an accused person in criminal trials. To our mind, these are the basic rights which each province should accord its English or French-speaking minority.

The P.Q. leaders explained that they were protecting their language and culture just as the Canadian government was taking steps to protect Canada from being swamped by the American culture. Those businesses that left the province were accused by the P.Q. of practising economic blackmail.

The Parti Québécois stressed the importance of gaining independence for Quebec. But despite their election victory in 1976, polls showed that only a small minority of Quebeckers wanted full independence from Canada. Most people seemed to draw back from asking for a complete break. Perhaps they feared that they would be swamped economically, culturally, and politically if they had to share the North American continent with the United States and Canada. Opinion surveys right through the 1970s have consistently shown that less than twenty per cent of Quebeckers favoured independence. However, as many as eighty-four per cent said they wanted some kind of change.

Lévesque was not able to move far ahead of public opinion. For one thing, he promised that his government would hold a referendum before making any move toward independence. He said he would abide by the results of the referendum even if independence was rejected. Lévesque told the Canadian Jewish Congress, 'Whatever is going to happen is going to happen as democratically as we have acted the last ten years ... We will do our best to win that referendum. But if we lose, it goes without saying that we'll respect that decision.' Some other senior P.Q. members have since disagreed with the Premier. They have said that referendums would continue to be held until an affirmative vote is achieved.

OPTIONS FOR THE FUTURE OF QUEBEC

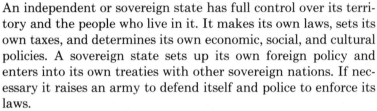

At the time of the writing of this book, there seem to be three main options for Quebec:
1. complete independence,
2. sovereignty-association with Canada, and
3. a renewed federalism.

An Independent Quebec Nation

An independent or sovereign state has full control over its territory and the people who live in it. It makes its own laws, sets its own taxes, and determines its own economic, social, and cultural policies. A sovereign state sets up its own foreign policy and enters into its own treaties with other sovereign nations. If necessary it raises an army to defend itself and police to enforce its laws.

Independence for Quebec is not a simple affair. Hundreds of problems would come up over sharing and ownership. They would include territory, finance, economics, powers, and division of assets. But before these could be solved, there would be constitutional problems to iron out. *Could Quebec legally leave Canada? Would Canadians have to agree to Quebec separation?*

One of Canada's top authorities on the Canadian constitution is Senator Eugene Forsey. Forsey claims that no province has the legal right to secede from Canada. The British North America Act would have to be changed by the British Parliament. Forsey believes that Parliament in Britain would not do this until it was absolutely sure that the government of Canada and all the provinces of Canada had a chance to be consulted.

Senator Forsey suggests that no Canadian government would even begin to negotiate independence for Quebec until it had held its own vote (referendum) in that province. Ottawa might even refuse to negotiate until it had submitted the whole question to all Canadians in a general election. Suppose the Quebec and Canadian governments managed to agree on the details of separation – even then the Canadian government might decide to submit the agreement for approval to the whole Canadian nation.

Many English-speaking participants who came before the Task Force on Unity argued that Quebec could not leave Confederation without consulting the rest of Canada. Premier Davis of Ontario presented a viewpoint along this line. He told the commissioners, 'It is utterly unrealistic to argue that for Quebeckers the only issue is the determination of their own future.

Protesters in Quebec.

No such fundamental decision can be taken without profoundly affecting us all.'

There are, of course, other opinions. A Winnipeg lawyer suggests that Quebec separation would not affect other provinces' constitutions, or the division of powers between them and the federal government.

Many citizens hold that the people of Quebec have the right to determine their own destiny. They recall how Newfoundland came into Confederation in 1949. The people of Newfoundland decided in a referendum that they wished to join Canada. No national referendum was held in the rest of Canada. If the people of a region can decide to *enter* Confederation, the people of Quebec should be allowed by a referendum to vote to *leave* Confederation.

Some citizens argue that Canada must abide by the Charter of the United Nations. The U.N. charter guarantees nations the right to determine their own future. Canada supports that right in the Third World. Can we now deny it to Quebec? Nearly all French-speaking Canadians live on Quebec soil. An independent Quebec would be better off economically than many member states of the U.N. Its vast territory would make Quebec 18th in size among 150 nations, and its population would place it in the first 55 states.

But this argument also has another side. Some citizens before the Task Force on Unity pointed out that if French-speaking Quebec has the right to self-determination, then so do the Inuit. The Inuit in the northern part of the province have said repeatedly that they do not want to be citizens of an independent Quebec. The area in which they live was not a part of Quebec when it joined Confederation in 1867. The government of Canada could challenge the right of an independent Quebec to that territory.

A break between Canada and Quebec might not be without violence. A few Anglophones in Montreal have already said that they are ready to call on the Canadian Armed Forces or even volunteers to defend their right to be part of Canada. *If civil war broke out in Quebec, would English-speaking people in Canada be prepared to go to the defence of the English minority in Quebec?*

If Quebec became an independent nation, where would its boundaries be located? Would an agreement be made to provide a land link connecting Atlantic Canada and the rest of the country? Who would control the St. Lawrence Seaway which is jointly owned with the United States? Then there is the matter of what would be done with northern Quebec. In 1912 the federal government gave Ungava, which was part of the Northwest Territories, to Quebec. Canada would probably demand that this territory be given back. Similarly in 1927 Britain's highest court, the Privy Council, awarded Labrador to Newfoundland. Newfoundland has already indicated that it is determined to hold on to its mainland territory. Quebec outside Confederation might have to accept very different boundaries than it has today. It could be limited to the boundaries that Lower Canada had when it joined Confederation in 1867. This would exclude the site of the present James Bay Power Project, as well as vast mineral and forest resources.

Sovereignty-Association with Canada

Lévesque says he wants a Quebec that is independent or sovereign, but closely joined to Canada in a kind of common market. Quebec would have its own citizenship and immigration laws, which Lévesque regards as essential to preserve the French culture. However, Quebec and Canada would have a common trade policy with the same tariffs and rules, and possibly the same currency. Lévesque calls this sovereignty-association. On 25 January 1977 Lévesque outlined this idea to a group of prominent

American bankers at the Economic Club in New York. 'This new partnership could take the form, essentially, of a common market based on a customs union, permitting free passage of persons, goods, and capital, as in the countries of Western Europe. Additionally, if the desire is mutual, we are ready to go further, as far as monetary union (use of the same currency).'

It is important to note that official policy of the Parti Québécois has not always agreed with Lévesque's idea of sovereignty-association.

In a speech to the Quebec Parliament, Lévesque said, 'There will be no question of gaining our independence and then asking for association. We will negotiate the two at the same time: sovereignty and association with the rest of Canada.' The referendum will probably be built around this idea of sovereignty-association.

This in itself immediately raises questions. A province can demand independence all by itself, but it takes two sides to negotiate. There is no certainty that the federal government would be willing to negotiate sovereignty-association for Quebec, or that the other provinces will let it. There has already been some indication that the provinces will not. Some provincial premiers have said if Quebec becomes independent, they do not necessarily want an economic union with it. Premier Blakeney of Saskatchewan has said, 'If Quebec decided to separate, we would have to ask ourselves what advantages there would be in maintaining links with a Quebec which is unwilling to continue supporting a federal government, but which would continue to benefit from our tariff structure. I cannot imagine very many in Saskatchewan being interested in such a proposition.'

The federal government is issuing a series of reports written by a team of economists. The reports concluded that sovereignty-association would not be profitable for the rest of Canada. They also warned that Quebec is much more dependent on the rest of Canada for its manufactured goods than the rest of Canada is on Quebec. The Ottawa experts say that the separation of Quebec would cause economic hardships for all the provinces. But the impact on Quebec would be particularly severe. Quebec is heavily dependent on sales to the rest of Canada, and therefore hundreds of thousands of jobs in Quebec could be at stake.

Shipments of manufactured goods, 1974

From Quebec to the rest of Canada (29.8%)

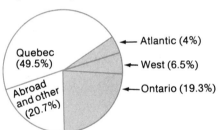

Quebec (49.5%)

Abroad and other (20.7%)

Atlantic (4%)

West (6.5%)

Ontario (19.3%)

From Ontario to Quebec — 11.2%

From the Atlantic region to Quebec — 9.0%

Lévesque has dismissed this as federal propaganda. He believes that the provinces of Canada will negotiate with an independent Quebec because it will be in their own interests to do so. Experts on Lévesque's team maintain that it will cost Canada dearly if its provinces do not have an economic association with Quebec. 'Just for instance,' says Lévesque, 'at least 100 000 jobs in Ontario depend immediately on the Quebec market.'

Aside from how Quebec and the rest of Canada could weather the split up of the country, a number of other issues must be solved. Here are a few examples. *How would the assets and debts of the federal government be divided between an independent Quebec and the rest of Canada?* The Parti Québécois has suggested that assets could be divided on the basis of population and personal income. Quebec's share would be about twenty-seven per cent. However, one Quebec minister has already warned that Quebec might not pay any share of Canada's war debts or debts to build special projects in other provinces.

Dividing up the assets of Canadian National Railways and Air Canada, for example, would be extremely complicated. Settling Quebec's share of the St. Lawrence Seaway or federal properties in Canada or overseas would involve long and bitter negotiating.

How would the currency issue be resolved? Would Quebec have its own currency? Or, would it be possible, as Lévesque has suggested, for Quebec and Canada to have a joint currency and a central bank? This question is of critical importance. Until it is decided, the value of the Canadian dollar will be uncertain in the eyes of the world.

Then there are questions about manpower. *Would Quebeckers be allowed to come into Canada to work?* What would happen to the employees of large Canadian companies whose head offices are in Montreal? Would they be permitted to work in Quebec?

These are just some of the questions that would have to be worked out if the sovereignty-association option between Canada and Quebec is chosen.

A Changed Federal System of Government

No matter which political party is in power in Quebec, the independence issue will not go away. A whole generation of students in Quebec is being taught by teachers who are often filled with the separatist spirit. Many of these students will believe deeply in separatism. But perhaps independence is not inevitable. Lévesque himself has said, 'It is not a question of ending our relationship with the rest of Canada, but of transforming it radically.'

Even those people in Quebec opposed to separation say that things cannot remain as they are. An organization called the Positive Action Committee was formed in Quebec to fight separatism. That committee has warned Canadians outside Quebec that change must come and come fast if Canada is not only to survive, but to flourish.

Quebec is not alone in wanting to change the relationship of the provinces to the federal government. Many English-speaking Canadians are also critical of the way our political system has been working. According to the Task Force on Canadian Unity,

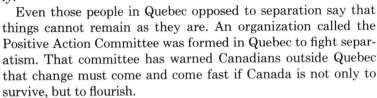

Although the B.N.A. Act has served Canada well for 111 years, in a variety of changing circumstances unforeseen by the Fathers of Confederation, and although there have been numerous slight adjustments over the years, there is a growing gap between the structure created in 1867, and the social, economic, and political realities of the vastly different Canada of 1979. *We believe therefore that there should be a new Canadian constitution to meet the aspirations and future needs of all the people of Canada.*

Canadian provinces other than Quebec also want more political powers for themselves. The western provinces are demanding more control over their natural resources. Alberta wants to set its own price for Alberta oil, not Ottawa. Ontario and Atlantic Canada likewise have complaints. Ontario talks about wanting to control cable television. It would like to be able to put up trade barriers on goods from other provinces that compete with Ontario products. Atlantic Canada insists that oil found off its coasts belongs to the provinces and not to all of Canada. Atlantic Canada thinks it deserves more say in transportation decisions affecting its ports and railways.

There are moves underway to give Canada a new constitution and replace the B.N.A. Act of 1867. If a new Canadian constitution could be worked out, it might still be possible to persuade Quebec to remain part of Canada. The new constitution would have to recognize the partnership between the French and English in the history of Canada and the distinctiveness of Quebec. It would also have to give much greater power to all the provinces to run their own affairs. This suggestion is sometimes called the 'third option.' It is a way of preserving Canada as a nation that includes Quebec. At the same time it is a way of satisfying the various groups within the country.

One of the key features of the third option is a new division of powers between the federal and provincial governments. One way of re-assigning the powers of these governments has been suggested by the Task Force on Unity. The chief roles and responsibilities of the central government should be:

- to strengthen the Canadian identity and pride in Canada;
- to defend Canada and keep it secure;
- to be responsibile for dealings with foreign nations;
- to plan for the economic development of all regions of Canada;
- to make certain that people in all parts of Canada have equal economic opportunities and an adequate standard of living.

The chief roles and responsibilities of the provincial governments should be:

- to have control over the social and cultural well-being of their citizens (education, health, social services, and immigration);
- to be responsible for provincial economic affairs, including the development of natural resources and trade within the province;
- to have responsibility over property and civil rights (provincial justice, urban affairs, marriage and divorce, housing and land use, and the environment);
- to manage their own provincial territory;

In addition Quebec should have full power to preserve and strengthen its French heritage in its own territory.

The ideas of the Task Force are one suggestion about the division of federal and provincial powers. Other people will have their own ideas. But any division of powers must consider the fact that Canada has changed greatly since the B.N.A. Act was accepted in 1867.

Will there be a future for Canada? Or, more accurately, will Quebec separate? What will happen if Quebec does separate? What will the new confederation be like if Quebec does not separate? These are the questions that dominate any discussion about the future of Canada. The answers to these questions will not be decided in Quebec alone. Much will depend on English Canada. The questions asked more than ten years ago by the Bi and Bi Commission are still valid. *Can English and French Canadians live together, and do they want to live together?* If they do, under what conditions are they prepared to do so? Now is the time for all Canadians to think about the answers to these questions.

Read and think about the following student's comment on Canadian unity. It was written by Connie Corner, a grade 11 student at an Ottawa high school.

FORUM

CANADIAN UNITY: THE TIME TO THINK ABOUT IT IS NOW

BY CONNIE CORNER

Canadian unity. We are forever hearing about the situation in Quebec: on television, the radio, in newspapers and magazines and even on our city streets. Having lived in both Quebec and Ontario, I have had the opportunity to experience the various thoughts and feelings of students in each province.

I am an English Canadian and I had always lived in English speaking communities in Quebec. It was not often that I was faced with speaking French because I did not often meet French people. Perhaps the milkman would be French, or the woman who worked at

the dry-cleaners, but otherwise I seldom met Francophones.

Although I went to French immersion schools for two years, I was still with my English friends and we spoke very little French amongst ourselves. Even though I studied more French in grades eight and nine, I never spoke in French because there was no need to when I lived in a basically English town. Nevertheless, at times my friends and I were involved in some French Canadian festivities such as St. John Baptiste Day. On these occasions, we enjoyed ourselves immensely. The French

Canadian culture is fascinating and their "*joie de vivre*" is irresistible and contagious.

Aside from such events, however, we had very little contact with Francophones. With so little exposure, we were not overly conscious or concerned with the issue of Canadian unity. However, we could not totally ignore it. Especially as it became increasingly noticeable that many of our close friends and their families were moving to other provinces. We also could not help but realize that it was our parents who were being affected; therefore, we were being affected. We also realized that once we left high school, we would have to seriously consider the possibility of going to university or seeking employment outside of Quebec because of language legislation and lack of job opportunities.

There were various attitudes toward Canadian unity amongst my friends in Quebec. At times we would be bitter that the *Parti Québécois* was upsetting our lives; occasionally some of my friends would make caustic remarks about René Lévesque. In general however, we took it in our stride. I was very happy living in Quebec. I was content to live from day to day with my friends in a city I loved.

In September 1977, my parents and I relocated in Ottawa, Ontario, although the move had nothing to do with the unity situation. I have been in Ottawa for almost a year now

attending an English school. At first, some students, upon hearing that I came from Quebec, would remark about those "French frogs" and ask me if I was one of them, or they would make other such derogatory comments. The first couple of weeks at school, I got very angry. I wanted to tell them that they were just being ignorant and knew nothing about the situation. Eventually I learned to ignore them and soon their talk died down. These people, however, were the exception.

Many of my confrères in Ottawa know very little about the situation in Quebec and yet they have a decidedly negative attitude toward the French. I often wonder if these students are influenced by their parents' thoughts and maybe even their prejudices. Perhaps also, they are influenced by the media and some of its biased reporting.

The majority of my classmates however, say nothing about Canadian unity. Many of them do not seem to care one way or the other what becomes of Quebec. If, however, the present condition results in separation then everyone will be very much concerned.

It is my impression that most high school students in Canada, not just those in Quebec and Ontario, do not realize the full importance of Canadian unity. There is no understanding of the problem. In the future, we will be affected and we will have to seriously think about Canadian unity and form our own educated opinions on the issue. We should start to understand now and not be influenced by others. After all, our decisions will help in forming our own future.

What do you think?

1. Do you think it is important to speak both of Canada's official languages?   yes ☐   no ☐

2. Would Quebec's economic situation be improved if it separates from Canada?   yes ☐   no ☐

3. Would Quebec's separation from Canada hurt the economy of your province?   yes ☐   no ☐

4. Will the other provinces of Canada stay together if Quebec separates?   yes ☐   no ☐

5. Should the government of Canada hold a national vote on Quebec independence?   yes ☐   no ☐

6. Should Ottawa use force if Quebec tries to separate?   yes ☐   no ☐

7. Are you in favour of sovereignty-association between an independent Quebec and Canada?   yes ☐   no ☐

8. Do you favour increasing the powers of the provinces?   yes ☐   no ☐

9. In a new constitution, do you think Quebec should have powers the other provinces do not have?   yes ☐   no ☐

10. Do you want Quebec to remain as part of Canada?   yes ☐   no ☐

HOLD A POLL

Hold a poll in your school or neighbourhood. Let your friends mark a ballot like this one, or add other questions to make up your own. Analyse and discuss the results your class collects.

A 1978 national poll found that sixty-three per cent of Canadians felt it was important to speak both languages. In Quebec the figure was ninety-three per cent.

The French Canadians Outside Quebec

According to the 1971 census, more than 1 400 000 French Canadians lived outside the province of Quebec. Though Canada became officially bilingual in 1969, the French outside Quebec feared that their culture was in danger of becoming extinct. The 1978 report, *Heirs of Lord Durham*, drew attention to the difficulties in keeping the French culture alive outside Quebec. Some of the problems were:

- assimilation (being absorbed into the English culture);
- decline of the French language outside Quebec;
- decline of the French culture as more people moved from smaller French communities into larger cities;
- fear that if Quebec separated, the bitterness in the rest of Canada would mark the end of any special rights for French Canadians.

Ontario

- the 1971 population of French origin: 737 360
- these people lived mainly in northern Ontario, the Ottawa-Carlton area, southwestern Ontario, and the eastern Ontario counties
- the population speaking French in the home: 352 465

What the Ontario government has done about bilingualism:

- For ten years French-language education has been possible when the parents of twenty-five elementary or secondary school children ask their local school board for it. More than 100 000 Ontario students are now enrolled in French-language classes or schools.

- Letters in French to the government are answered in French.
- All forms used by the public are being issued in English and French and more and more government publications are being printed in both languages.
- Signs on government buildings will become bilingual.

Franco-Ontarians complained that it was not always possible to get a French school built. For example, in the Windsor area, French Canadians had demanded a highschool for ten years. The predominantly English school board opposed the building of the school. Finally in 1977 the province of Ontario forced the school board to build the school.

FRENCH CANADIAN CULTURE ALIVE AND WELL IN TORONTO

100 000 FRENCH-SPEAKING RESIDENTS

- 2 French-speaking churches
- 10 elementary schools
- public highschools
- bilingual Glendon College, York University
- weekly newspaper
- television and radio station
- French theatres, restaurants, bookstores, cultural centres

Atlantic Canada

	1971 POPULATION OF FRENCH ORIGIN	POPULATION SPEAKING FRENCH IN THE HOME
Newfoundland	15 410	2 295
Prince Edward Island	15 325	4 410
Nova Scotia	80 220	27 215
New Brunswick	235 025	199 085

- areas where the French lived in Atlantic Canada

Newfoundland – along the western shore and in isolated central areas.

Prince Edward Island – the southwestern part of the island near Summerside.

Nova Scotia – in pockets along coastal areas.

New Brunswick – in areas along the Quebec border, across northern New Brunswick, and along the shores of the Bay of Chaleur, the Gulf of St. Lawrence, and the Northumberland Strait.

Le Parti Acadien

Canada's newest political party was organized in 1972 in those parts of New Brunswick where the French population ranges from fifty to ninety per cent. Le Parti Acadien is concerned with the loss of cultural identity and the economic problems faced by many French in New Brunswick. They claim that the traditional political parties neglected them. In February 1978 a bomb exploded in a federal government building in St. Quentin. A note at the scene threatened, 'This is the first warning to the federal and provincial governments to take seriously the demands of the Acadians.'

Economics

The feeling has long been strong in New Brunswick that the English were bosses and the French were workers. A survey in the *Globe and Mail* in 1977 revealed that two-thirds of the 575 workers at Consolidated Bathurst were French-speaking. However, the language of business was English. Collective agreements were printed only in English. Of 49 people in supervisory jobs, only 14 were French-speaking.

New Brunswick

New Brunswick is the only official bilingual province, guaranteeing education and court proceedings in the French language.

Western Canada

	1971 POPULATION OF FRENCH ORIGIN	POPULATION SPEAKING FRENCH IN THE HOME
Manitoba	86 510	29 600
Saskatchewan	56 200	15 935
Alberta	96 665	22 695
British Columbia	96 550	11 510

- Across the West, towns with French names are evidence of early French settlement: Dauphin, St. Boniface, Gravelbourg, Morinville, and Maillardville. Survival, however, has not been easy. One hundred years ago, for example, Francophones were in the majority in Saskatchewan. In 1971, they made up only six per cent of Saskatchewan's population. Many of the French Canadians in western Canada have never even been to Quebec.

- One of the major complaints of French Canadians in the West concerned getting services using the French language. A man in Ponteix, Saskatchewan tried to call long distance to Gravelbourg, Saskatchewan, sixty-four kilometres away. Even though these two towns are French communities, there was no French-speaking operator! The operator had to call Montreal, and the Montreal operator translated for her so she could call Gravelbourg for the customer.
- French-speaking people in western Canada complained that being surrounded by English-speaking people and English radio and television made it particularly difficult for their children to retain the French language. In Alberta a study was done on students between ten and eighteen attending bilingual schools. An astonishing fifty-one per cent said they never or rarely spoke French to their friends.

Questions:

1. Debate:
   Because Canada is a bilingual country, students should demonstrate the ability to speak both English and French before receiving a high school graduation diploma.

2. Do you think it is important for the French culture to thrive in Canada outside Quebec? Why?

3. Roleplay. Divide the class into three groups – Francophones outside Quebec, English-speaking people, and Italians (or another cultural group common to your area). Let the group discuss the pros and cons of bilingualism in your region of Canada. Should the English be forced to learn French? Should Italians be given equal status with French? Should the French be forced to learn English? What other problems of bilingualism do you see?

Digging Deeper

1

a) Suppose your family had to move to Quebec because your mother or father was transferred there. Under Bill 101, would you be allowed to continue your education in an English-language school? Do you feel this is fair? Explain your answer.

b) A French-speaking family from Quebec has just been transferred into your community. Are French schools available for the children to continue their education? Find out what education, health, and court facilities are available in your community for the French-speaking minority. Do you feel this is fair? Explain your answer.

c) Compare the treatment of the French-Canadian minority in your province and the English-speaking minority in the province of Quebec.

2

Explain why many immigrants to Quebec prefer to send their children to English schools.

3

Why is a person's language important? Why did the province of Quebec feel it was so necessary to protect the French language?

4

Roleplay: You are one of the following persons. Explain the reasons why you would or would not support the Parti Québécois in the election of 1976.

a) manager of an American branch plant based in Montreal;

b) a recent Italian immigrant with school-age children;

c) an English-speaking Quebecker;

d) a middle-class French-speaking businesswoman;

e) a French-speaking university student;

f) a person held for eight days by the police during the F.L.Q. crisis (1970).

5

Three language groups live in harmony in Switzerland. Do some research to explain the Swiss success. Compare Switzerland's political, geographic, and language situation with Canada's.

39

THE BEAVER AND THE ELEPHANT: CANADIAN-AMERICAN RELATIONS

CANADIAN INDENTITY?

THURSDAY, NOV. 10, 1977

'Living next door to the United States,' said Prime Minister Trudeau, 'is like sleeping in the same bed as an elephant. No matter how friendly and even-tempered is the beast, one is affected by every twitch and grunt.' If the elephant rolls over in its sleep, the Canadian 'beaver' must be ready to jump. Nine times out of ten the elephant and beaver get along very well together. Once in a while, however, the elephant gets a little grumpy, or the beaver feels threatened. When this happens these oddly-matched neighbours sit down and talk together about their problems. In many ways the comparison made by Trudeau was a good one. The United States is certainly a giant – the richest and most powerful nation in the world. It has ten times our population and economic production. As a military power the United States greatly overshadows Canada.

The American superpower is Canada's nearest neighbour. In fact Canada shares a border with only one foreign power, the United States. Almost seventy per cent of our trade is with the United States and more than seventy per cent of foreign investment in Canada is made by Americans. Of course the United States is Canada's most important military ally through our NORAD and NATO agreements.

As Canada entered its second century, many people became increasingly alarmed over the amount of control the American 'elephant' had on our lives. Our economy, our foreign policy, and our culture were each affected by the twitches and grunts of the United States.

The American Influence on the Canadian Economy

As a young country Canada welcomed foreign investment. First it was British money that got the wheels of industry started in Canada. Gradually more and more American money poured into Canada to keep the wheels turning. Throughout the 1950s and early 1960s, most Canadians thought foreign investment was of great and unquestionable benefit. But by the early 1970s, Canadians discovered just how much of their economy was owned by foreign investors, especially Americans. Several government studies made at this time made Canadians more aware of the seriousness of the situation (The Watkins Report of 1968, the Wahn Report of 1970, and the Gray Report of 1971). Many Canadians became concerned about how much control the Americans did have over our economy. It was felt by some that if this trend continued Canada would reach a point of no return. These people were known as 'economic nationalists'. They believed that Canada could not go on selling its resources and industries to foreigners without eventually losing political independence as well. They wanted the economy run by Canadians for Canadians. Otherwise not only the economy, but also Canada's cultural identity, would become completely dominated by the United States.

On the other hand, a large number of Canadians favoured American investment in Canada. They pointed out that the Americans were willing to invest their money in businesses in Canada when many Canadians were not prepared to take the risk. The high standard of living many Canadians enjoyed was one of the benefits of having American investment in our economy. Those who favoured American investment often lived in Atlantic Canada and the West. They were prepared to welcome even more American investment into Canada.

How serious a situation is foreign ownership in Canada? Facts about American investment in Canada are now well known. Since this information has been made public, Canadians have debated the pros and cons of foreign investment in our country. Newspapers conducted polls to find out how Canadians felt about American investment in Canada. People who believed that American investment was a good thing for Canada felt that it:

1. created thousands of jobs for Canadians;
2. provided money to help develop Canadian resources and industries when Canadians were unwilling to take the risk to do it;
3. helped raise the standard of living in Canada to almost the same high level as the United States;
4. brought advanced technical knowledge and machinery into Canada;
5. American-owned companies paid taxes to the Canadian government;
6. gave business to Canadian-owned companies;
7. profited Canadians who bought shares in American-owned businesses;
8. provided Canadians with a greater variety and the highest quality of manufactured goods;
9. made for friendly relations between Canada and the United States.

People who believed that American investment was a bad thing for Canada, such as the economic nationalists, felt that it:

1. led to American takeover of Canadian economy (Canadians should have control over their own economy);
2. made profits leave the country and go to the United States;
3. made top jobs often go to Americans;

4. took Canada's natural resources out of the country for processing. Canada had to buy back the resources as expensive manufactured goods.
5. made us more 'American' in our tastes and production methods;
6. discouraged technological advances in Canada (it was easier to borrow technological advances from the Americans);
7. caused key decisions about expanding or shutting down a plant to be made outside the country;
8. sometimes restricted the trade of Canadian branch plants with countries considered unacceptable by the United States (an example is Cuba);
9. brought American-based unions into Canada.

Question:
1. Which reasons seem to you to be the most serious? Why?

Case Study: The Denison Mines Case

In 1970 much of Canada's uranium was controlled by foreign-owned companies. Canada possessed some of the richest uranium fields in the world. Denison Mines Limited of Toronto controlled about forty per cent of the known reserves of uranium in Canada. The rest of Canada's uranium was owned by foreign companies. It became known in 1970 that Stephen B. Roman planned to sell his stocks in Denison Mines to an American firm, the Continental Oil Company of Delaware. This sale would have left less than ten per cent of Canada's uranium resources in Canadian hands. Therefore the Canadian government took action to block the sale. Trudeau surprised the business community by announcing that uranium was too important a resource to be controlled by foreigners. The government took further steps to limit foreign ownership of the uranium industry to thirty-three per cent or less. At least two-thirds of the shares of the uranium companies must be owned by Canadians.

Roman was amazed and upset by the government action. He claimed that he needed the money from the Denison Mines sale for his other investments. He said that the government was discriminating against him while allowing foreign interests to control other Canadian resources. He even tried to sue the Prime Minister and the Minister of Energy for damages in the amount of $104 million. The Ontario Supreme Court, however, dismissed Roman's

≫→

case, saying that the government was acting in the 'best interests of Canada'.

The economic nationalists were happy with the Denison Mines decision. They said it showed what the government could do about foreign ownership. However, the government did not continue this policy of strong action. Foreigners continued to buy Canadian industries as well as land and resources.

What Has the Canadian Government Done to Control Foreign Investment in the Economy?

1. Foreign Investment Review Agency 1974

This agency was set up to screen foreign investment coming into Canada. Any takeover of a Canadian company or the starting of a foreign-owned business must first be approved by this agency. The government emphasized that the agency was not trying to block foreign investment, or to discourage it. Its purpose, however, was to make sure that the foreign investment would be a significant benefit to Canada. The agency would ask such questions as:

- *Will the takeover provide jobs for Canadians?*
- *Will there be additional exports?*
- *Will it improve production and industrial efficiency?*
- *Will Canadians be involved as shareholders and managers?*
- *Will this investment be a good thing for Canada?*

In its first year of operation the F.I.R.A. examined eighty bids by foreigners to take over Canadian companies. Eleven of the bids were turned down.

Some business leaders and provincial governments were worried that the F.I.R.A. might cut off the flow of much-needed foreign money into the country. The provinces were afraid that the government might cut off foreign development of resource industries. Therefore the provinces pressed Ottawa to have a say in the review of future investors from outside Canada.

2. Canada Development Corporation 1972

As early as 1963, Walter Gordon, Finance Minister of the Pearson government, had suggested setting up the Canada Development Corporation. It was almost ten years later before the idea was carried out. The C.D.C. was given $250 million by the government to invest in Canadian businesses. It also raised money by selling shares in the C.D.C. to the Canadian people. With the money, the C.D.C. has invested in private Canadian companies in petrochemicals, mining, gas pipelines, and pharmaceutical products. Thus the C.D.C. helps to develop and maintain strong companies controlled and managed by Canadians.

3. Special Laws

The federal and provincial governments have passed specific laws regarding foreign ownership of certain important industries. For example, no more than twenty-five per cent of Canadian banks can be owned by non-Canadians. Only companies with at least eight per cent Canadian ownership can be granted television or radio broadcasting licences. Direct government participation in rail and air transportation, nuclear energy, and Arctic oil and gas exploration is another way of maintaining Canadian control in important economic areas. The government of Saskatchewan took steps to buy back American-owned potash mines in the province. Potash is used in fertilizer, and one of the world's largest deposits of potash is in Saskatchewan. Since 1976 the government-owned Potash Corporation of Saskatchewan (P.C.S.) has bought thirty-four per cent of the potash industry in Saskatchewan. In 1971 in Ontario the government granted the book publishers, McClelland and Stewart Limited, a million dollar loan in order to keep the business Canadian-owned. This was done to keep one of the two remaining large Canadian publishing companies under Canadian control.

4. Special Income Tax Deductions

To encourage investment in Canadian-owned industries, citizens were allowed to make an income tax deduction on profits earned in these companies.

The Energy Crisis

In the summer of 1979 many American states faced severe gasoline shortages. Signs saying 'Out of Gas' became a common sight in many service stations. Where there was a supply of gasoline, strict rationing had to be enforced. Lineups at the gas pumps often stretched for blocks as weary motorists waited to buy their $5 limit. Travellers were sometimes stranded on American highways and some trucking companies could not operate their vehicles because of the lack of fuel.

Until the early 1970s, Canada and the United States had taken all forms of energy (oil, gas, electricity, coal) very much for granted. North Americans were the greatest energy consumers in the world, and both Canada and the United States were

"HOWDY NEIGHBOR — YA'LL SPARE A CUP OF ENERGY? "

major energy producers. But in 1973 the Arab oil producers began to limit the export of oil (embargo) and increase its price. At the height of this Arab oil embargo, Canada was shipping 1.3 billion barrels of oil daily to the United States. During this crisis, the Canadian government re-examined its reserves. Canadians were shocked to find out that Canada was not the oil-rich nation we thought it was. Experts predicted that Canadian oil supplies would not be adequate to meet home needs much beyond 1982.

People called continentalists on both sides of the border have argued that Canadian energy resources should be shared with the United States. Since Canada and the United States make up North America, they believed the riches of the continent should be shared. Continentalists also believed in free trade. That is, all goods, including energy, should travel freely over the border without being taxed.

The Canadian government, however, held a different point of view. At the risk of upsetting our American neighbours, the government decided to phase out our oil exports. The export level of oil to the United States was therefore reduced as of January 1975 to 800 000 barrels a day. In 1976 the allowable amount was set at 460 000 barrels daily, and in 1977 it was reduced to 260 000 barrels a day. Americans at first found it hard to adjust to this policy. They were accustomed to importing Canadian oil at low prices. However, gradually they came to understand and accept Canada's export policies. Canada was of course ready to help the United States with energy in times of emergency. During the severe winter of 1976-1977, Canada approved additional exports of oil and gas to the United States on an emergency basis.

An example of co-operation between Canada and the United States in energy resource sharing was the northern gas pipeline agreement of 1977.

After weeks of tough negotiations, Canada and the United States have agreed on a gas pipeline route to bring Arctic natural gas to southern markets in the United States and Canada. Both the National Energy Board in Canada and President Carter in the United States have agreed on the pipeline route beginning at Prudhoe Bay in Alaska. The privately-financed pipeline will wind through Alaska, parts of the Yukon, British Columbia, and Alberta. It will then make its way into the lower forty-eight states. There is the possibility that eventually a spur line (the Demster line) will be built through Dawson to connect to the main pipeline. The Demster line will carry Canadian natural gas from the Mackenzie River delta area. The United States will pay up to a hundred per cent of the cost of the spur line. The builders (Foothills Pipe Lines Limited) will pay property tax to the Yukon of $30 million maximum annually for the life of the pipeline. This tax will pay for any environmental damage done to the land or the livelihood of the native peoples by the construction of the pipeline. Construction will start in the early 1980s. The project will cost around $10 billion.

Co-operation between the United States and Canada will be very much the theme of energy relations in the future.

The Future?

What will Canada's economic relations with the United States be in the future? There seem to be three general approaches suggested by Canadians.

1. Nationalization of the Canadian Economy under Public Ownership

The New Democratic Party has continually drawn the attention of Canadians to the increasing control of our economy by non-Canadians. Some members of the N.D.P. known as the Waffle Group, proposed complete nationalization of foreign-owned businesses in Canada. This means that foreign companies would be taken over directly by the government, or foreign owners would be forced to sell their companies to the government. The more moderate majority of the N.D.P. were not willing to go this far. The radical Waffle arguments were voted down by the N.D.P. It was thought that complete nationalization of our economy would anger the Americans and hurt Canada's trade partnership with the United States.

2. Continentalism

The exact opposite of the Waffle proposal is the suggestion that the economies of Canada and the United States should be more fully merged. This action would involve free trade between the two countries. It would set up a North American Common Market. A poll held in the summer of 1979 found that two out of three Canadians favoured free trade with the United States. Support was strongest in the Atlantic region (73%) and on the prairies (71%). In Ontario and Quebec, and British Columbia the results were slightly lower (66%, 65% and 64% respectively). The chief reasons given by Canadians for supporting free trade were lower prices for consumers and an increased number of jobs for Canadians.

3. Government Control to Check Foreign Takeovers and Increase Canadian Ownership

Somewhere between the two points of view – nationalization and continentalism – is a third approach. This plan suggests limiting the amount of foreign ownership allowed in the Canadian economy. The Committee for an Independent Canada was founded in 1970 by several prominent Canadians. Its purpose was to put pressure on the government and make Canadians aware of the extent of foreign ownership in Canada. Walter Gordon, the former Finance Minister, was one of the founding members. In an article in the *Toronto Star* in 1977, Gordon presented his point of view. He suggested that Canadians should get control of the thirty-two largest foreign-owned companies in Canada. The government should limit these companies to twenty-five per cent foreign ownership. The companies should be required to sell the remaining seventy-five per cent to Canadians over a ten-year period. Gordon claimed that if Canadians controlled these thirty-two large companies, it would mean that we had independent control over most of our economy. By means of government regulations Canadian investors could buy back these major industries. A large share of the Canadian economy would be restored to Canadian hands.

Which of these three approaches do you think would be best for Canada in the long run? Why? Which do you think is most likely to happen? Why?

Digging Deeper

Who would get more out of continentalism, Canada or the United States? State your reasons.

1

Make a poster to show your point of view on the American influence on the Canadian economy. Use one of the following topics, or one of your own choice.
a) continentalism;
b) nationalization of American-owned companies;
c) buying back Canada from foreigners;
d) American branch plants;
e) Committee for an Independent Canada.

2

The issue of Canada's relationship with the United States has been an important theme in Canadian history. Prepare a timeline outlining this theme historically. Note on the timeline those periods when Canadian-American relations were a critical issue in Canadian history. Indicate on the timeline when Canadian-American relations were friendly and when they were strained.

3

What Canadian natural resources does the United States seem most interested in at the present time? Discuss the reasons for selling resources and for not selling resources to the United States. Draft a policy for the Canadian government to follow with respect to the sale of Canadian resources.

4

Do some research on the Canada-United States Auto Trade Pact signed in 1965. Find out why the pact was set up in the first place, and how it was meant to work. Who benefits most from this pact? Why? In 1977 a special government study made some serious criticisms of the Auto Trade Pact. Try to find out what these criticisms were. You can contact the New Democratic Party to find out where this party stands on this economic agreement.

5

6

Some people have suggested that as a way of strengthening the Canadian economy, individuals and governments should buy Canadian products whenever they are available. How would a 'Buy Canadian' policy benefit the economy? Examine your own buying pattern over the last year. When faced with the choice of a Canadian-made or foreign-made product, which did you choose? Plan a 'Buy Canadian' project to make the whole school aware of what you have discovered.

7

In August 1978 the Canadian Senate published a two-year study of Canadian-American trade relations. A major recommendation was that Canadians should consider a free trade arrangement with the United States. Obtain copies of this report for your class and study the Senate's recommendations.

8

Discuss Trudeau's comment that living next door to the United States is like sleeping with an elephant. Do you think this is an accurate description of the two countries and their relationship?

40
DEVELOPING OUR CANADIAN IDENTITY

How does the United States affect your life? To what extent is your lifestyle influenced by patterns that have been 'made in the U.S.A.'? Do you resent this influence, or do you welcome it? Make a profile of your tastes and attitudes by answering the following questions. The results will help to show you how much the United States influences your life. What do you think the results will show?

Favourite movie of the last year —
Favourite actress —
Favourite actor —
Two favourite television programs —

Favourite television news program —
T.V. channel watched most often —
Radio station listened to most often —
Favourite musical group —
Favourite female singer —
Favourite male singer —
Two favourite magazines —

Favourite professional hockey team —
Favourite professional football team —
Favourite female athlete —
Favourite male athlete —
Most admired political figure, living or dead —
Most admired woman —
Most admired man —
City in North America you would most like to visit —
Place you spent your last vacation —
Favourite breakfast cereal —
Favourite brand of jeans —
Make of family car —

Analyse your responses to the questionnaire.

a) Go through your answers and sort out which are American and which are Canadian.
b) How 'American' is your lifestyle? How do you feel about this? Why?
c) What parts of your lifestyle did your answers reveal you to be 'Canadian'? Suggest possible reasons for this.
d) How 'Americanized' do you think Canadian life is? Suggest reasons for this.
e) Do you think the results of your questionnaire would have been different ten years ago? Do you think they will be different in the future? Explain your answer.

Culture consists of everything that we believe, do, and make. It includes all the ideas, religious beliefs, and knowledge that has been gained through time. It involves everything we create and pass on to future generations. It contains all the things we have made – our technology, buildings, cities, poems, and games. In other words, our culture includes art, music, religion, language, work, play – everything that makes one group of people different from another.

In a Canadian high school literature class, a student was asked to identify Margaret Laurence and Earle Birney, two of Canada's most popular writers. The student replied, 'Never heard of them. They must be Canadian.' This incident tells us a lot about Canada's culture. Nowhere else in the world is the culture of one country so dominated by another as is Canada's by that of the United States.

Consider the following facts that illustrate the American cultural influence on Canada. Three out of every four books and magazines bought in Canada are foreign (mostly American). Only four per cent of the records sold in Canada have Canadian content. Canadian movies in 1978 earned less than two per cent of the total North American movie box office receipts. Three out of every four hours of television watched by Canadians are taken up with American programs.

Now consider the American domination of one aspect of your life – television. Research scientists have estimated that in your first eighteen years you will have watched 20 000 hours of television. This means that before you graduate from high school, you will have spent twice as many hours in front of television sets as you spent in the classroom. If you are typical of Canadians, 15 000 of those hours will be spent watching American programs. To put it another way, for almost three hours of each and every day of your life, you have been exposed to American culture and American values.

Many Canadians argue that they prefer American shows. Of

course, with a population ten times the size of Canada, American producers can afford to spend much more money on television production. Their programs are often slicker and therefore more appealing to the audiences. However, American television can have a tremendous impact on our lives. If we spend most of our time watching American shows, it follows that we will learn more about American society and become more like Americans. Canadians might begin to look on our society as if it were American. American values might become our values. Canadian society might gradually be taken over by the United States. Culturally we could cease to exist as a separate nation.

Canadian nationalists have worried about the effect of American television on Canadian life. The government has already taken steps to tackle the problem. In 1968 the Canadian Radio-Television and Telecommunications Commission (C.R.T.C.) was set up to supervise radio and television broadcasting in Canada. This government agency issued broadcasting licences to Canadian-owned companies. It made sure that sixty per cent of prime time television (6:30-11:00 p.m.) and thirty per cent of AM radio were Canadian in content. Commercials were limited to twelve minutes per hour. Cable television was seen as a major cause of American domination. When cable television moved into an area, people were able to watch more American shows. The number of people watching Canadian shows went down. Since $50 million was being spent by Canadian companies advertising on U.S. border stations, in 1976 the Canadian government took action. They passed a law that stopped Canadian advertisers from deducting from their income tax the cost of advertising on American television.

The electronic media probably had more impact on Canadians than any other form of American influence. Radio and television flooded Canada with American programs and advertising. The C.R.T.C. was the government's attempt to increase the amount of Canadian content in the media.

Joe Clark.

What is the Canadian National Identity?

Foreigners often have trouble distinguishing Canadians from Americans. Yet Canadians travelling overseas do not like to be mistaken for Americans. They usually wear a maple leaf symbol on their jacket or backpack to identify themselves as Canadians. *What makes Canadians different from Americans? What is the Canadian national identity?*

Suppose your school was twinned with a school in a newly-independent nation in Africa. Your principal has asked your class to put together some sort of presentation about Canada that could be sent to the African school. The audio-visual presentation should describe for the Africans what Canada and Canadians are like. You should try to make clear to the Africans how Canadians differ from Americans. You should show some elements of the Canadian national identity. The following comments will help you put together your presentation on the Canadian identity.

The Land: One of the strongest feelings uniting Canadians is the land itself. The vastness and grandeur of the landscape is distinctively Canadian. Although more than half of the population live in cities of over 100 000, the land is still an inescapable influence. Even the city dweller does not have far to travel to get back to the open and rugged beauty of the land.

Tom Thomson and the Group of Seven were the first artists to express in their paintings the Canadian feeling for the land. Their art expressed what many Canadians felt – a sense of belonging to the rugged northern environment we call Canada.

Take a look at the coins and paper currency of Canada and the United States. The Americans have on their money pictures of national heroes, monuments, or symbols of power and authority, such as the eagle with bolts of lightning in its talons. Canadians, on the other hand, picture the land – prairies, mountains, rivers, schooners, moose, and beaver.

Regional Differences: Canada is a large country, one of the world's largest, but nature has subdivided it into many regions. Each of these regions retains certain unique features and claims strong loyalties from those who live there. Regional differences are often visible. Westerners and Maritimers complain about the people in prosperous central Canada. Central Canada ignores these comments, except to come back with an occasional joke about 'Newfies' or Westerners. People in northern Ontario mutter about 'Hogtown' (Toronto) in the south – unless of course they have already moved there themselves. Maritimers sometimes feel forgotten; Westerners think they are ignored by Ottawa. There are English Canadians who grumble that the country is being run by the French, and there are French Canadians who gripe that business is dominated by the English.

Collect pictures, maps, charts, and slides that illustrate the land and the regions of Canada. (Be sure you take into account Canada's cities and its northern climate.)

The People: The most distinctive feature of Canadian society is that it is the joining together of French and English. The two official languages and cultures of the founding nations have continued to survive side-by-side. The American humourist Henry Morgan lived for a while in Canada. The biggest difference he noticed between Canada and the United States was the bilingual characteristic. 'I have been here for almost ten weeks now and the only difference I've found is that when you pick up a jar that says "peanut butter" the other side says "beurre d'arachides".' Many people think it is this official bilingual and bicultural quality of Canada that will save it from being swallowed up by the United States. They feel that French-Canadian culture makes Canada unique and helps protect the Canadian identity from American influence.

Because two official languages already existed in Canada, more recent immigrants have kept many aspects of their cultural heritage. Government policy has encouraged them to keep customs brought from their homelands. We sometimes call this the Canadian 'mosaic'. A mosaic is made by placing small pieces of tile or glass in mortar. Canadian society is a mosaic because people from different lands contribute a variety and richness to the whole country, but remain distinct. In Canada the many languages and cultures do not weaken the Canadian identity, but in fact make it strong and unique.

Include with your presentation visuals that illustrate the two founding cultures, the native people, and Canada's multicultural heritage.

Canadians not Americans: In many parts of the world people do not distinguish Canadians from Americans. Yet most Canadians resent being called Americans. There is the touch of anti-Americanism in our Canadian identity. Canadians worry about American economic control and cultural influence. This feeling goes way back in the history of our country. In the late 1700s, after the American Revolution, many settlers came from the

United States to the Maritimes and Ontario. They were known as the 'United Empire Loyalists' because they wished to stay loyal to Britain. They did not want to be Americans. When the Americans briefly invaded Canada during the War of 1812, both English and French fought together to keep their land free of American economic and political control. At the time of Confederation, the Fathers looked closely at the American model of government and decided it was not for Canada. The founders of modern Canada decided in 1867 to keep the British system of government. Unlike the United States, Canada kept the British monarch as head of the new country. It was a deliberate decision that showed the rest of the world that we were not Americans.

In your presentation you should make it clear that Canadians are not Americans. You will want to show the things both countries hold in common, but the ways we are different too. You should emphasize the friendly relations that exist between the two nations.

Olympic village under construction.

Sports: Sport is the popular form of entertainment that best demonstrates the Canadian spirit. In Canada the most popular sport is hockey. Even the smallest community will build a hockey arena and support a hockey team. The 1972 Canada-U.S.S.R. hockey series illustrates this hockey enthusiasm. In the closing minutes of the last game Paul Henderson scored the winning goal. English Canadians, French Canadians and

Canadians of all other backgrounds rushed into the streets cheering and shouting, 'We beat them!'. Bruce Kidd, once an outstanding Canadian world-class runner, has written, 'If the C.P.R. held the country together during the early years of Confederation, certainly "Hockey Night in Canada" has done so in recent years.'

Gordon Lightfoot.

Tom Connors.

Performing Arts (music, dance, drama): The music of Canada has always been part of its identity. The early folksongs were those of the *habitants* and *voyageurs*. In songs they described the routine of the fishermen, the backbreaking toil of the railway builders, and the loneliness of the pioneer settlers. Recently singers such as Gordon Lightfoot and Tom Connors have continued to tell the story of Canada in song. The building of the railroad was the theme of Lightfoot's 'Canadian Railroad Trilogy'. 'The Wreck of the Edmond Fitzgerald' dealt with the loss of a lake freighter on Lake Superior. Stompin' Tom Connors was official Ambassador of Good Will for Prince Edward Island during its centennial in 1973. Connors sings about the people, places, and things of Canada, such as 'Black Donnelly's Massacre', 'Bud the Spud', and 'Sudbury Saturday Night'. Connor's ambition is to sing about Canada to the world.

Music has always helped keep alive the distinctive culture of French Canada. Popular singers in Quebec do not simply translate American songs, but write lyrics and compose music that emphasize the French-Canadian way of life. Pauline Julien,

Gilles Vigneault, and Robert Charlebois each express a strong French identity in their music.

Popular singers are also making Canada known elsewhere. Anne Murray, Joni Mitchell, Paul Anka, René Simard, Patsy Gallant, and David Clayton Thomas are well-recognized artists on both sides of the border. Classical performers such as the pianists Glenn Gould and André Gagnon, singers Maureen Forrester and Jon Vickers, the Canadian Brass Quintet, and symphony orchestras from several major Canadian cities have won international respect for Canada.

Maureen Forrester.

Since World War II more Canadians than ever before have been exposed to theatre in English and French. The theatre scene in Toronto has become one of the most dynamic in North America. Only in New York City are more plays produced than in Toronto. New theatre companies such as the Tarragon and Passe Muraille have introduced important Canadian plays to Canadian audiences. Among them have been *1837: The Farmer's Revolt*, a dramatization of the Mackenzie rebellion; *Ten Lost Years*, a picture of life in Canada during the Depression; and *Billy Bishop Goes to War*, the story of one of Canada's World War I heroes.

Literary and Visual Arts (literature, painting, sculpture, architecture): Any list of literary and visual artists is bound to leave out more than it includes. Many of our writers and artists have won international recognition for their work.

A unique theme that runs through Canadian literature is 'survival'. Canadian writers have been fascinated by the idea of people trying to survive in the Canadian environment. Hugh MacLennan and Gabrielle Roy have traced our English and French roots in their novels. W.O. Mitchell has spoken for the West while Thomas Raddall has spoken for the East. Mordecai Richler has given us Montreal through the eyes of Duddy Kravitz and John Marlyn has portrayed what it was like to be an immigrant growing up in Winnipeg. Pierre Berton has told the

Margaret Laurence.

tales of the C.P.R. and the Gold Rush days of the Klondike. Modern poets Leonard Cohen, Irving Layton, Raymond Souster, Margaret Atwood, and Earle Birney, to name a few, have given us a picture of Canada in poetic images.

In the 1960s and 1970s Canadian artists attracted national and international attention. From French Canada the names included Paul-Emile Borduas and Jean-Paul Riopelle. In English Canada some of the more influential painters included Jack Bush, Harold Towne, Alex Colville, Ken Danby, and William Kurelek.

Perhaps no group has contributed more to the Canadian identity than the native craftsmen. The Inuit in particular have portrayed everyday life among their people with soapstone carvings of seal hunts and family scenes.

French-Canadian film-makers have continued to thrive, probably because they do not have to compete with English-speaking films from Hollywood. Films made in Quebec have promoted French culture, and have won important Canadian and international awards. Claude Jutra has won attention for his films *Kamouraska* and *Mon Oncle Antoine*. In 1975 Michel Brault's film *Les Ordres* won an important award at the Cannes Film Festival. The following year, *J.A. Martin, Photographe* won the award for the best Canadian film.

The English commercial film industry and the National Film Board have produced some important Canadian films. These include *Goin' Down the Road*, the story of two Maritimers trying to establish themselves in Toronto; *The Battle of Crowfoot*, about an early Blackfoot chief; and *Why Shoot the Teacher*, a story of a teacher in a one-room school in the prairies of the 1930s.

Gather materials that show Canadian sports, performing arts, literary arts and visual arts. You might rehearse carefully and record some excerpts from Canadian poems, novels, or plays. You could collect the lyrics of folk songs or include the music of popular singers. Postcard reproductions of famous Canadian paintings can usually be purchased inexpensively from museums. A collection of these, or coloured slides, could be worked into an historical presentation on Canadian art. Select material that you feel portrays the Canadian identity.

Changing Roles for the Family and Women

During the last few years changes have occurred in the nature of the Canadian family unit. The typical Canadian family is made up of a mother, father, and one or more children. Experts call this a 'nuclear' family. In the nuclear family both parents share in household tasks and child-rearing. Fathers take on responsibility for raising the children and helping with the housework. Mothers frequently work outside the home and assist with the financial support of the family. But this type of family was not always typical in Canada.

In the earlier years of this century, most Canadians lived in 'extended' families. That meant that parents and children lived with grandparents, or close to relatives. Aunts, uncles, cousins, and grandparents were usually close by and everyone worked together to make life easier. But times changed. More people moved into cities in search of work and a better living standard. Relatives were gradually left behind. The extended family was replaced by the nuclear family because of changes in society.

The role of women has also changed in Canadian life. Women in Canada today do not struggle for the right to vote or for the freedom to work. Today's struggle is to bring about a change in attitudes and greater opportunities for women to be involved in the mainstream of Canadian society.

For example, according to *Women in the Labour Force 1975*, from 1964 to 1974 the number of Canadian women working increased by 68%. Women now make up over 40% of the labour force, and more than half of these women are married. Yet it is in employment that women are most discriminated against and hindered for being women. Some occupations open to women are still limited by social custom. Based on 1971 census information, 93.7% of nurses were female, but only 7.7% of physicians were women. An estimated 88.2% of tellers and cashiers were women, but only 6% of those who found their way into financial management positions were women. Nor can women who do make it into managerial or professional positions hope to make the same salaries as men. Between women and men doctors, there was a gap of between $6000 to $17 000 in salary. Equal pay for equal work is still not necessarily a reality for some Canadian women. Yet change will come because Canadian women are no longer content to sit quietly in the wings to wait for it to happen.

Along with pictures of women in today's Canadian society, write a short essay on the part Canadian women play in the life of the nation. You could also include descriptions of your school, homes and community, and accounts of local industry.

Teachers or others who have travelled overseas may be able to help you to arrange an exchange with a commonwealth school, or contact
Commonwealth Secretariat
Marlborough House
London, England.

Digging Deeper

Keep a record of the television viewing habits of your class. What percentage of your viewing was American?

1

Do you think the C.R.T.C. rules on Canadian content in broadcasting are fair? Explain your answer.

2

3   What impact does American culture have on other countries? Why is the Canadian experience unique?

4   In 1976 the government passed Bill C-58. It banned tax deductions for ads placed in non-Canadian publications. Its purpose was to encourage Canadian advertisers to use Canadian magazines instead of *Time* and *Newsweek*. Try to find out how effective the legislation has been. Check some recent editions of *Time* and *Newsweek* to verify your findings.

5   It has been said that Canadians dislike being mistaken for Americans, but will defend Americans to the British. Why do Canadians work so hard trying to show the rest of the world we are not Americans? Why would Canadians defend Americans to other countries of the world?

6   Do you feel that French Canada helps to protect the Canadian identity from American influence? How?

Refer back to the summary chart of themes at the end of Unit One (page 54). Using the chart as a model, make a chart for Unit Seven. On the chart trace the development of those themes through this unit.

WRAPPING IT UP
WHAT WOULD LAURIER THINK?

If the ghost of Sir Wilfrid Laurier were to return to Canada today, how do you think he would react? What changes would he notice? What would he think of present-day Canada? Consider these famous remarks that Laurier made in his lifetime:

'The best and most effective way to maintain friendship with our American neighbours is to be absolutely independent of them.'

'My object is to consolidate Confederation and to bring our people, long separated from each other, gradually to become a nation. This is the supreme issue. Everything else is subordinate to that idea.'

'The nineteenth century was the century of the United States, the twentieth century will be the century of Canada.'

To what extent do you think Laurier was correct when he predicted that the twentieth century would belong to Canada? Would Laurier be happy with the present state of French-English relations in Canada? What would be his opinion of Canadian-American relations today?

Digging Deeper

1 Slogans are brief, catchy phrases that get people excited about an idea. They are important because people use them as rallying cries for all sorts of things, from fighting wars to winning votes for a political party. Below is a list of slogans. Match each slogan with the idea, event, or person that it refers to. After you have done the matching, choose three of the slogans and discuss what they mean.

SLOGANS

1. Iron Curtain
2. No truck or trade with the Yankees
3. The Just Society
4. Maîtres chez nous
5. Peace in our time
6. The last best west
7. Vive le Québec libre
8. Conscription if necessary but not necessarily conscription

a) Prime Minister Chamberlain
b) General De Gaulle
c) Clifford Sifton
d) Pierre Trudeau
e) W.L. Mackenzie King
f) The quiet revolution
g) The election of 1911
h) Winston Churchill

2 Now that you have discussed these slogans, make a collection of others. Bumper stickers are one place to look. Discuss the collection in class. Which slogans are used most frequently? Classify the collection according to which ones have to do with politics, social problems, and religion.

3 Think back across the Canadian history you have read in this book.
a) Which decade in this century would you most like to live through? Why?
b) What do you think of the times you are living in now?
c) Do you think that this decade will be remembered as one of the most important in Canadian history?

4 Imagine you had the chance to put ten objects into a time capsule to be opened by Canadians in the year 2500 A.D. What would you place in it to show people of the future what life is like today?

5 What do you think Canada will be like in the year 2000? Write a short essay describing your ideas.

6 This text was published early in 1980. Prepare a time-line of major events in Canadian history since then. You may decide to use a long roll of paper and put it on the bulletin board of your classroom. Include political, social and economic events as well as any that illustrate the major themes of this book.

7 Styles of art change from one period to another. Make a collection of Canadian art in different periods of this century. Write a short report describing these styles.

8 Make a fashion history of Canada. Collect pictures of clothing styles from Canada's past. Mount the pictures on large sheets of paper and write a short essay to explain the changes and what they reveal about Canadian lifestyles.

9 In groups of five, prepare pantomimes which illustrate dramatic events in Canadian history. Let the rest of the class identify the event being dramatized.

10 Some historians have pointed out that Canada has struggled since its beginning to form a nation independent from the United States. This struggle has continually involved some kind of American challenge and a Canadian response to that challenge. In the period 1860-1880 the Americans seemed to be threatening a political takeover of Canada. This challenge certainly helped to hasten Confederation and our birth as a nation. It also encouraged the building of the C.P.R. and the settlement of the West.

From 1920-1940 there came the American cultural challenge. The influence of the American media was having a growing effect on Canadian styles, sports, and entertainment. From 1950 to the present a strong economic challenge has been felt in Canada.

Do you agree with the 'challenge and response' theory? What do you think was the Canadian response to the American cultural and economic challenges?

11 Discuss the truth of the following comment by Wilfrid Laurier: 'Compromise created this nation, nothing but compromise will hold it together.' Think of as many examples from our history as you can in which compromises have played a part in keeping Canada together.

BIBLIOGRAPHY

FOR FURTHER STUDENT READING

AUTHOR, TITLE, PUBLISHER	DESCRIPTION
TOPIC: THE LAURIER ERA	
Berton, Laura, *I Married the Klondike*, McClelland and Stewart Limited.	An exciting account of a school-teacher in the Yukon early this century.
Broadfoot, Barry, *The Pioneer Years 1895 - 1914*, Doubleday Canada Ltd.	*The Pioneer Years* is the story of the opening up of the Canadian West by settlers during those historic years between the turn of the century and 1914.
Bruce, Jean, *The Last Best West*, Fitzhenry and Whiteside Ltd.	This is a superb collection of photographs and quotations about the Canadian West 1896 - 1914
Marlyn, John, *Under the Ribs of Death*, McClelland and Stewart Limited.	This novel is the story of the son of a Hungarian family in Winnipeg. It describes many of the problems the newcomers faced as they tried to get established in the new land.
Robertson, Barbara, *Wilfrid Laurier*, Oxford University Press.	A well-illustrated brief biography of Sir Wilfrid Laurier, Canada's first French Canadian Prime Minister.
Smith, Margot and Pasternak, Carol *Pioneer Women of Western Canada*, Ontario Institute for Studies in Education, Curriculum Series 32.	This is a source book consisting of magazine and newspaper articles, stories, excerpts from books, and photographs. It explores the contribution of some women to Canadian history 1900 - 1940.
The Corrective Collective, *Never Done: Three Centuries of Women's Work in Canada*, Canadian Women's Educational Press.	*Never Done* is a picture and story album of the lives of women in Canada. The first part groups together women who pioneered in different times and in different parts of the country. The second half deals with the increasing variety of women's work outside the home.

TOPIC: WORLD WAR I

Bird, Michael J., *The Town That Died*, McGraw-Hill Ryerson Limited

The story of the Halifax explosion is told in gripping detail with many excellent photographs of the disaster.

Bishop, William A., *The Courage of the Early Morning*, McClelland and Stewart Limited.

The exciting story of Canada's flying hero and leading air ace, Billy Bishop, is told by his son.

Hannon, Leslie F., *Canada at War* McClelland and Stewart Limited.

An interesting illustrated look at Canada's involvement in World War I, World War II, and the Cold War.

Read, Daphne, *The Great War and Canadian Society: An Oral History*, New Hogtown Press.

The fascinating recollections of Canadian men and women who lived through the First World War and recall life in the trenches and on the homefront.

Robertson, Heather, *A Terrible Beauty*, James Lorimer & Co.

Paintings and letters reveal the war's impact on Canadian soldiers.

TOPIC: THE TWENTIES

Gray, James H., *Booze*, Macmillan Company of Canada Ltd.

This is a very readable account of prohibition in the West.

Skolnik, Peter L., *Fads*, Thomas Y. Crowell Company.

This is the story of North America's crazes, fevers, and fancies from the 1890s to the 1970s.

The Crazy Twenties, Canada's Illustrated Heritage.

The Crazy Twenties is one of the series published by Canada's Illustrated Heritage. This book pictures Canadian life in the decade of the 1920s.

TOPIC: THE DEPRESSION

Berton, Pierre, *The Dionne Years*, McClelland and Stewart Limited.

This is a journey back to the Canada of the 1930s.

Broadfoot, Barry, *Ten Lost Years 1929 - 1939*, Paper Jacks.

Broadfoot has gathered together moving stories of Canadians who survived the Depression.

Patton, Janice, *How the Depression Hit the West*, 　　McClelland and Stewart Limited.	A fascinating portrait of life on the Prairies during the Depression is presented in this book. It deals with the ways people lived through drought, dust, storms, grasshopper plagues, and killing frosts.
Stewart, Rod, *Bethune*, 　　Paper Jacks.	This is a fascinating biography of Dr. Norman Bethune.

TOPIC: WORLD WAR II

Broadfoot, Barry, *Years of Sorrow, Years of Shame*, 　　Doubleday Canada Ltd.	This book deals with the internment of Japanese Canadians during World War II.
Broadfoot, Barry, *Six War Years, 1939 - 1945*, 　　Paper Jacks.	This is a collection of the memories of Canadians about all aspects of the Second World War.
Douglas, W.A.B., and Greenhous, B. *Out of the Shadows*, 　　Oxford University Press.	This is the best general overview of all aspects of Canada's contribution to World War II.
Kuper, Jack, *Child of the Holocaust*, 　　Paper Jacks.	This is the true and terrible story of a young Jewish boy's fight for survival in the Polish countryside during World War II.
Takashima, Shizuye, *A Child in Prison Camp*, 　　Tundra Books of Montreal.	The author was a young Japanese girl when she and her family were interned during World War II. Her story is told through narrative, paintings, and poetry.

TOPIC: LIFE UNDER FOUR PRIME MINISTERS

Teatro, William, *Mackenzie King: Man of Mission*, 　　Personal Library for Nelson.	Hundreds of photographs are used to illustrate this biography of Canada's longest-serving Prime Minister. It is intended for the general reader.
Abella, Irving, *On Strike: Six Key Labour Struggles in Canada 1919 - 1940*, 　　James Lewis and Samuel.	This volume contains a good chapter on the Asbestos Strike in Quebec. Since other labour conflicts are also described, it offers a chance for comparison.

Thordarson, Bruce, *Lester Pearson*, Oxford University Press.

A lively biography on the life of Lester Pearson, an outstanding Canadian diplomat and politician.

TOPIC: LIFE BEGINS AT ONE HUNDRED

Butler, Rick, *Quebec: The People Speak*, Doubleday Canada Ltd.

This is a collection of the author's conversations with people in all parts of Quebec in 1977. They speak candidly about the future of Quebec and Canada.

Lévesque, René, *My Quebec*,

Lévesque states his views on Quebec and its future with the rest of Canada.

Levin, Malcolm, and Sylvester, C. *Foreign Ownership*, Paper Jacks.

The reader examines several detailed case studies that illustrate the nature and extent of foreign ownership in Canada.

Sylvester, Christine, and Harris, M. *On Strike*, Ontario Institute for Studies in Education.

Detailed case studies of some recent Canadian labour disputes invite reflection and discussion.

The Years of Protest, Canada's Illustrated Heritage .

Another volume in the series showing life in Canada in the 1960s.

Fowke, Edith, *Folklore of Canada*, McClelland and Stewart Limited.

Folk tales, legends, tall tales, riddles, myths, and sea shanties from every corner of Canada make up this classic collection.

ACKNOWLEDGEMENTS

CONRAD BLACK. Extract from Conrad Black, *Duplessis* (Toronto, McClelland and Stewart Ltd.). Reprinted by permission of the Canadian publishers.

ANNE AND MARIE BOURASSA. For extracts from pamphlets by Henri Bourassa.

BARRY BROADFOOT. Extracts from Barry Broadfoot, *Six War Years: 1939-1945* (Doubleday Canada). Copyright 1974 by Barry Broadfoot. Reprinted by permission of the publisher. Extracts from Barry Broadfoot, *Ten Lost Years* (Doubleday). Copyright 1973 by Barry Broadfoot. Reprinted by permission of the publisher. Extracts from Barry Broadfoot, *Years of Sorrow, Years of Shame* (Doubleday, Canada). Copyright 1977 by Barry Broadfoot. Reprinted by permission of the publisher.

MARCEL CHAPUT. Extracts from Marcel Chaput, *Why I Am a Separatist* (McGraw-Hill Ryerson Ltd. 1962).

RAMSAY COOK. Extract from Ramsay Cook with John Saywell and John Ricker, *Canada: A Modern Study* (Clarke, Irwin & Company Ltd. 1977). Used by permission of the publisher.

CONNIE CORNER. Connie Corner, *Canadian Unity: The Time to Think About It is Now* (Resourcebook, A Division of Special Interest Magazines Ltd. 1979).

LUCIEN DUMAIS. Extract from Lucien Dumais, *Un Canadien Français à Dieppe* (Editions France-Empire, Paris 1963).

B.J. ELLIOT. Extracts from B.J. Elliot, *Hitler and Germany* (London: Longman Inc.).

ANNE FRANK. Extracts from Anne Frank, *Diary of a Young Girl* (London: Valentine, Mitchell and Co. Ltd.).

JOYCE HIBBERT. Extracts from Joyce Hibbert, *The War Brides* (Toronto: PMA Books, 1978). Reprinted by permission of the publisher.

KINGSTON WHIG-STANDARD.

GERTRUDE LAING AND SOLANGE CHAPUT ROLLAND. Extracts from G. Laing and S.C. Rolland, *Face to Face* (New Press, 1972).

PIERRE LAPORTE. Extract from Pierre Laporte, *The True Face of Duplessis* (Montreal: Harvest House Limited, 1960).

JOHN MCLEISH. Extract from John A.B. McLeish, *September Gale: A Study of*

Arthur Lismer of the Group of Seven (J.M. Dent and Sons Ltd. 1973).

J.M. MILLMAN. Extract from J.M. Millman, *Press Comments on the Canadian Section of Fine Arts, British Empire Exhibition 1924-5* as quoted in J. Russell Harper, *Painting in Canada: a history* (University of Toronto Press, 1977 edition).

PUBLIC ARCHIVES OF CANADA.

DAPHNE READ. Extracts from Daphne Read (ed.), *The Great War and Canadian Society: an Oral History* (New Hogtown Press).

BARBARA ROBERTSON. Extracts from Barbara Robertson, *Wilfrid Laurier The Great Conciliator* (Toronto: Oxford University Press, 1971).

ROD STEWART. Extract from Rod Stewart, *Norman Bethune* from *The Canadians* series (Fitzhenry and Whiteside). *Time Capsules/1945* courtesy of Time-Life Books Inc. (Chicago).

UNITED PRESS INTERNATIONAL.

W.C. URQUHART. Extract from W.C. Urquhart and K.A. Buckley, *Historical Statistics of Canada.* Reprinted by permission of The Macmillan Company of Canada Limited.

THE WINNIPEG TRIBUNE.

STOCK MARKET GAME (Answers)

	Cycle 2	Cycle 3	Cycle 4	Cycle 5
Consolidated Mining and Smelting of Canada	$274.00	$575.00	$235.00	$9.50
Winnipeg Electric Light	$85.00	$110.00	$25.00	$2.00
International Nickel	$52.00	$72.50	$29.00	$4.50

PHOTO CREDITS

Page 10, City of Toronto Archives, James Collection;

p.11, City of Toronto Archives, James Collection;

p.13, Public Archives of Canada (hereafter called PAC), C-14090;

p.14, City of Toronto Archives, James Collection;

p.15, City of Toronto Archives, James Collection;

p.16, City of Toronto Archives, James Collection;

p.17, City of Toronto Archives, James Collection;

p.20, PAC, C-22106;

p.22, Metropolitan Toronto Library Board;

p.23, PAC, C-28727;

p.27, PAC, C-30621;

p.28, City of Toronto Archives, James Collection;

p.30, PAC, PA-10401;

p.32-33, PAC, C-14529;

p.37, City of Toronto Archives, James Collection;

p.39, Archives of Ontario;

p.40, PAC, PA-13399;

p.42, Archives of Ontario;

p.49, PAC, L 1054;

p.50, Provincial Archives of Manitoba;

p.55, private collection;

p.58, private collection;

p.59, private collection;

p.61, Royal Canadian Military Institute;

p.66, PAC, PA-1456;

p.71, Imperial War Museum, London, England;

p.77, PAC, PA-1654;

p.81, City of Toronto Archives;

p.83, City of Toronto Archives;

p.85, PAC, PA-364;

p.89, City of Toronto Archives;

p.90, City of Toronto Archives;

p.96, PAC, PAC, National Museums of Canada, and the Art Gallery of Ontario;

p.97, *Regina Leader Post*;

p.102, Metropolitan Toronto Library Board;

p.104, Archives of Ontario;

p.105, City of Toronto Archives;

p.111, City of Toronto Archives;

p.114, Metropolitan Toronto Library Board;

p.115, City of Toronto Archives, James Collection;

p.118, City of Toronto Archives;

p.121, Archives of Ontario;

p.122, City of Toronto Archives;

p.127, City of Toronto Archives;

p.128, Metropolitan Toronto Library Board;

p.131, Glenbow-Alberta Institute;

p.132, City of Toronto Archives;

p.133, City of Toronto Archives;

p.134, Provincial Archives of Alberta;

p.137, Provincial Archives of Alberta;

p.139, Archives of Ontario;

p.141, private collection;

p.146, City of Toronto Archives;

p.151, City of Toronto Archives;

p.153, Agriculture Canada;

p.155, PAC, C-30811;

p.158, Glenbow-Alberta Institute, NC-6-12955(b);

p.159, Glenbow-Alberta Institute, NA-771-3;

p.160, Glenbow-Alberta Institute, ND-3-6742;

p.160, City of Toronto Archives;

p.161, Glenbow-Alberta Institute, NA-2434-1;

p.162, PAC, PA-35133;

p.163, City of Toronto Archives;

p.165, Vancouver Public Library;

p.175, Archives of Ontario, S 4420;

p.177, Glenbow-Alberta Institute, NB-16-207;

p.181, Metropolitan Toronto Library Board;

p.181, Metropolitan Toronto Library Board;

p.183, Archives of Ontario, S 801;

p.184, Aviation and Space Division, National Museum of Science and Technology;

p.188, PAC, C 55451;

p.192, Metropolitan Toronto Library Board;

p.193, Metropolitan Toronto Library Board;

p.198, PAC, C-11452;

p.201, PAC, *The Gazette*, Montreal;

p.202, Canadian Forces Photo;

p.204, Canadian Forces Photo;

p.207, Canadian Forces Photo;

p.208, PAC, *The Gazette*, Montreal;

p.210, PAC;

p.211, Ullstein Bilderdienst, Berlin;

p.212, Canadian Forces Photo;

p.213, Canadian Forces Photo;

p.215, PAC;

p.216, Canadian Forces Photo;

p.225, City of Toronto Archives, James Collection;

p.227, Metropolitan Toronto Library Board, Metropolitan Toronto Library Board, PAC, C-90883, and the Library of Congress, Washington, D.C.;

p.228, Vancouver Public Library;

p.230, PAC;

p.235, PAC, C-46350;

p.237, Vancouver Public Library;

p.239, PAC, C-24452;

p.239, Vancouver Public Library;

p.240, PAC, C-47387;

p.244, Canadian Forces Photo;

p.249, United Nations;

p.253, PAC;

p.256, PAC, PA 113486;

p.258, Imperial Oil Ltd.;

p.260, Ontario Hydro;

p.261, Ontario Hydro;

p.264, Metropolitan Toronto

Library Board;

p.267, PAC, C-15160;

p.268, *Winnipeg Free Press*;

p.268, Canadian Forces Photo;

p.269, PAC, C-36219;

p.272, Photo Features Ltd.;

p.278, Metropolitan Toronto Library Board;

p.284, PAC, C 57897;

p.286, PAC, C-53641, *The Gazette*;

p.292, Metropolitan Toronto Library Board;

p.294, PAC, PA-113485;

p.295, PAC, PA-113484;

p.296, *Macleans*;

p.300, 301, Metropolitan Toronto Library Board;

p.301, PAC, C-35680;

p.303, Metropolitan Toronto Library Board;

p.304, 'Eagles Assist The Ascension' by Dennis Highway, Toronto Dance Theatre, Andrew Oxenham;

p.307, Metropolitan Toronto Library Board;

p.308, Metropolitan Toronto Library Board;

p.308, PAC;

p.309, Metropolitan Toronto Library Board;

p.309, PAC, PA-113483;

p.310, Metropolitan Toronto Library Board;

p.311, Reprinted with Permission: *The Toronto Star*;

p.313, Metropolitan Toronto Library Board;

p.328, Metropolitan Toronto Library Board;

p.329, PAC, PA-113488,

p.330, PAC, PA-113489;

p.334, Information Quebec;

p.340, Canadian Government Travel Bureau S-2622;

p.345, Metropolitan Toronto Library Board;

p.358, Reprinted with permission, *The Toronto Star*;

p.364, Reprinted with permission, *The Toronto Star*;

p.371, The *Varsity*, University of Toronto;

p.374, Metropolitan Toronto Library Board;

p.375, Imperial Oil Ltd.;

p.376, Metropolitan Toronto Library Board;

p.377, Imperial Oil Ltd.;

p.381, PAC.

Every effort has been made to determine copyright owners. In the case of any omissions, the publishers will be pleased to make suitable acknowledgements in future editions.

Cover photograph by Malak Photographs Ltd.

INDEX

A

B

C